Series Editor: Allan Luke
James Cook University of North Queensland
Australia

Literacy remains a contentious and polarized educational, media and political issue. What has emerged from the continuing debate is a recognition by many critical researchers and theorists that literacy in education is allied closely with matters of language and culture, ideology and discourse, knowledge and power.

This new series of monographs and anthologies draws together critical, cross-disciplinary work on language and literacy in a format accessible to researchers and students of education. Its aim is to provide competing discourses and alternative practices to the extant technical literature which offers 'state of the art' insights and 'how to' formulae for the achievement of literacy narrowly conceived as individual, psychological skills. Drawing perspectives variously from critical social theory and cultural studies, post-structuralism and feminisms, sociolinguistics and the ethnography of communication, social history and comparative education, the contributors to this series begin a critical interrogation of taken-for-granted assumptions which have guided educational policy, research and practice.

**Social Linguistics and Literacies:**
**Ideology in Discourses**
James Paul Gee, *University of Southern California, USA*

**With Literacy and Justice for All:**
**Rethinking the Social in Language and Education**
Carole Edelsky, *Arizona State University, USA*

**A Critical Theory of Public Life:**
**Knowledge, Discourse and Politics in an Age of Decline**
Ben Agger, *State University of New York, Buffalo, USA*

*Forthcoming Titles*

**Knowledge, Culture and Power:**
**International Perspectives on Literacy as Policy and Practice**
Edited by Anthony R. Welch and Peter Freebody, *The University of New England, Australia*

**Discourse, Gender and School Literacy:**
**Studies in the Social Organization of Classroom Knowledge**
Carolyn Baker, *The University of New England, Australia*

**Word Perfect:**
**Prospects for Literacy in the Computer Age**
Myron Tuman, *The University of Alabama, USA*

**The Insistence of the Letter:**
**Literacy Studies and Curriculum Theorizing**
Edited by Bill Green, *Deakin University, Australia*

**Texts of Desire:**
**Essays on Fiction, Femininity and Schooling**
Edited by Linda K. Christian-Smith, *The University of Wisconsin-Oshkosh, USA*

**Writing Science: Literacy and Discursive Power**
MAK Halliday and JR Martin, *University of Sydney, Australia*

**Morning News: Lessons in Learning How to Learn in School**
Francis Christie, *Northern Territory University, Australia*

**Television Literacy: Text and Context**
David Buckingham, *University of London, UK*

# A Critical Theory of Public Life:

## Knowledge, Discourse and Politics in an Age of Decline

Ben Agger

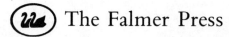 The Falmer Press

(A member of the Taylor & Francis Group)

London · New York · Philadelphia

UK    The Falmer Press, 4 John St., London WC1N 2ET
USA   The Falmer Press, Taylor & Francis Inc., 1900 Frost Road, Suite 101, Bristol, PA 19007

---

First published 1991

**A catalogue record for this book is available from the British Library**

**Library of Congress Cataloguing in Publication Data are available on request**

Typeset in 11/11.5pt Bembo
by Graphicraft Typesetters Ltd., Hong Kong

Printed in Great Britain by Burgess Science Press, Basingstoke on paper which has a specified pH value on final paper manufacture of not less than 7.5 and is therefore 'acid free'.

# Contents

For Beth Anne...
again and again!

# Acknowledgments

I am extremely grateful to Allan Luke for including this book in his Falmer series on literacy as well as for helping me pull these chapters together into a coherent book. He challenged me to rethink (and rewrite) a variety of my theoretical positions in ways that helped strengthen my arguments.

I am indebted to Jacinta Evans at Falmer for her superb editorial help with this project. She is a model editor: patient, rigorous, sympathetic.

Kate Hausbeck helped check the proofs with her usual skill. Kate Miller did a fine job of copyediting the manuscript, helping turn critical theory into plain English.

In addition to Allan Luke's careful reading of the entire manuscript, the following people offered very helpful readings of particular chapters:

Richard Scott, Laurel Richardson, Norman Denzin, Douglas Kellner, Ray Morrow, Tim Luke, Larry Hazelrigg, John O'Neill, Mark Gottdiener, Beth Anne Shelton, Stanley Diamond, Mark Kann, Russell Jacoby, Robert Maniquis, Christine Gailey, John Forester, Allan Rachlin, Philip Wexler, Ted Waagenar, Lionel S. Lewis (and other anonymous reviewers). Thank you one and all!

**Ben Agger**
Buffalo, NY
December 1990

# Permissions

'Critical Theory, Poststructuralism, Postmodernism' is an amended version of a paper published in the *Annual Review of Sociology* and is reproduced, with permission, from the Annual Review of Sociology, volume 17, 1991 published by Annual Reviews Incorporated. 'Marxism, Feminism, Deconstruction: Writing the Social' is a revised version of a paper which first appeared in *Dialectical Anthropology* and is reproduced here with permission from the University Presses of Florida. 'Reading/Writing Otherwise: Radical Hermeneutics as Critical Theory' was first published in Agger, B., *Fast Capitalism*, University of Illinois Press and is reproduced with kind permission from Richard Wentworth. 'Do Books Write Authors? Textbooks and Disciplinary Hegemony' is a revised version of an article which appeared in *Teaching Sociology*, 1989, volume 17, pp. 365–69. It is reproduced here with kind permission from Theodor Wagenaar. 'The Dialectic of Deindustrialization' was first published in Forester, J. (Ed.) (1985) *Critical Theory and Public Life*, Cambridge, MA, MIT Press, pp. 3–21 and is reproduced with permission from MIT Press. 'The Dialectic of Desire' first appeared in *Dialectical Anthropology*, 1983, volume 8, pp. 75–86 and is reproduced with kind permission from Stanley Diamond.

# Series Editor's Introduction

The first volume of this series, James Gee's *Social Linguistics and Literacies* (1991), offers a reworking of sociolinguistics in light of contemporary theories of ideology and discourse. Carole Edelsky's *With Literacy and Justice for All* (1991) poses the question of the viability of a holistic, critical approach to literacy in light of postmodern 'crises' in social science, politics and culture. Works in progress examine the kinds of literate practices propagated by new modes of information, scientific discourse and literacy teaching, the place of popular 'texts of desire' in the educational construction of gender, literacy as policy and practice in non-Western national contexts, and talk and gender in literacy lessons.

These monographs, anthologies and textbooks offer alternative, cross-disciplinary perspectives to the academic and professional literature that defines literacy in terms of neutral, psychological 'skills' or 'processes' internal to the literate person. Several themes traverse these volumes: 1) a view that literacy is above all a social practice intricately tied to power and sociocultural reproduction in the contemporary nation state; and relatedly, 2) a recognition of the need for critique and reconfiguration of conventional disciplinary agendas for dealing with texts, representation and literacies in institutions.

Yet this move towards social and cultural analyses of educational work in universities, schools, research sites and publishing houses raises as many questions as it answers. Such calls can foster the shaky assumption that 'theory' exists as a unitary, finished entity, with a disinterested, outsiders' purchase on 'truths' of social and cultural life (Harding, 1986). In the case of literacy and education, the danger is that these alternative perspectives will be seen as the latest 'state of the art' in seminars, classrooms and clinics — and, like dominant psychological models, translated into new, improved and more 'efficient' institutional technologies.

To see literacy and education in terms of an incremental substitution and deployment of new science for old science — truth for

untruth, cognitive for behaviorist, Deconstruction for New Criticism, and so forth — would be to misconstrue their historical and
sociocultural character altogether (Baker and Luke, 1991). What
comes to count as theoretical, disciplinary or scientific 'truth', Ben
Agger here argues, is itself tied up in the politics and economics of
universities, publishers and other text industries. And yet it seems all
too easy for many commentators to ignore a glaring and telling
axiom: that theories of literacy are the products and representations of
the politics of the literate culture they attempt to theorize.

What then are we to make of this 'literate culture' which continually reappears as the benchmark of academic and popular debate
over education? Typically it is presented as a preserve of accumulated
scientific wisdom, 'timeless' literary expression of the human psyche,
spirit and so forth. Agger here offers an alternative account, an
ongoing inquiry into the political economy of textual labor which
centers on the constraints and consequences of 'writing for profit' and
'writing for tenure'. His case is that the character and limits of literate,
'information' culture are shaped by the commodification of texts and
truths for circulation in a public marketplace.

In this milieu, intellectual work (which teaching is) has become
more divided, devalued and risky. As many recent discussions have
noted, state economic and moral crises in the west, and the attendant
resurgence of conservatism, have greatly influenced government and
popular perceptions of the roles of universities and academics, and the
'usefulness' (or 'uselessness') of research and scholarly texts. Agger
argues that rampant commercialism and careerism among writers,
academics, publishers and others, combined with a growing distance
between intellectual texts and everyday language, have done little to
defend or revive academic work as critical social practice. The specialization and division of discourse thus poses the 'public' texts of
popular culture against the discourses of 'professional expertise' and
élite academics. It is in this public forum — a domain of 'all consuming images', of the 'primacy of style over substance' (Ewen, 1988) —
that contemporary political and moral debate is ostensibly waged and
adjudicated. And it is in specialized genres and texts (e.g., medical and
scientific journals, corporate reports and administrative memos, legal
briefs) — as unfamiliar and daunting to a 'universally literate' public as
Latin texts might have been to medieval laypeople — that substantive
decisions about peoples' bodies, desires and lives are enacted.

Responsibility for this state of affairs cannot be placed solely in
the not-so-hidden hands of advertising and 'public relations' agencies
(whether private or governmental), media multinationals and an audience of consumers, 'hungry for redundance' of image and product,
myth and pleasure (Eco, 1978). Agger maintains that the public 'decline of discourse' has been unintentionally supported by an increasing
'heterodoxy' among academic writers. Ironically, he notes, even trenchant social critics of the mid and late-twentieth century have tended

to write in increasingly obscure styles and vocabularies, accessible only to a privileged few, mostly other critics. Hence, between a powerful retailing of popular discourse and inaccessible academic writing is a dangerous gap, one which prevents effective social criticism and practice in either.

*A Critical Theory of Public Life* forwards a positive thesis for 'rewriting' public discourse in the interests of a radical, heteroglossic democracy, where texts and positions are scrutinized and adjudicated openly, on critical grounds (cf. Mouffe, 1988). Agger begins from a candid acknowledgment of his (or rather our) own participation in academic language games, and of the very real difficulties in making critical social theory accessible and available. What is needed, he argues, is a rethinking of the roles of academics, intellectuals and educators in light of feminist, poststructuralist and critical theories of textuality, discourse and dialogue.

As an illustrative case, Agger takes up his own work, the enterprise of 'doing sociology' in American universities. Social scientists, theorists and educators in effect engage in the 'literary production of discipline'. This production process, and its classroom practice, is done under the aegis of powerful culture industries of academic credentialling, promotion and publication, the latter clearly at work in the discourses of sociology textbooks and their singular ideological constructions of 'society', the (male) 'individual', and the 'discipline' itself.

As an alternative, Agger sets out a pedagogical agenda of dialogue and discourse critique which aims at the unmasking of the tricks that mass public and élite academic cultures alike have played on writers and readers. For instance, he describes some of the textual devices at work in the texts of sociology: the sublimation of authorial presence, the incantation of 'founding fathers', the status of the 'textbook' as authoritative, neutral truth, and so forth. The key here is a rediscovery of the role of critique and analysis as material textual and political practice. Drawing from Freire and Habermas, Agger argues that reading and writing need not be about transmitting a static disciplinary corpus nor about learning obscure stylistics, but can be remade into dialogic practice that renames and revalues social worlds.

The need for a critical, dialogic approach to education is, of course, at the heart of calls for radical and progressive educational reforms forwarded in the US and elsewhere. Yet Agger here provides a different entry point into critical social and discourse theory: a 'social textual theory of reproduction'. Social science, disciplinary study and research, and literacy research itself, are indeed literate practices: 'metatextual' activities which can be opened to deconstruction and critique. What Agger develops is a reconciliation of the prescriptive, ultimately moral agendas of neo-Marxian and critical theory with the textual, potentially relativist, turn of poststructuralism and postmodernism (Fraser, 1989). It is this critique of value freedom in social sciences which Agger marks out as a starting point for recovering consensus and humane social action.

Of what value, then, is a book about grounded, critical theory for educators and researchers concerned with literacy? For a start, we can return to Agger's question of 'who should write the texts for educating the educators?' If literate culture has become above all else an interest-bound, commercial enterprise, this is indeed crucial.

**Allan Luke**
San Diego, California
December, 1990

## References

BAKER, C.D. and LUKE, A. (Eds) (1991) *Towards a Critical Sociology of Reading Pedagogy*, Amsterdam and Philadelphia, John Benjamins.

ECO, U. (1978) *The Role of the Reader*, Bloomington, Indiana University Press.

EDELSKY, C. (1991) *With Literacy and Justice for All: Rethinking the Social in Language and Education*, London, Falmer Press.

EWEN, S. (1988) *All Consuming Images: The Politics of Style in Contemporary Culture*, New York, Basic Books.

FRASER, N. (1989) *Unruly Practices: Power, Discourse and Gender in Contemporary Social Theory*, Cambridge, England, Polity Press.

GEE, J.P. (1991) *Social Linguistics and Literacies: Ideology in Discourses*, London, Falmer Press.

HARDING, S. (1986) *The Science Question in Feminism*, Milton Keynes, Open University Press.

MOUFFE, C. (1989) 'Radical Democracy: Modern or Postmodern?', in ROSS, A. (Ed.) *Universal Abandon: The Politics of Postmodernism*, Edinburgh, Edinburgh University Press.

# Introduction:
# Critical Theory Goes Public

## The Book's Rationale:
## Toward an Applied Critical Theory

In this book I present a sustained argument for the redevelopment of critical theory, originally formulated in the 1930s by the founders of the Frankfurt School (Marcuse, Adorno, Horkheimer and others) and later extended by Habermas. Although I take my bearings from these thinkers, they do not provide a fully adequate foundation for applying critical theory to the problems of public life in the 1990s. For critical theory to become simply a method, to be used willy-nilly regardless of historical context, violates the original Frankfurt contention that critical social theory must above all be defined by its historicity, thus ensuring its adaptability. As critical theory enters its third generation (see Kellner, 1989b), it needs to be rejuvenated by theoretical sources outside of it, notably by poststructuralism (Jameson, 1981; Culler, 1982; Ryan, 1982), postmodernism (Harvey, 1989; Agger, 1990; Best and Kellner, 1990) and feminist theory (Jaggar, 1983; Donovan, 1985; Fraser, 1989). This is one of the tasks that I set for myself in this book.

My redevelopment of critical theory is necessary in order to analyze a number of social problems of modernity and postmodernity that have gone largely ignored by critical theorists. Broadly understood, these are problems of public life, including dilemmas of disciplinary knowledge, the use and abuse of scientific and technological expertise, deindustrialization, prejudice and discrimination and the loss of public discourse. I contend that loss of public discourse and the professionalization of social-problem solving erode democracy. Unfortunately, though, critical theory itself has been phrased in such an esoteric voice that its message has been lost on the very people whose lives it seeks to improve. In order to make sense of public life using insights from a redeveloped critical theory, I need to come to grips with critical theory's own élite discourse as well as with problems of socially critical pedagogy generally. In this introduction, I both state my book's problem and I attempt to rethink the timeworn problem of educating the educator. My thesis is that we need a new concept of radical intellectuality with which to address problems of public life in postmodern capitalism (see Agger, 1990).

This involves not only phrasing critical theory in relatively comprehensible ways for people untrained in recondite European philosophy and social thought. It also involves returning critical theory to the intellectual mode of Adorno, Horkheimer and Marcuse, who first applied the general theoretical logic of critical theory to emerging capitalism in the 1930s. The original members of the Frankfurt School did a great deal of important theoretically-informed empirical work relating political economy to cultural and ideological analysis. As Kellner (1989b) argues, this important focus of critical theory was largely lost with Habermas' linguistic turn in critical theory. Although Habermas (e.g., 1984, 1987b) plunders a wide variety of theoretical and research literatures in order to reconstruct Marxist historical materialism as a communication theory of society, his is more a philosophical project than an empirical and political one. Even Habermas' (1981b) attempt to address 'new social movements' in concrete terms has left a good deal to be desired in the way of an adequate theoretical model of public life; the eclecticism and decentered nature of his new social movements theory make it difficult to go beyond a simple iteration of groups and causes that left-leaning people may endorse.

Instead, critical theory needs to return to the mode of theoretically-informed empirical analysis of the Frankfurt School's first generation (e.g., Adorno, 1945, 1954, 1974b), albeit now fortified by theoretical insights from poststructuralism, postmodernism and feminism. In particular, poststructuralism, postmodernism and feminism afford *a social-textual theory of reproduction* that in significant ways improves the original neo–Marxian critique of ideology developed by Lukacs (1971) and the Frankfurt School (see Jay, 1973, 1984a). A feminist postmodern critical theory, outlined in the first section of this book, understands ideology as a process, practice and product imbedded in the material language games of everyday life and not simply imprinted on ideologizing texts that are read at a distance by stupefied readers. Poststructuralism and postmodernism show the dispersal of ideology beyond the covers of books *per se*; feminism shows how texts, much like sexuality, function as agents of social reproduction. In what I (1989a) have called fast capitalism, texts are dispersed into the texture of an everyday life in such a way that they are not read critically, at one remove, but are received and enacted vicariously. Hence texts turn into the disempowered lives they script. This has always been so in capitalism. But in fast capitalism the boundary between text and world has blurred to such an extent that it is nearly impossible to identify where text leaves off and world begins. This is the secret power of textuality today: *Texts write our lives without the apparent mediation of authoriality*; hence we are prevented from writing new texts. A critical theory of public life needs to understand how the public sphere has been taken over by these disguised tracts and treatises that silently advocate a range of behaviors inimical to freedom and justice.

In the first section of this book I explore what I call *the literary production of discipline*, beginning in chapter 1 with an overview of critical theory, poststructuralism and postmodernism for people unfamiliar with them. In the next chapter I develop the relevance of feminist theory for a postmodern critical theory. In chapter 3, I argue for a mode of critical theory that directly intervenes in everyday life as a mode of ideology-critique conceived as radical hermeneutic practice, decoding the dispersed texts commanding experience today. In my opening three chapters I theorize how texts in general reproduce a version of public life. I show how a blend of critical theory, postmodernism, poststructuralism and feminist theory helps us address the role of discourse in shaping our public environment. Necessarily, these first three chapters are involved in theoretical debate and clarification.

In chapter 4 I extend my argument in the opening chapters by addressing the literary production of academic discipline in terms of its organizational and discursive setting in the corporate university. In chapter 5 I examine the hegemonic assumptions about society contained in sociology textbooks as an exemplar of the literary production of discipline. These chapters together apply a feminist postmodern critical theory to the particular practices, products and problems of academic discourse constraining a genuinely public discussion of social purposes and social problems, the topic of much of the second section of the book.

In chapters 6 through 10, comprising the second section of the book, I apply a feminist postmodern critical theory to particular social problems of modernity and postmodernity, including deindustrialization (chapter 6), the intensification of prejudice and discrimination (chapter 7), the decline of public discourse (chapters 8 and 9) and the post-ideology of postmodernity theory (chapter 10). This extends my reading of positivist academic texts in the first section to a range of discourses and practices typically viewed as separate by social reformers. An integrated critical theory of public life shows convincingly that these social problems are not separable and must be understood in terms of their complex interrelationships, as well as in light of their obfuscation by traditional non-poststructural-Marxist approaches to social change. This second section examines *crises of social and economic reproduction* in capitalist modernity, arguing, with Marx, that we must view discrete social problems as outcomes of the irrational logic of capital (albeit without the millennarian optimism of Marx about the 'synthesis' of these structural contradictions at the 'end of history').

Postmodernism (e.g., Lyotard, 1984) counsels skepticism about millennarian philosophies of history. Yet, as I argue, a neo-Marxist version of postmodernism makes optimism possible by showing the ways in which critical theory can actively intervene in public life as a mode of critique and imagination, especially where feminist theory helps us reconceptualize public life to include crucial sexual-political issues of reproduction. Like the original members of the Frankfurt School, I am extremely uncomfortable with the Enlightenment's blind progressivism, especially where enlightenment and myth seem to be dialectically connected (Horkheimer and Adorno, 1972). But against Lyotard's (1984) influential version of postmodernism, this does not rule out the possibility of radical social change altogether. Indeed, my particular contribution in this book is to articulate the possibility of social change in terms of the establishment of authentic public life, in which societal priorities are formulated through open dialogue and debate and not imposed via technocratic engineering.

It is in this sense that I rely on Habermas' (1984, 1987b) notions of an ideal speech situation, communicative democracy and a quasi-transcendental framework of universal emancipatory interests, if not his Kantian restriction of emancipatory possibilities to the realm of communicative praxis as well as his undialectical approach to the public/private relationship (as Fraser, 1989, points out). Although Habermas stalls critical theory in philosophical argumentation, thus losing the applicability of critical theory to the empirical social world so characteristic of first-generation critical theory, he offers critical theory an important imagery of *communicative public life* characterized by dialogue, discourse and democracy. Habermas' reformulation of socialism as an ideal speech situation in which people possess roughly equal dialogue chances and in which they seek consensus and not monologue is an important component of my critical theory of public life. In interesting ways, Habermas' communication theory connects up with poststructural, postmodern and feminist themes of discourse, even though, as Habermas himself (1987a) points out, the philosophical discourse of postmodernity is driven by conservative political interests. My critical theory of public life blends Habermas' communication theory with discourse-theoretic concerns of postmodernism, poststructuralism and feminist theory. This complex synthesis of theoretical insights is in my opinion the best way to return to and extend the mode of empirically and politically engaged scholarship characteristic of Adorno's, Horkheimer's and Marcuse's work in the first generation of the Frankfurt School.

More than the original generation of Frankfurt School theorists (who otherwise usefully developed the model of an applied critical theory that transcended speculative philosophy), Habermas has developed a regulative concept of a future better society. He points the way toward a society of discourse in which power is shared, including the power of public language. Habermas' (1975) analysis of legitimation crises in late capitalism suggests principles and strategies of relegitimation within the framework of his overall communicative theory of society. More than anyone else today, he points the way toward a concrete engagement of critical theory with social problems conceived as *irruptions of the crises of modernity and postmodernity*, even if his own labored philosophical attempt to move from what he calls the paradigm of consciousness to the paradigm of communication does little empirical and political work. More than anyone else, Habermas has asked the right questions about relations among knowledge, discourse and politics in contemporary life.

## The Dilemma of Public Discourse

Habermas' questioning provokes my own attempt to develop a theory and critique of public life with the aid of insights from poststructuralism, postmodernism and feminism. But, in addition to these influences, critical theory in its third generation needs to go public, engaging with an audience largely unprepared in European philosophy and social theory. In chapter 9, I address the dilemma of theorizing about the decline of public discourse in language so obscure that it ironically hastens discourse's decline. That is a real concern in a book like this, where I use recondite theory in order to explain how technocratic élitism has gotten the better of public dialogue. I have crafted these essays deliberately to meet the standard of public speech, although I have not completely succeeded in this. One of the fundamental lessons of poststructural discourse theory is that one cannot unproblematically translate one text into another: meaning is always and inherently elusive. It is not enough to translate the words in this book into simpler ones, although that is a necessary beginning. Difficulty sometimes educates just as simplicity sometimes occludes.

It would take too many pages to introduce and clarify all of the disputes giving rise to the various theoretical traditions discussed in this book. Critical theory, postmodernism and poststructuralism would require whole volumes; I attempt to do them justice in my opening chapter! Although writing such volumes would be extremely useful (and others have already undertaken these tasks; e.g., Held, 1980; Culler, 1982), readers would be sidetracked here by these preparatory studies, which could expand endlessly. One digression would lead to another; the reader would go in circles vainly pursuing the question to which he or she already believes that we have an answer. Although this digressive hermeneutic circling is vitally necessary — it is best called *education* — we must also attend to the economy of our arguments.

Some of these essays were published before, where others were composed for this volume. I have revised all of them in order to suit my theme and to articulate well together. (As I said, chapter 1 serves as a primer for people totally unfamiliar with the theories discussed, although one can read virtually any of the essays in isolation from the others and without the theoretical stage-setting provided in chapter 1.) The chapters are structured sequentially so that readers can move from general to particular, although my sense of sequence might well be idiosyncratic and someone else would organize these chapters quite differently and equally legitimately. Such concerns are not immaterial. Titles, headings, sequence are all 'texts' in their own right, conveying meaning beyond the so-called content of the writings themselves. These issues must be carefully considered; too many theorists neglect the ways in which these contingent matters reflect, and inform, the substance of the whole.

Nancy Fraser in her (1989) book, *Unruly Practices*, begins with an apologia to academic radicals. She situates her academic concerns without pretending that she is speaking to a mass public. She notes the irony of academic radicalism without pretending that she somehow escapes it. I confront the same irony in this book; at least by acknowledging it, I avoid selling the reader a bill of goods — a crystalline analysis of our world's problems as well as definitive solutions. It is one of my theoretical claims that any analysis pretending to clarify and solve everything is bogus — that such claims must be deconstructed as the hubris they are. Nevertheless, not to clarify and explain redoubles prevailing academic obscurantism. I am caught in the same dilemma as Fraser. We are academics writing for other academics but desperately trying to change the norm of restricted academic codes that reproduce the hierarchy of writers over readers. In any case, deconstruction informs us that the meaning of words like *radical* and *radicalism* are up for grabs; frequently, *soi-disant* 'radicals' professing 'radicalism' are the least radical in their resistance to political and intellectual heterodoxy, a theme I take up in a forthcoming book, *Do Books Write Authors? Gender, Class and Critique in the Age of the Blockbuster* (1992).

I argue here that academic radicalism must be suspicious of all cults, including its own. Simply to rail against prevailing forms of discourse and practice ignores the tendency of radicalism itself to become a dead language conveying little more than the will to power. Although this is an avowedly political book, I argue throughout that the meaning of the political is problematic today. Politics is found everywhere but in the political arena, traditionally defined. This makes it hard on academic radicals who sincerely want to believe that their words matter. We are after all in the word business, which too often produces sheer wordiness that we transact as one type of cultural capital or another. In so doing we establish and advance our careers. But we run the risk of ignoring the textual politics of our own work. One of the main themes in this book is that disciplinary knowledge and discourse involve a politics of their own, notably in the way that academic practices are organized hierarchically and bureaucratically.

## Main Themes

Readers can gain access to the structure of my argument simply by inspecting the table of contents, where I divide the book into two units — the development of feminist postmodern critical theory as it informs my analysis of the literary production of discipline, followed by a discussion of the social problems of modernity and postmodernity seen through these theoretical lenses. These sections reflect different substantive themes, as I spelled out above. But certain integrating themes cut across these discrete sections and inform the whole book; these are less easy to decipher from the structure of the contents page. Three themes inform the book, surfacing in different configurations and combinations:

1 Texts/textuality; reading/writing;
2 The role of academic discourse and the organization of academic disciplines in the commodification of knowledge;
3 Public dialogue, discourse and critique as positive activities.

With respect to theme 1, I develop the argument, in different places and with different inflections, that the writing and reading of texts are important social practices. As such, I show how the interpretation of texts represents bona fide social analysis. This sort of work tells us a great deal about the societies in which writers write and readers read; it also tells us a great deal about the ways that textual practices constitute the social order. I show how social reality is reproduced through textual practices and I show how textual practices can help change society.

With respect to theme 2, I situate my analysis of textual practices in the contemporary research university, which for structural reasons commodifies knowledge. I am particularly concerned with the textual politics of disciplinary knowledge — how academic disciplines enforce discipline through the establishment of discourses closed to outsiders. I examine the literary production of discipline within the context of the state management of knowledge, a recurring theme throughout this book. A critical theory of public life needs to move beyond critique; better, it needs to formulate critique as a positive, constructive activity (theme 3). It is not enough to oppose disciplinary knowledge formulated in the state-managed university. Thus we must conceive of and engage in public dialogues that both deal with serious social problems of modernity and, in their own example, prefigure a democratic polity wherein the aim of public life is not only to create rational policy but to enjoy the vitality of public discourse for its own sake. All of these essays, no matter how critical in nature, celebrate dialogue and discourse as antidotes to the monologic disciplinary codes in which experts arrogate power to themselves and thus reproduce a hierarchical social order.

Like Fraser, I stop short of offering blueprints of a better society: any programmatism must already write in the voice it recommends, hence shortening the distance between the process of social change and its product. The product *is process* where the life and times of democracy are concerned. This is where Habermas' (1984, 1987b) communication theory of society, with its utopian *telos* of the ideal speech situation, is such a powerful model of democratic literacy and publicity in late capitalism. Habermas argues that the simple pursuit of enlightened consensus is a good in itself, following an ancient line of thought stretching back through Marx to the Greeks. I agree with Habermas completely that discourse is a regulative principle of the good society, worth insisting on in its own right. Without public discourse, democracy is undermined. Without discourse, the authority of expertise goes unchallenged as disciplinary knowledge simply reproduces itself. But to make this point stick, we must move critical theory beyond Nietzschean negativism toward a more positive construction of the good society, accepting the risk that in doing so we contribute to the affirmative culture in which cheerful positivity drowns out the cries of victims.

Nihilism is the outcome of cynicism installed as a sufficient political theory. But as I say in the course of this book, cynicism cannot be allowed to become political theory, nor is it appropriate political strategy. When so much is going wrong with the world, the temptation is nearly irresistible to compose critical theory in Adornoian terms. I have addressed and tried to resist this temptation (e.g., Agger, 1976a), remembering that critical theory, with Marx, wants to join theory and practice in a usefully transformative synthesis. Although Adorno's (1974a) contextual defense of pessimism in the wake of fascist extermination camps made eminent sense, as I argue in chapter 7, one wonders today whether German fascism was qualitatively different from atrocities committed in the meantime. Adorno ontologized the Holocaust in such a way that he lost the ability to recognize subsequent holocausts as well as to detect the stirrings of hope and resistance even amidst the ashes of nearly total devastation. Lampooning Adorno's seeming absolutism is easy. It is much more challenging to rethink Adorno's negative dialectics sympathetically, notably with the help of feminist theory, poststructuralism and postmodernism.

Critical theory until now has been phrased in pessimistic terms, largely in response to the integration of social criticism and dissent since the consolidation of welfare-state capitalism in the 1930s (see Kellner, 1989b). The original Frankfurt School theorists like Horkheimer, Adorno and Marcuse argued that late capitalism was capable of integrating dissent, although they also agreed with Marx that capitalism is an inherently self-contradictory social and economic system that irrationally plants the seeds of its own demise. Unlike Marx, they believed that state intervention and the culture industry could absorb radicalism as well as shore up the capitalist profit system, hence prolonging capitalism indefinitely. They formulated critical theory as a last-ditch attempt to keep the embers of critical thought glowing at a time of growing darkness — positivism, pluralism, post-Marxism.

Although my own version of critical theory derives from the original model of critical theory offered by these German thinkers in the 1930s, I am increasingly convinced that there are strategic points of possible resistance to the structurally irrational nature of capital's logic. This is not to say that my own critical theory of public life is bursting with optimism about the imminence of radical social change. Evidence of social and political regression abounds — the so-called pro-life movement, neoconservatism, the discourse of the 'end of Communism' as it fuels western mythology about the failures of socialism and Marxism, a degraded environment, a significant wealth gap between white males and women and people of color, uneven development that hierarchizes rich and poor nations, the nuclear threat, the depletion of fossil fuels, overpopulation, the scapegoating of minorities, including homosexuals...this list could be extended indefinitely. This is truly an age of decline, as evidenced by these social problems of modernity and postmodernity.

But this is not the one-dimensional world (Marcuse, 1964) portrayed by the original critical theorists. New categories need to be developed to identify and then foster critical resistance. I draw these categories partly from Habermas' critical communication theory (Habermas, 1984, 1987b), partly from feminist theory (e.g., Fraser, 1989) and partly from poststructuralism and postmodernism (e.g., Ryan, 1982; Agger, 1990, 1991b; Aronowitz, 1990; Harvey, 1989; Best and Kellner, 1990). These traditions afford original critical theory much-needed flexibility with respect to developing a non-deterministic portrait of the social world. Although I firmly ground my critical theory of public life in the first generation of the Frankfurt School's critical theory, I refresh critical theory of the 1930s with these diverse influences that together combine into what I call a feminist postmodern critical theory of public life.

This critical theory of public life identifies pockets and agents of resistance without romanticizing them. It analyzes social problems that reveal systemic contradictions and possible resolutions of them. Above all, it reformulates socialism as a *dialogic society*, a society of unfettered public speech that can only be achieved through discursive means. Although, as I said, Habermas' communication-theoretic reformulation of first-generation critical theory in certain respects regresses behind the sweeping utopianism of both Marx and the later Frankfurt thinkers (as I have argued; see Agger, 1976b, 1979b), in other respects he significantly advances traditional socialist thinking about a better society. In particular, Habermas' dialogic ethics coupled with his 'new social movements' theory offers an intriguing alternative to the earlier Frankfurt pessimism, notably in the way that he allows us to retain a dynamic, dialectical understanding of the relations between what he calls system and lifeworld.

It is overly mechanical to view my critical theory of public life as a simple addition of Habermas, feminist theory, poststructuralism and postmodernism to original critical theory. Yet we urgently need to move beyond a monochromatic portrayal of one-dimensional society if we are to assess rigorously the possibilities of radical social transformation. Just as Marxism itself had become a stale orthodoxy by the turn of the last century, so Adornoian critical theory has lost a good deal of its own dynamism over the past twenty years. Although critical theory cannot dispense with Adorno's extremely powerful understandings of capitalism's tendencies toward 'total administration', it is difficult to escape the impression that Adorno's negative totality was equally as metaphysical as the positive totality of Hegel and Marx. This is ironic inasmuch as Adorno was metaphysics' severest critic. Today, we must reject the metaphysical in Adorno's (1973a) own negative dialectic if we are to rethink the modalities and aporias of domination in empirically feasible terms.

My analysis of public life goes only so far. I do not solve all the theoretical or empirical problems before us. This book inevitably delivers less than it promises in the way of a systematic critical theory of public life. Today, it is virtually impossible to capture the complexity of the social totality without achieving a level of empirical specificity that somehow contradicts the purpose of a largely programmatic book like this. A theory that reduces the world to simple axial principles invariably misses the mark. Indeed, this is one of the problems, as I see it, with Habermas' (1984, 1987b) otherwise magisterial reformulation of historical materialism as communication theory. His system/lifeworld motif is too pat, ignoring such issues as the politics of reproduction, as Fraser (1989) notes. Nevertheless, Habermas helps critical theorists rethink some of their fundamental assumptions about the relationship between self and society, reinvigorating the attempt to apply critical theory to the present circumstance.

The ultimate question of whether my or Habermas' version of critical theory is faithful to first-generation critical theory, let alone to Marx, is quite irrelevant; such questions promote obscurantism and destine those who ask them to obscurity. This book is not a pedantic exercise in which I carefully delimit my own filiation to the theoretical founders. Although it is important to acknowledge one's debts, the question of whether my critical theory of public life is Adornoian, Habermasian or feminist-postmodern is much less important than the kind of work that such a theory does. That is the only important criterion by which we can judge a theory's validity. Good theory will illuminate aspects of social reality heretofore unseen or unexplained.

## Reformulating the Problem of Educating the Educator

My critical theory of public life raises perennial questions about the role of intellectuals in raising the level of political and cultural literacy. As Marx reminded us, educators need to be educated, too; they do not float freely in an ethereal stratosphere somehow unaffected by objective interests. Western Marxists since Marx (e.g., Merleau-Ponty, 1964a, 1964b; Lukács, 1971) have argued that educators — radical intellectuals — need to be inculcated with humble, humane and dialogical values lest, in Korsch's (1970) terms, the dictatorship of the proletariat become a dictatorship *over* the proletariat. The subsequent history of Bolshevik command economies has proven the western-Marxist circumspection about revolutionary élitism to have been well founded. *Perestroika* is not the capitulation of socialism to capitalism, as western pundits smugly believe, but simply a sign that statist socialism has dismally failed to reach a capitalist level of economic modernization let alone more substantive socialist justice.

This book is firmly within the western-Marxist tradition. All of my work since *Western Marxism: An Introduction* (Agger, 1979a) has opposed socialist élitism. But poststructuralism vitally helps me reframe the problem of educating-the-educator in more discursive terms: *Who shall write the public texts that educate educators and how should these texts be read?* The poststructural critique of transmission theories of education (e.g., see Wexler, 1987; A. Luke, 1988) makes it clear that it is not enough to analyze power relationships between teachers and students, mediated by the state apparatus. In addition, textuality itself must be interrogated for the ways in which texts become potent language games of their own in which power is encoded and through which it is transacted. Luke's (1988) *Literacy, Textbooks and Ideology* offers a critical-theoretical analysis of textbooks, much like the one I have presented in my (1989c) reading of sociology textbooks in *Socio(onto)logy: A Disciplinary Reading*.

These studies show that reading and writing are themselves problematic practices. Education is not transmission as much as construction and conversation; it is thoroughly textual and dialogical. Thus, for educators to be educated, in the western-Marxist sense, means that people deconstruct and demystify sacred canonical texts in what I call a permanent revisionism of dialogical ethics (chapter 2). One of the best ways to humble intellectuals in order to ensure radical democracy is to deprivilege their authoritative readings of canonical texts, hence empowering lay readings. Poststructural theories of the text suggest that textuality is inherently open to readings and rewritings, thus offering powerful political correctives to epistemological versions that privilege specialist texts. In this sense, Derrida's poststructuralism and populism go hand in hand, together opening Marxism itself to deconstructive, hence democratizing, readings.

Derrida suggests that every reading changes the text. There is no univocal or unilateral text apart from the corrigible interpretive practices of readers, who come to texts with all sorts of different interests and needs. Texts exist in con-texts; they are given their sense only by having readers participate in them as full authorial partners. This is not to say, with idealism, that 'texts are what we make them'. After all, as Fish (1980) argues, one cannot bend writing into any imaginable shape, only into determinate shapes made possible by readers' fidelity to their authors' directions of meaning. But meaning 'itself' (whatever that might mean) is a constructive and deconstructive product of the dialogical interventions of readers into the sense and sentience of texts. Often texts are canonized in ways that have very little to do with their authorial constitutions; over time they have become clichés, seldom read but often quoted. This is particularly true of political texts that endure across generations and take on liturgical qualities. Marxists are especially prone to removing their favorite writings from the deconstructive ebb and flow of dialogical interventions, instead approaching these cherished texts didactically, as if one could simply teach them without really knowing them.

Political education is either a tautology or an oxymoron today. When books acquire cultic status and readers cease to read them except as catechism to be repeated among the faithful in study groups or inscribed scholastically in essays and term papers, educators cease to educate as well as to be self-educated. The left's right prospers where we allow books to write authors and readers and not the other way around. A genuinely dialogical public sphere requires that people know how to read and write. Not only must they be basically literate; they must also be capable of understanding textuality poststructurally, if not in terms of Derrida's own analytic categories then in the way that *textuality is a constructive and deconstructive process that can never be decided logocentrically*. In plainer English, one might say that we need to learn that every reading strongly contributes to a text's meaning, just as every text is a powerful argument for one or another state of affairs. Writing is not neutral, inertly lying on the page or screen. Neither print nor pixels are pieces of nature in the sense that they have meaning apart from the sweat expended to formulate and interpret them. Dialogue and discourse depend on this understanding of textuality's contingent, sometimes capricious character. In a better society we would all become readers and writers.

In the last analysis, then, my preferred dialogic society depends on public literacy, both basic and deconstructive in kind. People must learn how to engage with texts technically, a skill rapidly being lost among members of the mass-mediated generation (see Bloom, 1987; Jacoby, 1987; Agger, 1990). They must also learn to engage with texts deconstructively, *in terms of their potential for being reformulated and hence relived*. Texts are not just units of information; they are also the lives they script for readers — the lives they recommend by their own example and content. Where ideology has been dispersed into a host of meta-texts of media, culture, journalism and science, defying ready interpretation, deconstructive literacy becomes an essential radical agenda item. Without this sort of literacy, people will remain in thrall to the texts and screens of power (see T. Luke, 1989) that appear to have neither authors nor literary artifice. These are the most powerful texts of all; they are secret writing.

The challenge for a feminist postmodern critical theory is to decode these secret texts, illuminating them for all to see. This is the sort of pedagogical work that radical intellectuals can do, filling the public sphere with all sorts of deconstructive dialogues that challenge the power of writers to script our lives for us. Although this deconstructive work is not a sufficient political contribution in itself, it is a good beginning especially where detextualized texts promoting adjustment and acquiescence litter the public sphere. Today, public life is dominated by mass-mediated entertainment and state-managed knowledge that further fatalize readers, who are passive receptacles into which these encoded messages are poured. Critical intellectuals help teach public literacy where they provide people with the tools with which to deconstruct deauthored texts as secret writings. When advertising as well as academic writing seems to flow from no pen or word processor, it is that much more difficult to confront it strongly as the silent advocacy it really is. Poststructural cultural theory affords lenses through which to view these covert texts as rhetorical vehicles, promoting not only entertainment or information but a whole world-view according to which people reproduce the present with an attitude of Nietzsche's *amor fati* — the love of fate.

Textuality is a political battleground in this postmodern era of capitalism. Intellectuals need to politicize textuality in order to open texts to public argumentation, contestation and reformulation. We can write different textbooks, script better television and essay science. To do this we need to approach these cultural products as authorial outcomes. Cultural texts like these do not fall from the sky unbidden; they are produced by the culture industry and knowledge industry in order to both create surplus value and stupefy intelligence. We need to struggle in the domain of textual politics in order to reclaim politics as a valuable public activity. This book helps us locate the political in surprising discourses and practices like culture and science. Once we identify the political, we can work to reformulate it — this is the sort of critical work that radical intellectuals should do. We must redefine public life through textually empowering activities that shed disciplinary argot and instead institute a dialogical version of politics according to which arguments will be decided on the basis of reason and not coercion or deception. This is precisely the sense of Habermas' ideal speech situation, although I add poststructural and feminist discourse theories to Habermas' otherwise overly rationalist understanding of communicative action.

Critical theory must not only theorize public life; it must go public itself. Intellectuals cannot avoid the region of the political, especially where, as Foucault notes, the microphysics of politics are found squarely in the midst of the quotidian. In late capitalism nothing goes uncolonized, in Habermas' (1984, 1987b) terms. There are no worlds apart, as Adorno (1973) recognized. This can be an occasion for doom and gloom, Adorno's predominant motif. Or it can be an energizing insight, showing the work people can do in many venues of discourse and practice. Nothing is irrelevant to the emancipatory project in postmodern capitalism: every practice is inflected by the disciplinary society (see O'Neill, 1986) and, accordingly, every practice must be reformulated. The economistic prejudice of orthodox Marxists is antediluvian. As Horkheimer (1972b) understood, in late capitalism base and superstructure are not sundered but increasingly intertwined. Or as feminists like Fraser (1989) argue, the realm of the personal is political precisely because sexuality has been politicized (and politics sexualized). Textual politics is a cultural version of sexual politics; both can be understood in terms of a larger critical theory that refuses to ignore sexuality or textuality out of male-economistic biases.

Ultimately, for critical theory to go public means more than that critical theorists write accessibly. They must also conceptualize their own theoretical practice as public activity itself and hence they must view their deconstructive work as a political contribution, if initially a local one. This is precisely what the left means by education; people's minds are opened to the possibility that they can participate in their own liberation, located in the lifeworlds that matter to them. Foucault's postmodern understanding of micropolitics blends with both the Frankfurt theory of total administration/colonization and the feminist notion of the personal as political. This dialectical understanding of the interpenetration of public and private lies at the heart of my feminist postmodern critical theory of public life. We discover that the realm of the private has become intensely political whereas the realm of traditional politics has been drained of relevance.

By going public, radical intellectuals change the public sphere. They transform the definition of what *public* means. This is not to say that writing is the most important human activity or the most essential. Writing authorizes seemingly authorless texts — what I call a radical hermeneutic in chapter 3. This authorization opens the world to new formulations of itself. Textuality is not everything, but neither is it nothing. Textuality is a potent medium of ideology, especially where books are no longer found between covers or on book shelves but in the simulations (Baudrillard, 1983) and figures (Harvey, 1989) of the electronic and built environments. At a time when books exist as archaic remainders of an era of industrial-age literacy, we must search for books far beyond the libraries and bookstores. And once we find the relevant texts of the time, whether television or science, we need to rewrite them, returning to the era of public literacy when a book was a book and authors could be identified, arguments made straightforwardly, and rebutted and reason advanced.

This seems like nostalgia at a time when literacy refers to one's stock of cultural capital (Bourdieu, 1984; Hirsch, 1987). But, as I argue in chapter 7, nostalgia can have a radicalizing function where it joins a solidarity with the dead and forgotten. Although perhaps the golden age of reason never existed (book culture being restricted to a tiny élite for most of world history), that is no reason to abjure reason in favor of the various fads and fetishes of the postmodern. As I argue in my concluding chapter, relativism is no more a viable political theory or strategy than it ever was. The relativity of values demonstrated by poststructuralism is no cause for celebration. Rather, deconstruction must lead to new constructions of the humane and the just. That is precisely the role for critical theory formulated in the great tradition of high-European intellectuals like Adorno and Marcuse.

This is not an endorsement of their mandarinism, either. The Frankfurt disdain for popular culture needs to be corrected, as I argue in my forthcoming *Cultural Studies as Critical Theory* (1991a). The popular does not exhaust populism — simply the belief that the people are important. Critical theory can theoretically and methodologically inform a cultural studies that attempts to plumb the popular both for symptoms of domination and for resonances of resistance and creativity. There can be no democracy without publicity. By the same token, publicity is insufficient in its own right; accessibility is not a sufficient epistemological criterion. The dilemma of educating educators remains unresolved; formulaic entreaties for plain language or passionate politics only reinforce thoughtlessness. Critical theory in trying to restore the public sphere must not renounce its theoreticity. The world is complex and must be theorized complexly. The postmodern aversion to theory is symptomatic of a stupid age. This is not to say that theorists should constitute a new vanguard but only to note that the attack on mandarinism and élitism must be tempered by the recognition that we have a very long way to go before we can use a genuinely critical public discourse unproblematically.

Theory and publicity are antonyms today. This can change if theory does its job well. A new public life can be created out of the ashes of the old, but this will not be easy. Political education cannot be accomplished by injection or indoctrination. The only genuine education is self-education, which sparks self-emancipation. This book challenges certain taken-for-granted assumptions about knowledge, discourse and politics today. Although I seek to stimulate self-education in readers, I do not cease to educate myself. We are all readers: I reread this book from the same perspective as readers who did not write the chapters with their own hands. In doing so, I realize that I could have said some things differently, perhaps more publicly.

Nevertheless, this book represents me well, in both its strengths and silences. Readers, too, are responsible for the sense of texts. Reading is work; it requires one to make changes in one's life — fetching a dictionary, rethinking cant, questioning one's values. These personal changes are precisely where social change begins.

# PART 1
# The Literary Production of Discipline

# Chapter 1

# Critical Theory, Poststructuralism, Postmodernism[1]

## Introduction: A Critical Theory of Public Life

This book has been crafted to move scholarship on critical social theory from the realm of explication and interpretation toward practical diagnoses of real social problems. As such, it moves critical theory into its third generation, extending the founding work of Adorno, Horkheimer and Marcuse and then the communication-theoretic revisions of Habermas. This third generation of critical theory is characterized by an active engagement with poststructuralism and postmodernism as well as with a feminist version of postmodernism. In this chapter, I introduce the contributions of these theoretical schools to an integrated critical theory of public life. Just as the founders of the Frankfurt School in the 1930s reinvigorated a stale Marxian orthodoxy with categories and research findings from outside of Marxism proper, here I rejuvenate critical theory with theoretical and empirical developments from a host of different sources heretofore deemed off limits to leftists. Only in this way can critical theory develop a coherent perspective on the problems and possibilities of public life near the beginning of the twenty-first century.

This opening chapter will prove useful to those who are relatively unfamiliar with critical theory and with some of the other theoretical perspectives discussed in this book. This chapter not only explains the main theoretical contributions of critical theory, poststructuralism and postmodernism but it also develops the sociological and political relevance of these perspectives in a concrete way. As such, this book can be read profitably by people without backgrounds in social theory but who are interested in a broader theoretical understanding of public life today. This introductory chapter is followed by two other essays that together develop a version of critical theory indebted to feminism, postmodernism and poststructuralism. These opening essays make way for the more concrete treatments of discourse and politics that follow in chapters 4 through 10. In chapters 4 and 5 I address the textual politics of disciplinary knowledge and discourse housed in the university. I argue that there are powerful forces inimical to critical literacy and social problem-solving in the modern university, including the academic division of labor and technical writing in the social sciences. In chapters 6 through 10 I extend critical theory's insights to key social problems of modernity, making good on my claim here that a conjoined feminist postmodern critical theory can do powerful empirical work in addressing social problems of late capitalism unforeseen by Marx.

### Sociology Meets German Critical Theory and New French Theory

Critical theory, poststructuralism and postmodernism are intellectual traditions most familiar to people who work in philosophy, aesthetic theory, literary criticism and women's studies. Yet a number of American sociologists are beginning to show productive familiarity with the three theoretical schools discussed in this paper (e.g., Lemert, 1980; Lemert and Gillan, 1982; Gottdiener, 1985; Gottdiener and Lagopoulos, 1986; Denzin, 1986, 1989, 1990, 1991; Brown, 1987; Richardson, 1988, 1990a, 1990b, 1990c, 1991; Agger, 1989a, 1989b, 1989c, 1990, 1991a, 1991b, 1991c, 1992; Hazelrigg, 1989; Antonio and Kellner, 1991). Outside of sociology, the interpretive literature on critical theory, poststructuralism and postmodernism is huge and growing (e.g., Jay, 1973, 1984a, 1984b; Eagleton, 1976, 1983, 1985; Held, 1980; Schoolman, 1980; Culler, 1982; Weedon, 1987; Aronowitz, 1988, 1990; Harvey, 1989; T. Luke, 1989, 1990; Best and Kellner, 1990). Any humanities-oriented bookstore is bursting with exegetical volumes on Derrida's deconstruction, the Frankfurt School, poststructural-feminist film criticism, French feminism and cultural studies. Derrida has become virtually a discipline in his own right, not least because he writes so densely and allusively (also because of his enormous intellectual charisma; Lamont (1987) has addressed the phenomenon of Derridean deconstruction sociologically).

I begin this book with a general introduction to critical theory, poststructuralism and postmodernism because these traditions orient many of the more substantive chapters that follow. This opening chapter introduces these three perspectives for theoretical newcomers, presenting their main arguments succinctly. In the following chapter, I introduce the contributions of feminism to this emerging synthesis. I also suggest some substantive applications of these perspectives in the realms of sociological and policy analysis, keeping with the general theme of this book as outlined in my introductory chapter. In addition, I make an argument for the compatibility (if not outright identity) of these perspectives, thus advancing my attempt to update critical theory, which was originally formulated in the 1920s and 1930s in response to a much more rudimentary stage of capitalism. As I see it, poststructuralism and postmodernism supplement critical theory with a variety of theoretical insights into the nature of the politics of discourse that emerge concretely in new research possibilities. This opening chapter is an argument for theoretical synthesis as much as anything else. This synthesis is not an eclectic combination of these three perspectives but an attempt to politicize the insights of Derrida, Foucault and Baudrillard in accord with the general critical program of the Frankfurt School, the broad outline of which I retain in my own attempt to develop a critical theory of public life.

Although the three theories discussed in this opening chapter are inherently and sometimes vigorously political, they are often ignored by empiricists not because they are leftist (after all, a good deal of the mainstream stratification and gender work published in *American Sociological Review* is vaguely leftish) but because they are incredibly, extravagantly convoluted — to the point of disastrous absurdity one would think, if reading Derrida's (1987) *Glas* or Lyotard's (1989) *The Differend* (no typographical error that!). One cannot help but wonder why these theorists do not write more clearly and in ways that show the empirical (political, cultural, existential) relevance of their work more directly. I intend this chapter largely as translation, explication and application. As I will argue below, the three theories are most relevant *for the methodological and empirical work they can do*, even if this is buried deep beneath the surface of some of these writings.

I begin by developing the main ideas of each of the three theories. I then summarize the relevance of these ideas for methodology, research and concept formation in mainstream sociology. Above all, critical theory, poststructuralism and postmodernism are effective as *critiques of positivism* (Stockman, 1984), interrogating taken-for-granted assumptions about the ways in which people write and read science. They also make potentially useful substantive contributions, as I discuss. Although most American sociologists are not wedded to positivist doctrine, the research and writing they do tend to embody the central positivist tenet that it is possible to reflect the world presuppositionlessly, without intruding philosophical and theoretical assumptions into one's work. All three theoretical perspectives discussed here reject presuppositionless representation, arguing explicitly that such representation is both politically undesirable and philosophically impossible.

Although all three theories mount an exhaustive frontal attack on positivism, they hold open the possibility of an empirical social science, albeit one that operates with decidedly non-positivist assumptions (see Diesing, 1991). Although neither poststructuralism nor postmodernism has produced a concrete version of this social science, the German critical theorists, during the exodus of the Frankfurt School in the US during and just after World War II (see Adorno,

1969; Arato and Gebhardt, 1978), did important empirical studies that adapted critical theory to the project of empirical social science, including but not limited to Adorno *et al.*'s (1950) study of the authoritarian personality (also see Adorno, 1945, 1954, 1974b). This work anticipates subsequent applications and adaptations of these three theories to mainstream sociology.

## Critical Theory: Main Ideas

Critical theory is associated with the Institute for Social Research, established in Germany in 1923 and staffed by Theodor W. Adorno, Max Horkheimer, Herbert Marcuse, Friedrich Pollock, Leo Lowenthal and Walter Benjamin (see Jay, 1973; Hughes, 1975; Kellner, 1989b). The most important recent representative of critical theory is Jürgen Habermas, Adorno and Horkheimer's student, who departed significantly from certain positions of the founders (see Habermas, 1970a, 1970b, 1971, 1973, 1975, 1979, 1981a, 1981b, 1984, 1987a, 1987b). For representative studies of the origins and meaning of critical theory, see Jay, 1973; Agger, 1979a; Connerton, 1980; Kellner, 1989b). Also see Slater (1977), who offers an orthodox-Marxist appraisal of the Frankfurt School.

Critical theory as developed by the original Frankfurt School attempted to explain why the socialist revolution prophesied by Marx in the mid-nineteenth century did not occur as expected. Marcuse, Adorno and Horkheimer felt that they had to reconstruct the logic and method of Marxism in order to develop a Marxism relevant to emerging twentieth-century capitalism. They did not believe that they were recanting Marx's basic understanding of capitalism as a self-contradictory social system (e.g., see Horkheimer's 1937 (1972b) essay on this issue, 'Traditional and Critical Theory', in which he spelled out the basic parameters of critical theory). In particular, the Frankfurt School theorists, following the Hungarian Marxist Georg Lukács (1971), attempted to link economic with cultural and ideological analysis in explaining why the revolution expected by Marx did not occur. Like Lukács (who used the term *reification* to refer to deepened alienation in an emerging 'late' capitalism), the Frankfurt theorists believed that Marx underestimated the extent to which workers' (and others') false consciousness could be exploited to keep the social and economic system running smoothly. Although Lukács and the Frankfurt thinkers agreed with Marx that capitalism over time develops internal economic irrationalities (e.g., the concentration and centralization of productive wealth at the expense of workers who are thrown out of work as a result and thus cannot consume the commodities that their labor produces), they felt that capitalism in the twentieth century was beginning to develop effective coping mechanisms allowing it to forestall the cataclysmic eruption of these periodic crises into a wholesale socialist revolution.

In particular, capitalism deepens false consciousness, suggesting to people that the existing social system is both inevitable and rational. Marx (n.d.: pp. 76–88) already provided for the possibility of false consciousness in his famous analysis of commodity fetishism in volume one of *Capital*. According to him, commodity fetishism (typically misunderstood to mean people's obsession with commodity consumption — consumerism) refers to the way in which the labor process is mystified, appearing not to be a purposeful construction of willful human beings. The particular character of false consciousness in a society founded on commodity fetishism — capitalism — is the inability to experience and recognize social relations as historical accomplishments that can be transformed. Instead, people 'falsely' experience their lives as products of a certain unchangeable social nature.

The deepening of commodity fetishism leads to what Lukács called reification and the Frankfurt theorists *domination*. Domination in Frankfurt terminology is a combination of external exploitation (e.g., the extraction of workers' surplus value, explored exhaustively in *Capital*) and internal self-disciplining that allows external exploitation to go unchecked. In sociological terms, people internalize certain values and norms that induce them to participate effectively in the division of productive and reproductive labor. Classical non-Marxist social theory (Comte, Durkheim, Weber, Parsons and now the neo-Parsonians) explores what Parsons (1937; see O'Neill, 1972a) called the Hobbesian problem of order: why do people obey in organized industrial societies? The Durkheimian-Weberian-Parsonian answer is that people obey because they share certain common values and beliefs (e.g., Durkheim's *collective consciousness*) that explain the world to them in a rational way. In particular, people believe that they can achieve modest personal betterment by complying with social norms but that large-scale social changes beyond this are impossible.

The Frankfurt thinkers argued that these common values inculcating obedience and discipline contradict people's objective interest in liberation. These values function ideologically to foreshorten people's imagination of what is really possible in an advanced technological society. Marcuse (1955) argues that domination must be redoubled in late capitalism in order to divert people from the increasingly realistic prospect of an end to scarcity and hence toil. What he (Marcuse, 1955: pp. 32–4) calls *surplus repression* imposes discipline from the inside, inducing people to keep their noses to the grindstone, have families and engage in busy consumerism. People are taught to fulfill their needs through *repressive desublimation*, exchanging substantive socio-political and economic liberties for the 'freedoms' of consumer choice so abundant today (see Marcuse, 1964: pp. 4–6).

The Frankfurt thinkers explained the surprising survival of capitalism in terms of deepened ideologies — domination, in Frankfurt terms. In particular, they target *positivism* as the most effective new form of capitalist ideology. In the 1940s Horkheimer and Adorno (1972) in *Dialectic of Enlightenment* trace this new ideology all the way back to the Enlightenment. Although they support the Enlightenment's effort to demystify religion and mythology, the particular model of enlightenment grounded in positive science was insufficient to banish mythology once and for all. They argue instead that the positivist theory of science has become a new mythology and ideology in the sense that it fails to understand its own investment in the *status quo*. But they do more than contest positivism as a theory of scientific investigation; they argue that positivism has become the most dominant form of ideology in late capitalism in the sense that people everywhere are taught to accept the world 'as it is', thus unthinkingly perpetuating it.

Horkheimer and Adorno, like Marcuse (1964), reject positivism as a worldview of adjustment. Positivism suggests that one can perceive the world without making assumptions about the nature of the phenomena under investigation. Its notion that knowledge can simply reflect the world leads to the uncritical identification of reality and rationality. One experiences the world as rational and necessary, thus deflating attempts to change it. Instead, the critical theorists attempt to develop a mode of consciousness and cognition that breaks the identity of reality and rationality, viewing social facts not as inevitable constraints on human freedom (as they were for Durkheim [1950: pp. 1–13] — social facts) but as pieces of history that can be changed. Dialectical imagination (Jay, 1973) is the ability to view the world in terms of its potential for being changed in the future, a hard-won ability in a world that promotes positivist habits of mind acquiescing to the *status quo*.

Positivism functions ideologically where it reinforces passivity and fatalism. Critical theory targets positivism both on the level of everyday life and in social theories that reduce the social world to patterns of cause and effect. In this sense, a good deal of bourgeois social science comes under sharp attack by the Frankfurt School (e.g., Institute for Social Research, 1972) for lacking the sort of dialectical imagination enabling social scientists to look beyond the appearance of given social facts toward (and as a way of achieving) new social facts — the end of class society, patriarchy, racism and the domination of nature. Even Marxism has become too positivist, according to the Frankfurt School, where it has portrayed the downfall of capitalism as inevitable according to what Marx called economic 'laws of motion'. Whether Marx himself was a positivist is difficult to establish, given the range of his expressions on epistemology (e.g., Marx, 1961). Very much a child of the Enlightenment, Marx suggested that science could conquer uncertainty and thus bring about a better world. What is also clear is that Marxists after Marx (especially those who dominated the Second and Third, or Communist, Internationals) reconstructed Marx's more dialectical social theory along the lines of positivist materialism (see Lichtheim, 1961; Agger, 1979a). This began with Marx's close collaborator, Friedrich Engels (1935), who inaugurated a tradition that gathered momentum (see Lenin, 1952 and Stalin, 1940) until the death of Stalin and until Marxists in the west had access to Marx's (1961) early *Economic and Philosophic Manuscripts* (see Marcuse, 1973) in which he more fully articulated a non-determinist historical materialism.

Frankfurt critical theory positioned itself against positivism of all kinds, notably the Marxist variety. For his part, Habermas (1971), more decisively than his earlier Frankfurt colleagues, found positivism writ large in Marx's own *oeuvre*. Habermas argued that Marx failed to distinguish carefully enough between knowledge gained from causal analysis and knowledge gained from self-reflection and interaction. As a result, Marxism has not been able to secure an adequate ground in voluntarism, instead falling back on the fatalism of positivist determinism. Habermas disagrees with Horkheimer, Adorno and Marcuse over whether Marx was actually an opponent of positivism himself. As a result, he argues, we must work even harder to reconstruct Marx's historical materialism in a way that gives more credence than Marx did to the categorical difference between knowledge gained from self-reflection and knowledge gained from causal analysis and technique. For Habermas, this reconstructed historical materialism has taken the form of his (1984, 1987b) communication theory, in which he attempts to shift critical social theory, like all western philosophy, from what he calls the paradigm of consciousness to the paradigm of communication, thus enabling workable strategies of ideology-critique, community building and social-movement formation to be developed.

Habermas' reconstruction of critical theory has been especially compelling for critical social theorists because he has mastered and integrated a wide range of theoretical and empirical insights, all the way from traditional Marxism and psychoanalysis to Parsonian functionalism and speech-act theory (see McCarthy, 1978). Habermas has helped legitimize German critical theory in the university through his enormous erudition as well as his willingness to engage with diverse theoretical and political traditions (where his earlier Frankfurt cohorts were much more dismissive of bourgeois philosophy and social science for their accommodationism). Some (Agger, 1976b; but see Wellmer, 1976; Benhabib, 1987) argue that Habermas has seriously truncated the emancipatory agenda by drawing a heavy line between self-reflection/communication and causality/technical rationality, an issue to which I return in chapter 8. One upshot of Habermas' categorical distinction has been to limit agendas of social change to the realm of self-reflection/communication, in which people rationally discuss alternative social policies and attempt to build consensuses about them. His Frankfurt colleagues, like early Marx, wanted to change not only deliberative policy processes but also the social organization of science and technology. Habermas (1971) rejects Marcuse, Adorno and Horkheimer's view that we can change not only social policy but our whole technological interaction with nature. He (Habermas, 1971: pp. 32–3) calls this view 'a heritage of mysticism'. His resulting critical communication theory is closer to the parliamentary social democracy of Eduard Bernstein (1961) and, later, the Scandinavians, than it is to traditional Marxist concepts of class struggle.

That is not a sufficient reason in itself to reject Habermas' reconstruction of historical materialism, especially at a time when orthodox-Marxist certainties about the inevitability of socialism's triumph over capitalism are being severely tested. One might reasonably respond that Soviet statism since Lenin (1973, n.d.) never resembled the mature socialism or communism advocated by Marx. And one might also acknowledge that Habermas' (1981b) 'new social movements' theory is a fruitful empirical as well as political contribution to an ossified Marxism that excludes consideration of aspects of domination typically ignored by the white male left, notably domination based on sex and race. This is also a potentially significant substantive contribution to sociology, along with the other Frankfurt contributions in the realms of state theory and cultural analysis.

Critical theory's most lasting methodological contribution to social science is the way it attunes empirical social researchers to the assumptions underlying their own busy empiricism. Sometimes, as Horkheimer and Adorno (1972) indicate in *Dialectic of Enlightenment*, the seeming avoidance of values is the strongest value commitment of all, exempting one's empirical claims from rigorous self-reflection and self-criticism. It is in this sense that the Frankfurt School's analysis of mythology and ideology can be applied to a positivist social science that purports to transcend myth and value but, in its own methodological obsessions, is mythological to the very core.

## Poststructuralism: Main Ideas

A brief discussion of the main ideas of poststructuralism assumes that we can cleanly separate poststructuralism from postmodernism. Unfortunately, we cannot. Primers (e.g., Culler, 1982; Sarup, 1989; Best and Kellner, 1990) on the subject(s) cut the theoretical pie in any number of ways: although most agree that Derrida is a poststructuralist (even though he does not identify himself as such), Foucault, Barthes and Lyotard can be claimed by either camp and often are. And the French feminists (Kristeva, 1980; Irigaray, 1985; Cixous, 1986) are sometimes viewed as proponents of poststructuralism (e.g.,

Weedon, 1987). The lack of clear definition reflects the purposeful elusiveness of work that can be variously classified as poststructural and/or postmodern. Perhaps the most important hallmark of all this work is its aversion to clean positivist definitions and categories. For Derrida (1976, 1978, 1981, 1987), the leading poststructural writer, every definition 'deconstructs' itself — that is, it tends to unravel when one probes deeper into its foundational assumptions and literary gestures (but see Fraser, 1984).

There is substantial overlap between poststructuralism and post-modernism. Although here I distinguish poststructuralism and post-modernism, throughout the rest of this book I generally use the term postmodernism to include poststructuralism, in line with Best and Kellner's (1990) argument that poststructuralism is a subspecies of postmodern theory that relates specifically to language, writing and knowledge. For my purposes here, poststructuralism (Derrida, the French feminists) is a theory of textuality and knowledge, whereas postmodernism (Foucault, Barthes, Lyotard, Baudrillard) is a theory of society, culture and history. Derrida's influence in the realms of literary criticism, literary theory and cultural analysis has been sub-stantial (A. Berman, 1988). Literary critics prise out of Derrida a methodology of textual reading called *deconstruction* (Culler, 1982). This deconstructive method has spread like wildfire through American humanities departments, offering a serious challenge to traditional literary and cultural criticism dominated by textual objectivism (e.g., see Ransom, 1941 on the New Criticism; also see Fekete, 1978 and Lentricchia, 1980).

Although Derrida does not elaborate a single deconstructive method, refusing programmatism in favor of his own exemplary literary, cultural and philosophical readings, it is easy to see that literary deconstruction challenges traditional assumptions about how we read and write (Fischer, 1985). Indeed, some of these deconstruc-tive insights have begun to fertilize social-science disciplines (e.g., in anthropology Marcus and Fischer, 1986; in sociology Lemert, 1980; Brown, 1987; Agger, 1989c), especially with regard to the examina-tion of cultural works and practices. I have argued for a blending of poststructuralism and critical theory that trades heavily on Derrida's model of textual analysis (see Callinicos, 1985; Agger, 1989a; Poster, 1989). Derrida's insights into reading and writing disqualify the posi-tivist model of a researcher who simply reflects the world 'out there', suggesting new ways of writing and reading science.

Derrida insists that every text is *undecidable* in the sense that it conceals conflicts within it between different authorial voices (some-times termed the text and subtext/s). Every text is a contested terrain in the sense that what it appears to 'say' on the surface cannot be understood without reference to the concealments and contextualiza-tions of meaning going on simultaneously to mark the text's signi-ficance (e.g., the use of specialized jargon). These concealments and contextualizations might be viewed as the assumptions that every text makes in presuming that it will be understood. But these assumptions are suppressed and thus the reader's attention is diverted from them. A sociological example is pertinent here: where Blau-Duncan (Blau and Duncan, 1978) generation status-attainment researchers defined mobility with respect to one's father's occupational status, a deconstructive reading would reveal the profound assumptions about the gendered nature of work as well as about male supremacy that underlie this methodological choice. More recent feminist scholars (e.g., Bose, 1985) challenge the operationalization of occupational status in terms of father's occupation because, they argue, this represents a powerfully ideologizing subtext that (a) leads people to think that only men work, or should work, and (b) misrepresents reality where, in fact, women work outside the home for wages.

Feminist deconstruction of this aspect of status-attainment work shows, in Derrida's terms, that the operationalization of occupational status is 'undecidable' in the sense that it engages in certain exclusions that imperil its own claim to fixed and final meaning. There is no univocal or unchallengeable measure of occupational status; there are only competing versions, each of which is incomplete because it engages in certain exclusions. For Derrida, deconstructive reading prises open inevitable, unavoidable gaps of meaning that readers fill with their own interpolative sense. In this way, reading is a strong activity, not merely passive reflection of an objective text with singular meaning. Readers help give writing its sense by filling in these gaps and conflicts of meaning, even becoming writers themselves and hence challenging the hierarchy of writing over reading, cultural production over cultural reception.

Derrida's concept of undecidability rests on his notions of *difference* and *differance*. Essentially, he argues that it is in the nature of language to produce meaning only with reference to other meanings against which it takes on its own significance. Thus, we can never establish stable meanings by attempting correspondence between language and the world addressed by language. Instead, meaning is a result of the differential significances that we attach to words. Thus, for example, Weber's notion of 'status' acquires meaning with reference to his concept of 'class', not in terms of a fixed reality that his word 'status' supposedly reflects. Derrida plays on the French word *differance* to show that one cannot hope to arrive at a fixed or transparent meaning as long as one uses a necessarily deferring as well as differing language. Every definition and clarification needs to be defined and clarified in turn; meaning always lies elusively in the future.

Word choice cannot do our thinking for us, nor solve major intellectual controversies. One is fated to improve on the undecidability (and sometimes sheer muddleheadedness) of language *through* more language, which creates its own problems of difference/differance and thus occasions its own deconstruction (see Coward and Ellis, 1977). Although (Agger, 1989c: pp. 335–44) the best writing anticipates and acknowledges its own undecidability forthrightly, refusing the positivist pretense of transparency once and for all, Derrida is not particularly concerned to strategize about how to write better (or, in the case of social science, to do better empirical work). He is more concerned to puncture the balloon of those who believe that language is simply a technical device for establishing singular, stable meanings instead of the deeply constitutional act that it is. In itself, this powerfully demystifies positivism by calling attention to positivism's own imbeddedness in language (and, in the case of science, method). There is no royal road to meaning except through the meaning–constitutive practices of language that, in turn, provoke new confusions, contradictions and conflicts. Derrida can be read as a gloomy relativist where he seems to despair of the possibility of enlightenment. He believes that we are destined to remain locked up in the prison house of language, as Nietzsche called it (see Jameson, 1972). But the fact that Derrida bothers to write at all shows his conviction that language can be clarified, even if we do this playfully, allusively and ironically.

Derrida (e.g., 1976) would defend his own density by arguing that difficulty educates. He would also say that simplicity brings false clarity, suppressing the difficulties of making oneself clear that are intrinsic to language's undecidability. In this sense, Derrida joins the Frankfurt School's attack on positivism, albeit from a particularly linguistic and literary direction. Where the Frankfurt School argued that positivism wrongly exempts itself from its own critique of mythology and ideology (value-freedom being a value stance, after all), Derrida shows how this works on the level of rhetoric. One can read his *oeuvre* as a rhetorical analysis of what he calls the philosophy of presence (another name for positivism; see Hartman, 1981). He shows how the process of differing/deferring works on the page, and underneath it, just as he also suggests his own work as an example of genuinely deconstructive reading that subverts the false simplicity and closure claimed by positivists.

Derrida's relevance to social science is potentially enormous (Agger, 1989c). His poststructural notions of literary criticism suggest ways of reading and reformulating the densely technical and methodological discourses of the empirical social sciences. Must methodology mystify way out of proportion to its intellectual accomplishments as well as intrinsic difficulty? A Derridean would not only crack the code of densely technical and figural work characteristic of quantitative social science but would, in this, exemplify a more accessible mode of reading and writing. Methodology can be read as rhetoric, encoding certain assumptions and values about the social world. Deconstruction refuses to view methodology simply as a set of technical procedures with which to manipulate data. Rather, methodology can be opened up to readers intrigued by its deep assumptions and its empirical findings but otherwise daunted by its densely technical and figural nature.

To put this generically, deconstruction can help reveal the values and interests suppressed far beneath the surface of science. This politicizes and democratizes science by opening its text to outsiders, allowing them to engage with science's surface rhetoric more capably as well as to contest science's deep assumptions where necessary (e.g., in the case of my previous example about how to operationalize occupational status). Science written from the perspective of deconstruction avoids overreliance on technical and figural gestures, instead continually raising its assumptions to full view and thus inviting readers to join or challenge them. Of course, a deconstructive science text will never solve all problems of opacity and undecidability. Science no more than fiction can attain absolute truth, no matter how reflexive it is about its own values, assumptions and methodological choices; every deconstruction can be deconstructed.

Poststructuralism helps science readers and writers recognize their own literary involvements and investments in the text of science. No matter how seemingly insignificant, every rhetorical gesture of the text contributes to its overall meaning. How we arrange our footnotes, title our paper, describe our problem, establish the legitimacy of our topic through literature reviews and use the gestures of quantitative method in presenting our results all contribute to the overall sense of the text. We can learn to read these gestures not simply as embellishing 'subtext' but also as a central text in their own right, making an important contribution to the argument of science. We can also rewrite science by *authorizing* these seemingly marginal gestures, turning them into the discursive arguments they really are. Poststructuralism calls into question a variety of literary norms of empirical science, suggesting that we read science not as a mirror of the world but as a strong, imaginative, sometimes duplicitous literary intervention in its own right. Methodology tells a story in spite of itself; it can be read rhetorically and hence rewritten in less technically compulsive ways, both affording greater access and raising its encoded assumptions to view (see Richardson, 1990c).

For the most part, poststructuralists have concentrated on literary and cultural texts (although, as I am arguing, there is no necessary reason for doing so, given the susceptibility of science to deconstructive analysis). Derrida is averse to science because science almost always claims an exemption from the rule of undecidability; he equates positivism with all empirical science. There is a certain prejudice against science on the part of deconstructors, who reject all objective analysis and not only the falsely presuppositional objectivism of positivism. This had made it somewhat difficult (if not impossible) for sociologists to recognize the potential sociological contributions of deconstruction.

## Postmodernism: Main Ideas

More than Derrida's poststructuralism, postmodernism, especially in the work of Foucault (1970, 1976, 1977, 1978, 1980), makes evident connections with mainstream social science, particularly in the realms of cultural and discourse analysis, the sociology of social control and the study of sexuality. I will discuss these contributions after I clarify some of the general tenets of postmodernism.

Although postmodernism arguably arose as an architectural movement (see Portoghesi, 1983; Jencks, 1987) the most explicit philosophical postmodernist is Lyotard. His (1984) *The Postmodern Condition: A Report on Knowledge* represents the core of postmodern thinking on central issues of modernity and postmodernity (also see Newman, 1985; Huyssen, 1986; Hassan, 1987; Featherstone, 1988; Klinkowitz, 1988; Harvey, 1989; Sarup, 1989; Best and Kellner, 1990; Turner, 1990). Lyotard rejects totalizing perspectives on history and society, what he calls *grand narratives* like Marxism that attempt to explain the world in terms of patterned interrelationships. His postmodernism is an explicit rejection of the totalizing tendencies as well as political radicalism of Marxism. Like most postmodernists, Lyotard suspects Marxists of self-aggrandizing motives. He maintains that one cannot tell large stories about the world but only small stories from the heterogeneous 'subject positions' of individuals and plural social groups. Jameson (1972, 1976–77, 1981, 1984a; see Dowling, 1984), an important literary theorist who examines postmodernism through neo-Marxist lenses, suggests that postmodernism ('the cultural logic of late capitalism') is fundamentally conservative (Jameson, 1984b); Habermas (1981a, 1987a) argues that postmodernism is neoconservative (also see Raulet, 1984; Wolin, 1984). I (Agger, 1990) have split postmodernism into apologetic and critical versions, extending the angry modernist impulse of certain postmodernisms (e.g., Huyssen, 1986) toward a merger with critical theory. Typifying the majority of American affiliates of postmodernism, Kroker and Cook (1986) attempt to depoliticize postmodernism, viewing it simply as a cultural movement (or 'scene'; see Gitlin, 1988).

A postmodern social theory (see Benhabib, 1984; Kellner, 1988) would examine the social world from the multiple perspectives of class, race, gender and other identifying group affiliations. At the same time, this social theory would refuse the totalizing claims of grand narratives like Marxism that attempt to identify axial structural principles explaining all manner of disparate social phenomena (e.g., Marx's theory of the logic of capital). Postmodernism is anti-reductionist and pluralist, both in its causal priorities and in its politics, which are more liberal than radical (see Arac, 1986). Postmodernism mistrusts radicals and radicalism, preferring the decentered knowledges available not only to a central knowledge commissar but also to people who engage with the world from the irreducible perspectives of their own experience.

Foucault (1976, 1980) insists that knowledge must be traced to different *discourse/practices* that frame the knowledge formulated from within them. Sociologists of science will recognize Foucault's view of discourse/practice as a version of Kuhn's (1970) paradigm notion, although Foucault makes more use of everyday experience and ordinary language with which to define the parameters of these paradigmatic knowledges. Foucault has made direct empirical contributions to social science where he has studied the discourse/practices of prisons (1977) and sexuality (1978), offering rich and varied accounts of how these modes of knowledge and practice were constituted historically by way of the discourses through which they were problematized. Although clearly influenced by Marxism, Foucault rejects Marxist class analysis for its simple dualities (see Poster, 1989; but see Dews, 1984, 1987 and Fraser, 1989). Instead, he argues that potential power is to be found everywhere, in the lot of the disenfranchised as well as with the wealthy (see O'Neill, 1986).

Like poststructuralism, postmodernism is profoundly mistrustful of social sciences that conceal their own investment in a particular view of the world. Like poststructuralism and critical theory, postmodernism rejects the possibility of presuppositionless representation, instead arguing that every knowledge is contextualized by its historical and cultural nature. At some level, a universal social science is judged impossible because people's and groups' different subject positions cannot be measured against each other: for example, there is no way to adjudicate the issue of who is more oppressed — women or people of color. Instead, it is important to recognize how their differential experiences of the world are framed by the discourse/practices constituting the experience of being a woman or a person of color at a given historical moment. Social science becomes an accounting of social experience from these multiple perspectives of discourse/practice, rather than a larger cumulative enterprise committed to the inference of general principles of social structure and organization.

Thus, like poststructuralism, postmodernism rejects the project of a universal social science, falling back on the particular modes of knowledge defined by the multiplicity of people's subject positions. In many respects, this is highly reminiscent of social phenomenology and ethnomethodology (e.g., Schutz, 1967; O'Neill, 1974), both of which emphasize the irreducibility of experience and reject social-structural analysis. This should not be surprising because postmodernism, phenomenology and ethnomethodology emerge from some of the same sources, notably the philosophies of Nietzsche and Heidegger, both of whom rejected the Enlightenment's attempt to create a universal knowledge. Although phenomenology and ethnomethodology are more methodologically inclined than postmodernism,

Foucault clearly converges with Garfinkel (1967) and others (e.g., Cicourel, 1973; Douglas, 1981) in his tradition (see Mehan and Wood, 1975). Their main difference is that ethnomethodology, unlike post-modernism, affiliated itself to the disciplinary project of sociology during and after the 1960s. Postmodernism remains a largely French perspective on cultural and historical analysis that bears little explicit relationship to French or American sociology.

But while postmodernists tend to reject the project of science, a postmodern social science is possible, especially if one extrapolates creatively from the work of Barthes (1970, 1974, 1975) who, like Foucault, suggests new ways to view the socio-cultural world. For example, he (1975: p. 92) argues that 'the city is a discourse', suggest-ing that by reading the city we can do useful social science, albeit of a type barely recognizable to positivist urban sociologists. Gottdiener (1991) and Gottdiener and Lagopoulos (1986) further develop a post-modern semiotics of urban life, showing the relevance of the post-modern project to empirical social science. (As I will discuss later, Gottdiener's postmodern sociology has drawn fire from establishment sociologists who judge the contribution of French theory to be scanty.)

After Lyotard, Foucault and Barthes, the fourth major post-modernist thinker is Baudrillard (1975, 1981, 1983), who offers the most sociological version of postmodernism to date (see Kellner, 1989a). In his early analysis of late capitalism, Baudrillard (1975, 1981) suggests that in a consumer society commodities acquire a certain *sign value* that people covet. Instead of consuming designer-labeled com-modities for their use values (Guess jeans functioning as clothes and Honda cars as transportation), people buy them for their sign value, a notion akin to Weber and Veblen's notions of status value, albeit grounded in a dense semiotic theory that builds on the work of Saussure (1960) and Eco (1979). In later work, Baudrillard (e.g., 1983) suggests that reality (he calls it *hyperreality*) is increasingly *simulated* for people, constructed by powerful media and other cultural sources. People lose the ability to distinguish between these simulations and reality, a precondition of all social criticism. This analysis closely resembles the neo-Marxian Frankfurt analyses of false consciousness and suggests lines of research in the sociology of culture, media and advertising.

## Using Critical Theory, Poststructuralism and Postmodernism: Methodology, Research and Concept Formation

I have already pointed to ways in which critical theory, poststructural-ism and postmodernism are used, and can be used, by empirical sociologists. There are also important ways in which these traditions are inimical to the concept of a social science. They would transform the concept and practice of social science to an extent to which most sociologists would scarcely recognize it. Let me summarize the explicit contributions of these three theoretical perspectives to methodology, empirical research and concept formation in sociology, before I conclude by offering some cautions about these integrations.

The sociological contributions of critical theory, poststructuralism and postmodernism fall into two broad categories. They are *methodologically* relevant to the ways in which people write and read sociology (1–5, below). This mainly involves their critique of positivism. They are also relevant *substantively* in their various contributions to the study of the state, ideology, culture, discourse, social control and social movements (6–10, below).

### Methodological Implications

1 *Critical theory forces sociological empiricism to interrogate its own taken-for-granted exemption from the sullying interests of perspective, passion, polemic and politics.* As Horkheimer and Adorno (1972) argue, positive science is no less susceptible to mythification and mystification than theology. The unquestioned belief in value-freedom is no less problematic than the belief in God or spirit. The researcher is perhaps even more vulnerable to self-serving self-deception where research is conducted with an obliviousness to the powerful forces of what Habermas (1971) calls interest as these frame and form the research act as well as the interpretation of findings. This is another way of saying that social science should be reflexive, Gouldner's (1970; also see O'Neill, 1972c) term for the studied self-reflection necessary to deflate the hubris of scientists about the unquestioned superiority of their methods over the non-sciences, from literature to philosophy. As Gouldner showed (heavily influenced by the Frankfurt School), a non-reflexive sociology ignores its own contamination by political interests in preserving the *status quo* (see also Boggs, 1983).

2 *Critical theory contributes to the development of a post-positivist philosophy of science.* Although the Vienna Circle's unreconstructed logical positivism has been defunct for decades, many working methodologists in the social sciences, especially sociology, are practicing positivists, even where they have not read systematically in the positivist philosophy of science. Habermas (1971) opposes the positivist dichotomy of knowledge and interest, arguing that the most valid science recognizes its own grounding in interest, hence controlling for the muddying effect of context on one's scientific text. The Frankfurt theorists argue that positivism is not only a flawed philosophy of science but also a flawed political theory that reproduces the *status quo* by encouraging conformity with alleged social and economic laws. In this sense, the Frankfurt theorists broaden the critique of positivism

from epistemology *per se* to broader issues of political and social theory, hence overcoming the differentiation of epistemology from substantive social theory. In this sense, they help deconstruct methodology, showing that method, like the philosophy of science, is not simply a technical apparatus but a rhetorical means for concealing metaphysically and politically freighted arguments in the densely technical discourse/practice of quantitative analysis and figural gesture. Horkheimer and Adorno's (1972) argument against unthinking quantification and methodologization in the social sciences is a contribution to this deconstruction of methodology, although, as I argue below, poststructuralism offers an equally fruitful critique of methodologism by showing how method can be read and hence rewritten as a passionate, perspectival and political text in its own right.

3 *Poststructuralism completes the Frankfurt critique of science by showing that we can read all sorts of non-discursive texts as rhetoric* — arguments for a certain state of social being. By drawing attention to the subtexts of science's literary presentation (e.g., acknowledgments, citation practices, preliminary literature reviews, the use of number and figure, how discussion/conclusion sections of research articles are phrased, endnotes, footnotes and appendixes etc.), poststructuralism helps read and hence democratize science. Methodology can be cracked open and laid bare to outsiders. It can also be written differently, less technically, without sacrificing important technical detail. Unfortunately, few poststructuralists have attempted this deconstruction of methodology, preferring to concentrate their critical attention on cultural and literary texts. But this is beginning to change, as the ethnographic sociology of science (Latour and Woolgar, 1979; Knorr-Cetina, 1981; Gilbert and Mulkay, 1984) is buttressed by this poststructural underpinning in discourse analysis (Agger, 1989b; T. Luke, 1991).

4 *Poststructuralism reveals how language itself helps constitute reality* — thus offering new ways to read and write science. Its critique of presuppositionless representation — texts mirroring a world 'out there' — suggests non–positivist literary strategies for writers who deconstruct their own work and thus heighten their reflexivity. This both filters out subjective contaminants, and, where perspective cannot (and should not) be eliminated altogether, it raises an author's deep investments to full view and thus allows readers to enter dialogue with them. Habermas (1984, 1987b) argues for a universal speech situation governed by norms of dialogical equality and reciprocity wherein the goal of consensus formation guides many dehierarchizing social practices. Where writers learn how to bring their own foundational assumptions to the surface, not concealing them underneath the methodological artifice of science (which counsels dispassion as well as technical solutions to substantive problems), they enhance democracy by opening science to public debate.

Blending with critical theory, the poststructural critique of science suggests new sciences (Marcuse, 1969) that are formulated in different terms. This is not simply an argument 'for' first-person writing, as if that would solve all problems. The occasional intrusion of the author in the text may only disguise a deeper commitment to positivist representation, in which the author's voice is filtered out after initial stage-setting prolegomena. The poststructural critique of science *reauthorizes* the science text where scientists have lost their own voices. In so doing, it challenges the authority of objectivist science, interrogating the most basic assumptions of mainstream sociology, notably the view that substantive analytical problems can be solved methodologically. The poststructural critique of science leads to new writing and reading practices. Writers excavate their own, often unconscious, predilections and readers learn to do this excavation where writing is couched in hardened objectivist prose.

5 *Postmodernism rejects the view that science can be spoken in a singular universal voice* (e.g., Lyotard's [1984] critique of the grand meta-narratives of western reason). Although this risks losing the global perspective of the Enlightenment (including Marxism), it enables readers to deconstruct the universal reason of the Enlightenment as the particularistic posture of Eurocentric rationality, which contains class, race and gender biases. Postmodernism makes it possible to read universal reason as secret partisanship just as it suggests ways of detotalizing the voices of science more accurately to reflect the variety of so-called subject positions from which ordinary people can speak knowledgeably about the world.

This has the advantage of challenging singular methodologies, whether quantitative or qualitative. It would seem to argue for multiple methodologies as well as multiple class, race and gender perspectives on problems. This has the additional advantage of empowering a variety of heretofore muted speakers to join discussions about social issues, legitimating their non-credentialed interventions into the scientific field and depriviliging the mainstream positivist voice. Postmodern and poststructural ethnographers (e.g., Marcus and Fischer, 1986) are highly self-conscious about the ways in which their own narrative practices impose distorting interpretive frames on people's experience. Although this has been a perennial concern of positivist ethnographers as well, the postmodern and poststructural attention to issues of discursive politics has significantly advanced the ways in which ethnography is composed (e.g., Richardson, 1988, 1990a, 1990b, 1990c; Denzin, 1990, 1991), especially among those who link discourse theory with larger socio-political questions of colonialism and imperialism (e.g., Said, 1979).

These five methodological contributions can be summarized by saying that *critical theory, postmodernism and poststructuralism attune work-*

ing empiricists to the ways in which their own analytical and literary practices encode and conceal value positions that need to be brought to light. Although critical theory, stemming from Marxism, is decidedly the most political of these three perspectives, it is possible to forge links among critical theory, poststructuralism and postmodernism, as a number of scholars have begun to do (e.g., Ryan, 1982, 1989; Smart, 1983; Agger, 1989a, 1989c, 1990; Kellner, 1989b; Aronowitz, 1990). But even without this leftist political underpinning deriving from one or another version of neo-Marxism, the theoretical critique of the *encoding of value* affects everyone who rejects the positivist posture of value-freedom, whether from the standpoints of liberalism or radicalism.

The primary encoding of value in empiricist social science occurs through an uncritical reliance on methodology as a purely technical device for solving intellectual problems. Ironically, many empirical sociologists either ignore the philosophy of science altogether, as I noted above, or they explicitly reject positivism and claim that they are sensitive to Kuhnian concerns about framework and paradigm. Unfortunately, even a casual reading of mainstream sociology journals suggests that most empiricist sociologists privilege methodology over theory and concept formation, even if they disavow this in their methodology classes, where they expose graduate students to compulsory readings in Kuhn and other post-positivist historians, sociologists and philosophers of science. Most empirical articles published in *ASR* and *Social Forces* rely on the rituals of methodology in order to legitimate a certain form of knowledge. In these formulaic journal articles methodology is not written or read as the perspectival text it is. Instead, the technical and figural gestures of quantitative method are used to suppress the deconstructive recognition of the undecidability of the arguments/analyses being presented. Whether or not the authors of these articles talk about causality explicitly, using the vernacular of positivism, virtually all of these empirical articles deploy methodological techniques as a rhetorical device to enhance the *science aura* (Agger, 1989b: pp. 70–2) of the text in question.

The three theoretical perspectives discussed here help strip away the appearance of science's representationality in order to show the creative authorship underlying every gesture of the science text. We learn that science is a literary practice that could be done differently — more democratically and less technically. The real author underneath the leaden objectifying prose attempts to cover his or her own footprints lest the scientificity of the text come into question. Critical theory, poststructuralism and postmodernism expose science's apparent authorlessness as one possible rhetorical stance among many.

This helps demystify and democratize not only journal science but the whole institution of science, which Foucault (1977) astutely likens to the disciplining discourse/practice of the prison, in which surveillance comes from the inside as well as the outside. It also suggests new ways of writing science, exposing science's authorial artifice directly in the body of the text and not suppressing it with the apparatus of methodology. This is not an argument against method (see Feyerabend, 1975) but an argument for the literary deconstruction and reconstruction of method as a persuasive, public text in its own right. We learn to use the discourse of method where it is really integral to our arguments, which we do not cast in positivist terms of pure representation but which we recognize are undecidably subject to revision and improvement.

## Substantive Implications

6 *Critical theory suggests new ways of theorizing the role of the state and culture in advanced capitalism* (e.g., Neumann, 1942, 1957; Horkheimer, 1973; Habermas, 1975). The state today intervenes in protecting capitalism against its own contradictory nature. Capitalism outlives Marx's expectation of its demise because the state massively intervenes to alleviate economic crisis and popular culture forestalls psychic crisis (see Kellner, 1984–85, 1989b). The Frankfurt theorists contributed both theoretical and empirical analyses of state and cultural intervention, culminating in works like Horkheimer and Adorno's (1972) *Dialectic of Enlightenment*, Marcuse's (1964) *One-Dimensional Man* and Habermas' (1984, 1987b) *The Theory of Communicative Action*, probably the three most systematic statements of critical theory.

The critical theorists do not abandon Marx's analysis of the contradictory nature of the logic of capital. But Marx could not have foreseen the huge growth of the state and mass culture in late capitalism. These studies provoke important theoretical and empirical work on the state (Offe, 1984, 1985) as well as critical analyses of mass culture (Miller, 1988; T. Luke, 1989). In this sense, Frankfurt critical theory joins more traditional Marxian and neo-Marxian economic theory (e.g., O'Connor, 1973; Poulantzas, 1973) as well as the cultural-studies traditions of the Birmingham School, poststructuralism, postmodernism and feminist cultural studies (especially cinefeminism; see Agger, 1991a). Although the Frankfurt School's political economy was not as reductionist as that of more economistic neo-Marxists (e.g., Althusser, 1969) and although their approach to popular culture was more mandarin than that of other cultural-studies analysts (e.g., Marcuse, 1978; Adorno, 1984), there are important empirical and theoretical convergences here that are relevant to sociologists of culture who view culture as a structural and hence political factor in late capitalism (see Johnson, 1986–87).

7 *Foucault's postmodernism offers valuable insights to students of social control.* His *Discipline and Punish* (1977) revolutionizes the study of crime and punishment, particularly in his argument that criminology

is a discourse/practice that in a sense creates the category of criminality. This category is then imposed punitively on behaviors that formerly were viewed as socially legitimate or simply ignored as bizarre. This analysis converges with labeling theory (e.g., Goffman, 1961, 1974; Becker, 1966), although it gives labeling theory a firmer historical and political foundation. Foucault helps sociologists view deviance in terms of the experiences and meanings that construct it. But unlike labeling and social-control theories, Foucault's postmodern theory of discipline stresses the inherent resistances that people mount against their labeling and differential treatment. This is a theme that emerges very clearly in his (1978) work on *The History of Sexuality*, where he discusses ways in which women and homosexuals resist their societal disapprobation. Although Foucault is sometimes accused of having a sloppy method, he makes up for this in his extraordinarily imaginative use of historical and cultural data, which he assembles into a theory of social control that neglects neither macro-level nor micro-level phenomena.

8 *Derrida's poststructuralism and Baudrillard's postmodernism offer valuable contributions to the sociological study of discourses*, potentially enriching a wide range of sociological subfields including the sociology of mass communication and media, the sociology of knowledge and the sociology of science. Derrida's deconstructive program contributes substantively to the interpretation of cultural and linguistic forms. Using semiotic theory, Baudrillard decodes cultural images and works for their socio-political meanings. His (1981) *For a Critique of the Political Economy of the Sign* moves the Marxist theory of culture a significant step beyond orthodox-Marxist cultural and aesthetic theory, arguing that historical materialists now need to consider the relative autonomy of symbolic and cultural systems without giving up the traditional political-economic focus of Marxism. Baudrillard, like the Frankfurt School (e.g., Horkheimer and Adorno, 1972), gives cultural sociology a stronger theoretical foundation as well as critical resources with which to decode cultural simulations as false representations of reality.

Critical theory and poststructuralism both generate deconstructive readings of cultural works and practices like television (Kellner, 1981; Best and Kellner, 1988a, 1988b), journalism (Hallin, 1985; Rachlin, 1988) and advertising (Kline and Leiss, 1978; Williamson, 1978; Wernick, 1983; Ewen, 1974; Leiss, Kline and Jhally, 1986) as literary works encoding powerful authorial claims about the social world. For example, Denzin (1989) has read films in which alcoholics and alcoholism are depicted. The growing literature on poststructural literary and cultural interpretation (e.g., Mulvey, 1989) can illuminate sociological studies of cultural practice and meaning, helping reverse their sociologically reductionist tendencies by showing the interplay between expression and interpretation. In this sense, poststructuralist discourse theory could converge with non-Derridean approaches to discourse (e.g., Wuthnow, 1987) in a fruitful way.

9 *A postmodern and poststructural feminism suggests concrete empirical studies of the ways in which discourses like film are structured by gendered themes* (Kristeva, 1980; Irigaray, 1985; Cixous, 1986; Weedon, 1987; Mulvey, 1989; Walters, 1992). In particular, feminist cultural studies focuses on the different power positions of women and men as these influence writing and reading. With Lyotard, these feminisms reject the notion of a singular (male) vantage point from which knowledge and discourse are developed. They attune us empirically to the ways in which knowledge of the world is structured by discourses (e.g., pornography) that reflect conflict over power; they decode these discourses as politically salient. Richardson (1988, 1990a, 1990b, 1990c) has systematically developed the sociological implications of poststructural and postmodern feminism with respect to the ways social scientists tell their research stories. Fraser (1984, 1989) has blended critical theory, feminist theory and poststructuralism in her development of a theory of practice relevant to women as well as men.

10 *Habermas' (1981b) 'new social movements' theory offers theoretical insights to scholars of social movements who otherwise lack a larger theoretical perspective that explains where these movements come from and what sort of structural impact they might have* (see also Boggs, 1986). Finding a course between orthodox-Marxist theories of class struggle and non-Marxist perspectives on social movements, Habermas retains the Marxist vision of transformational socio-political action while significantly altering left-wing orthodoxy with respect to movements deemed irrelevant by traditional Marxists, especially movements of people of color, women, anticolonialists, antinuclearists, environmentalists, etc. Here, as in his (1975) analysis of the state's legitimation crisis, Habermas makes contact with venerable sociological concerns and places them in a larger historical-materialist framework, recouping their most radical insights in spite of themselves (e.g., his reading of Parsons in *The Theory of Communicative Action* (1987b: pp. 199–299). Unlike most sociological students of social movements (and like Foucault in this respect), Habermas locates points of resistance against systemic domination that give his overall critical social theory a certain practical intent (see Kellner, 1989b).

## What Counts as Sociology?: A Cautionary Note

For American sociology to adopt, and thus adapt to, these three theoretical perspectives would substantially change the nature of the discipline. At some level, the notions of poststructural and postmodern sociology are oxymorons. Postmodernism and poststructuralism, like critical theory, resist their integration into a highly differentiated, hierarchized, technical discipline that defines itself largely with reference to the original sociologies of Comte, Durkheim and Weber, who established the positivist study of social facts and separated the vocations of science and politics. These three theoretical perspectives question the rights of academic disciplines to exist apart, especially within the frame of positivism.

Critical theory, poststructuralism and postmodernism challenge the territoriality of sociology, including its differentiation from other disciplines in the human sciences as well as its heavy reliance on method with which to solve intellectual problems. All three perspectives oppose the mathematization of the world, even if they logically allow for mathematics as one discourse among many. This is not to privilege qualitative methodology. After all, qualitative methods can be as positivist as the quantitative kind. The poststructural critique of language casts doubt on ethnographies which rely on subjects' accounts of their own experience as if these accounts, like the accounts of experts, are not already encoded with undecidable meaning.

These three theoretical perspectives redefine the human sciences and cultural studies in ways that blur traditional disciplinary boundaries (Brodkey, 1987). They are all committed to interdisciplinarity (see Klein, 1989), deconstructing disciplinary differentiation as arbitrary. Derrida's strategy of reading emphasizes the *intertextuality* of writings that attempt to seal themselves off from the contaminating influences of other versions, other writers, other disciplines. He argues that all texts are infected and inflected by other texts to the point of genuine interdisciplinarity. In other words, these three theoretical perspectives open up the question of *what counts as sociology*.

Sociology has progressed far beyond (or regressed far behind, depending on one's perspective!) the sweeping speculation that characterized sociology in the classical tradition. This classical tradition has been enshrined as Grand Theory (see Agger, 1989b: pp. 181–6) in order to legitimate the subsequent technical discipline; witness the telling publication of an obscure Parsons paper (Parsons, 1990) as a lead article in a recent *ASR*, as well as sympathetic commentaries on it by two disciplinary luminaries (Alexander, 1990; Coleman, 1990). The Parsons article is positioned in order to add canonical value to the technical articles following it, enhancing disciplinary territoriality and identity at a time when mainstream sociology risks becoming mathematics.

The theoretical challenge to sociological territoriality posed by critical theory, poststructuralism and postmodernism is resented in some quarters. Rebutting Gottdiener (1990), Randall Collins (1990: p. 462) dismisses Foucault as a theoretical 'amateur'. Collins does not recognize that *Foucault would have loved to be called an amateur*. Foucault implies that the professional/amateur distinction is a peculiar product of the discourse/practice of late capitalism, wherein unofficial knowledges are disqualified as unrigorous, undisciplined, unprofessional. Foucault's amateurism positions itself outside of disciplinary mainstreams so that he can gain a useful vantage on them from the outside, as it were. Similarly, Habermas' encyclopedic grasp of a huge range of disciplinary literatures, from psychology and political theory to economics and sociology, threatens the narrow professionalism of disciplinary academics.

Critical theorists, poststructuralists and postmodernists rethink the prevailing definition of what counts as sociology; they would enlarge that definition considerably. In so doing, they risk losing productive disciplinary identity and a workable professional division of labor but stand to gain an enriched perspective on the literary and substantive practices of sociology. Whether or not mainstream sociology will countenance theoretical and political interrogation of the kinds provided by the three theories discussed here has yet to be determined.

In the next chapter, I further examine the convergence of Marxism, postmodernism and poststructuralism as they fertilize modern critical theory. As well, I more fully explore the contribution of feminism to critical theory than I have done in this chapter. The addition of feminist insights into the nature of social reproduction makes way for the application of critical theory to a host of issues of gender, family, sexuality, intimacy and discourse heretofore ignored by the original Frankfurt School.

### Note

1  Reproduced, with permission, from the Annual Review of Sociology, volume 17, 1991 published by Annual Reviews Inc.

# Chapter 2

# Marxism, Feminism, Deconstruction: Writing the Social

In chapter 1, I argued that critical theory, poststructuralism and post-modernism offer a combined critique of positivism as well as other substantive insights into the nature of modern society. Here, I particularly develop the contribution of a poststructural and postmodern feminism to the redevelopment of critical theory, using the critique of positivist social science as a point of departure. In this chapter, I hope to secure the legitimacy of a postmodern feminist critical theory that will be of use later in this book where I examine particular social problems heretofore ignored by critical theory.

In much of my past work, I have attempted to understand how mainstream American social science functions ideologically, beyond its ostensible surface commitment to making the world a better place to live, reflecting its liberalism if nothing else (see Agger, 1989c). Under sway of positivism, science sharply separates the alleged objectivity of its validity claims from moral sentimentality, whether evoked in images of concerned scientists protesting the military uses of technologies that they themselves invented or in terms of their vigorous electoral participation as private citizens. I am interested in this schizophrenia between science and politics as a validity claim *in its own right* or, to put this differently, I want to rethink the issue of value-freedom in the social sciences. Although I come from Marxism among other places, Marxism is too often either a theoretical cult of personality, lacking any empirical referent in an emerging capitalism, or it is simply denied any specificity by being swallowed in specialized disciplines. This problem is especially acute now that *perestroika* in the Soviet Union has further delegitimized western Marxism (Agger, 1979a). Thus, to be a Marxist today signifies one's canonical investment in a biblical reading of *Capital* along with an idolatry of various state-socialist countries and Third World political regimes that, in Susan Sontag's terms, are fascist with a human face.

This is not to begin with a tired neoconservative confession that I sinned in my youth and now come to atone, for I still believe that one cannot be a critical intellectual today without having some commerce with Marxism, whether the aesthetic theorizing and dense philosophy of Theodor Adorno or the byzantine constructs of Jürgen Habermas, not forgetting my own struggles to work through *Capital* and, even worse, Hegel's *Phenomenology of Mind*! I apply Marxism to one of the most imperious and entwining discourses of our time, the positivist behavioral sciences, exemplified particularly by American sociology. The fateful dominion of positivism in sociology at a time when even the philosophy of natural science is maturely post-positivist requires Marxism to rethink its own unreflexive claim to be a science.

So in beginning let me regress about thirty years to some of the first left criticisms of the notion of scientific value-freedom, notably from within American sociology. Indeed the books by C. Wright Mills (1959) and Alvin Gouldner (1970) that attack Parsons' celebration of Eisenhower's America only scratch the surface of what is insidiously political about a mainstream social science embracing Parsons' (1951) contention that industrial society — capitalism — is held together by the common values of patriarchy, free enterprise, Judaeo-Christianity and the work ethic. While the critique of structural functionalism, the dominant sociological theory framing most research, is certainly not wrong or ill-intended as such (Parsons metaphysically gilding the so-called iron cage that his hero, Max Weber, lamented as the rigid purposelessness of a bureaucratized society), the standard left critique of structural functionalism does not go far enough toward an adequate understanding of the politics of science. Here I read science, especially positivist social sciences like sociology, as writing that methodically suppresses its own literariness in order to provoke the enactment of a world it describes and thereby would reproduce — Marx's notion of ideology understood through Derridean lenses as a textual practice (see Jameson, 1981; Eagleton, 1983).

My basic premise is that the suppressed subtext of positivist social science aims secretly to reproduce the supposedly nature-like necessity of the extant social order by reflecting it in a text that intends to be enacted by disempowered, hence self-disempowering, readers. Positivist sociologists model a world 'as such' that they know is incomplete, running a deficit of obedience that they hope to make up in the ingenious replication of a putatively unalterable social nature. The 'truth' of social science on this understanding is the extent to which it can provoke what Nietzsche called a love of fate among readers who quite literally bring into being the alleged truth of a reflected, patterned world, vindicating the text of social science ironically by acting it out, in particular its supposed 'laws' of hierarchy, inequality, sexism, racism, the domination of nature and scientism itself.

Sociology as a paradigm of the positivist social sciences portrays, and thus hopes to provoke, a heteronomous, closed world governed by overarching laws of adjustment and adaptation, adjustment being the reasonable person's response to the invisible hand of market economies and the visible hand of the interventionist welfare state. I read the text of empiricist social science, modeled on a sociology written by Comte, Durkheim and Weber, *as a literary production that fatefully conceals its own authorship in the cleansing processes of methodology, thus denying the problematic nature of its own intelligibility.* This reduction of thought to method reproduces the world frozen in the lens of science — reproduction used here in the tellingly double sense of reflection/ imitation, on the one hand, and reenactment/reiteration, on the other. Although positivist sociology has been written by some scribbling or keyboarding author, it methodically suppresses its literary nature, notably the self-recognition of its own authorial artifice and thus its politicizing non-identity to the world to which it is an address. Method postures as writing done by no perspectival, passionate, pouting author; instead, it freezes the world on the page of science, hence freezing the world enacted by readers duped to believe that science's world is ontologically unalterable. Ontology utilizes the idea of a static or finished history to reproduce itself as history.

Positivist social science in this sense is a *social text* (see Agger, 1989c), a notion extending the concept of ideology by drawing on but not simply synthesizing the complex lineage of western Marxism, including the Frankfurt School's critical theory, poststructuralism, postmodernism and feminist theory. Less mechanically than Marx's original notion of ideology as false representation, a social text interposes itself as a text between readers and the world as the world's reflection, thus hoping to reproduce it in fact. Social texts are written on the occasion of deficits in the compliance of people with the supposedly iron-clad patterns of postulated social laws; authors of these texts recognize that *there are no laws* but only an open historicity. This happens in spite of the fact that on the surface, at least, science disavows politics as the bane of a transcendental disinterest that it claims for itself, a value-freedom it ensures by disabling and thus disempowering both author and reader, thus precluding their constructive hermeneutic work. Precluding this constituting hermeneutic work required of people who are confronted with social texts that they must interpret, social texts in effect dictate their own receptions by concealing their literary nature. Instead, positivist texts clean themselves of the dirty fingerprints left by busy authors, notably through the apparatus of methodology, which vouchsafes the verisimilitude of science (see Agger, 1989b). Science deeply represses its subtext of desire not simply to reflect but also to reproduce the world in a political way. A postured objectivity is a secret vehicle for an imperial subjectivity that is the more potent the more it disguises itself merely as a disinterested quest for knowledge, science for science's sake. Science pretends not to be a piece of fiction concocted to produce social and political conformity with its story of social lawfulness that it disguises underneath the appurtenances of methodology.

45

Science claims no deeper political interest — no animating desire, passion or need — that warrants its facile depiction of the world as a generic one, thus eternalizing domination as a veritable social fact in Durkheim's (1950) sense. That people suffer the world does not, however, exemplify an eternal essence of our subordination before an overwhelming social structure as such; there are no historical essences but only contingencies. Subordination only defines a particular, inherently alterable history in which texts like sociology reinforce powerlessness by portraying the power of the social as inescapable. Sociology thus encourages the enactment of these alleged social laws of inequality by readers who do not realize that they are actually reading ideologizing texts and claims, which they turn into their own disempowered 'everyday' lives. This offers the peculiar image of a social science that in effect *scripts* a ritualistic obedience to authority simply by appearing to reflect authority's ubiquity, the essence of the power of the social declaimed by Durkheim as the essence of modernity.

Science denies its own authoriality in this sense, its own political project of closing an open world by fatalizing readers. Using the textless text of methodology, science puts distance between itself and what it constructs as an inappropriate nonscience inferior to the disciplinarily vouchsafed and methodologically guaranteed knowledge of the normative community of science. Sociology is an authorless text; better, it is secret writing, the source of its hegemonizing power over readers who do not realize that they are participating dumbly in a scripted everyday life. Critical theory, of which this version of what I call a critical theory of public life is a local example, attempts to disclose the secret authors of sociology's social texts, educating people to their own needless disempowering by texts that could be read and written differently. A deconstructive reading of science excavates the author's desire to write and thus it deflates science's false authority as a text beyond perspective, empowering readers to become writers themselves — authors of their own history. This version of critical theory extends Habermas' communication theory of society by deploying some of the tools of postmodernism, poststructuralism and feminism (see Morrow, 1991).

This effort to read positivist social sciences as ideologizing social texts belongs to my general effort to create a third-generation critical theory that demonstrates how social texts reproduce a certain capitalist version of public life. Positivist texts in particular reproduce a version of public life, extending the programmatic analysis presented in this chapter. My general thesis is that public life is reproduced textually and discursively through cultural works and practices like disciplinary social science that defy their ready reading as ideologizing claims. This builds on my argument in *Fast Capitalism* (Agger, 1989a) that ideology has now been effectively dispersed into the disciplinary, built and figural environment in such a way that it suppresses its own critical interrogation. What I call a radical hermeneutics in chapter 3 is a mode of critical theory that *reauthorizes* hidden texts by exposing their explosive ideological content, notably their positivist representation of a lawful social world that freezes the fluid historicity of social life. Here I introduce this argument by suggesting that the social-textual reproduction of a capitalist public life suggests new theoretical syntheses of critical theory, deconstruction and feminism.

Today's discourses are yesterday's ideologies that disable not simply by freezing a heartless, hopeless world somewhat palliated by the emoluments of leisure, mobility and spiritual plenitude. Instead, these discourses disqualify any intellectual construction out of hand and so require us to accept science's secret constructions as the only uncontaminated writing in the world. Science's message is quite literally its medium — methodology. Method functions as secret political theory by offering seemingly disinterested descriptions of a generic social nature imitating the laws physicists impose on their version of inanimate nature. Social texts like positivism deceive not simply where they proclaim the wrong laws but lawfulness at all. The social world cannot be represented outside of history and people's desire to change history by understanding it, hence giving it a new direction. Science makes history by seeming only to reflect it, thus usurping literary competence from readers who are rendered mute before the seemingly given, the numerous socio-historical indignities that litter history, blown into an unavoidable fate as History. Sociology becomes socio(onto)logy, a version of metaphysics concealed and hence conveyed in the technical apparatus of methodology.

Textuality comprises embryonic political relationships between writers and readers that social theory only ignores out of an unexamined belief in the primacy of the productive. Critical theory since the 1920s rejected economism for its political fatalism. It is possible to understand the disempowering production and reproduction of the supposedly iron laws of a generic social history as a power relationship between writers and readers that, I contend, is the modal power relationship today, under which other power relationships between capital and labor, men and women, and white and colored can be subsumed as specific exemplifications of this general logic of domination. This general logic is the domination of production over reproduction, value over alleged valuelessness, including both the hierarchy of valued labor over unwaged household labor and the hierarchy of work in general over textuality.

Building on a heterodox version of Marxism mediated through iterations of the Frankfurt School's critical theory as well as feminism, poststructuralism and postmodernism, *a critical theory of the text* addresses the crucial social relationship between production and reproduction that traditional Marxism ignores out of masculinist biases, subordinating textual and sexual politics to the allegedly more real, more political politics of productive activities — men's work, accessible at best to male science and theory. My version of this critical theory of the text addresses a whole host of issues of public life that necessarily redefine as public aspects of sexuality and textuality that have been ignored for too long by the male left. A critical theory informed by feminism, poststructuralism and postmodernism interrogates all dualities of public/private, reading them for the secret hierarchies encoded in them. Feminism takes the lead here in politicizing aspects of the putatively 'personal' (e.g., sexuality, housework, childcare, emotional intimacy) that are, in fact, intensely political (see Elshtain, 1981). Feminism helps reconstruct Marxist critical theory in light of its deconstruction of the public/private duality. In this context, I want to draw attention to the telling parallel between social reproduction and sexual reproduction as these are achieved through a mode of domination that I call *heterotextuality* — the privileging of central over marginal terms in any duality like public/private, man/woman or productive/unproductive.

Social science heterotextually encourages the enactment of alleged fate from readers by describing seemingly incontrovertible laws of social motion like inequality, bureaucracy, division of labor and patriarchy. Readers are to enact these supposed laws as 'necessity', unavoidable in modernity, which is metaphysically constrained by immense structures requiring obedience and duty (the essence of Kant's sense of morality). A postulated 'necessity' becomes necessary when seen from the vantage of a history in which subordination is the empirical rule. The text of science inculcates the love of fate in concealing its own authorial subjectivity as the political possibility of any free subjectivity.

This is more complex than Marx's original notion of ideology, although Marx's apparent mechanism is not in the nature of Marxism but only reflects Marx's con-textual debt to physics, the most credible text of science in the nineteenth century and one shared by Comte when he called sociology 'social physics'. While Marx in his own terms wrote a natural science of history, I want to understand all textual practices, including Marxism, as world-constitutive engagements among author, readers, other writers, nature and topic — text in Wittgenstein's (1953: pp. 8, 11, 88, 174, 226) terms read as a form of life or language game encoding all sorts of political and social meaning. While all life is not a text, every text is a life, a form of society through which power is transacted and accumulated. Broadening ideology in this way from an imposed false consciousness, with Marx, to a discursive writer-reader relationship opens all sorts of questions about social, political, sexual and textual reproduction that bring together discourse theory, feminism, critical theory, postmodernism and poststructuralist literary theory, all of which interrogate the nature of the relationship between hierarchies of valued and devalued terms: production/reproduction, writer/reader, man/woman, capital/labor, white/colored, etc. Marx presaged a critical discourse theory in this sense in his deconstructions of religion and bourgeois economic theory as enmeshing, occluding forms of mystification. *Avant la lettre* of poststructuralism and feminism, Marx's semiotic reading of money in *Capital* anticipated later discursive developments in critical theory of the kind I am proposing here. He did not fully understand the ruse of science, including his own, that purports not to be a literary practice or product at all but simply a presuppositionless reflection of inert social nature. Marx thus denied himself a crucial foundation for a new textual practice that avoids science's suppressed will to power by admitting socialism's fiction as a purposeful piece of authorial artifice — an intersubjective, intertextual practice reflecting the elemental desire to shape the text of one's own life.

Understanding science as a literary practice weakens its spell over readers by revealing its artifice as the possibility of different versions of itself and thus of a genuine political community characterized by openness, heterogeneity and peace. The notion of intertextuality functions here as a utopian political imagery, adding deconstructive velocity to Habermas' (1984, 1987b) own notion of the ideal speech situation, now broadened to include all sorts of literary relationships and not just those of politics proper. This is especially necessary at a time when politics is found everywhere but in the political arena *per se*, one of the central insights of postmodernists like Baudrillard (1975, 1981, 1983). The literary comprises science in spite of the fact that science methodically conceals its own authorial mediation of concepts and the world.

Yet there can be a non-positivist version of science (see Marcuse, 1969; Agger, 1989b) that refuses to blush at its own fiction but instead regards its literary artifice as an occasion for making intertextual connections, unabashedly writing its version of versions as a mode of self-expression soliciting its gentle correction by other writers — community. While literature comprises science, unlike literature science claims validity methodically, arguing for its verisimilitude through a practiced proceduralism. In this sense, methodology functions as the subtext making good on science's presumption to be heard as a truthful account. *King Lear* has no subtext; Shakespeare intended his fiction to be read as a truthful account of the world, unsupported by the display of his credentials as a playwright or the grounding of his script in the accoutrements of literary method. *King Lear* succeeds as a truthful account if we can be convinced to believe that people behave the way Shakespeare suggests they do. This is not to say that *King Lear* does not in its own way intend to persuade, arguing its version of a perfidious world, but only to observe that science is the special case of a discourse whose fiction is heuristically suppressed *for the sake of argument* — making science seem like science to the skeptical. This is so even if good science never forgets its ground in the perspectivity of the text, indeed foregrounding that perspectivity as the text's main topic. Good science self-consciously argues for its version of the world, its validity claims made available for deconstruction, or simply rewriting, where other literary forms — novel, poem, autobiography — dispense with validity claims altogether but rather gamble on validity to emerge in the play of text and subtext. In other words, we do not doubt for a moment that *King Lear* expresses Shakespeare's world, the world that he intends. But under sway of positivism and its pretense not to be a literary account, we are unclear about whether Margaret Mead's anthropology and Parsons' sociology also intend worlds in the same way or indeed are autobiographical, as all literature is. One might say that good literature, including science, allows readers access to the sense of the text understood as the author's argument for this or that state of affairs, the *text's echo of itself writing*, whether Graham Greene's demythified world in which no one is innocent or Marx's world that he would create out of the ashes of the old.

## Durkheim's Socio(onto)logy: A Disciplinary Reading

One of the biggest contributions of a critical theory of public life lies in its ability to read back and forth across traditionally differentiated academic disciplines for the deep assumptions concealed within their methodological protocols. Sociology is paradigmatic of the positivist social sciences in the way it encodes its political and social assumptions within the technical apparatus of its methodology, which is highly quantitative and figural in nature. A critical theory informed by feminist postmodern literary criticism can productively decode disciplines by examining their texts in ways traditionally ignored by sociologies of sociology (e.g., Friedrichs, 1970). This contributes to a better understanding of public knowledge largely dominated by its academic definition and iteration. It is crucial to understand the literary production of discipline for its political echoes and suppressions. Here, I want to outline the possibility of disciplinary reading through my blend of critical theory, postmodernism and poststructuralism as well as feminism (see Agger, 1989c). In particular, I want to examine the grounding assumptions that Durkheim (1950) made about the nature of the social, particularly about what he took to be its essentially heteronomous quality. By historicizing his sociological reading, showing it to be socio(onto)logical, we help historicize the patterns frozen by positivist sociology, thawing them into open political possibility.

Scientific sociology as a paradigm case of positivist behavioral science functions covertly as an enmeshing, disempowering social text, developed in the first thirteen pages of Durkheim's (1950) *Rules of Sociological Method*, where he demarcated sociology from psychology as a legitimate discipline through his definition of social facts. For Durkheim, sociology's object domain was to be the study of social facts understood as the billion pieces of history marked by our sub-ordination to an impinging social reality (e.g., the force of religion over suicidal behavior, the theme of Durkheim's methodologically pioneering study, *Suicide*). He exemplified these social facts in his study of the religious correlates of suicide, showing that in fact people are conditioned by various religious affiliations to commit suicide at varying rates. Far from an ultimate existential act unexplainable with reference to social correlates, suicide for Durkheim is structurally determined through religion. The example of his study of suicide is now repeated in the extraordinary busyness of a discipline that maps the numerous correlations expressing the causality that Durkheim first suggested as the essence of organized social life — poverty causing crime, unemployment divorce, stress unhappiness, anomie suicide.

Sociology for him was to map exhaustively the numerous epi-sodes of our subordination to the social world's *generic* power over individuals. This is to reinforce the notion, by now second nature among social scientists as well as the lay public, that the seemingly unalterable necessities of industrial-age society such as inequality, hierarchy and bureaucracy require what an earlier speculative idealism called Reason to be reduced to a conventionalized reasonableness — the capitulation and conformity to putative necessity *written into the text of social science*. The reasonable person lives and hopes within the constraints of the allegedly given, the untranscendable horizon of Durkheim's social-factual, embracing our metaphysical susceptibility to a society that for sociology always overdetermines us. In charting the terrain of the social-factual through a representational science, Durkheim wanted to reproduce the subordinate behavior that he froze as the essence of organized social life. Thus, our acquiescence to an overwhelming social structure would be played out in exigencies of everyday life, in which we allow ourselves to be imprinted with the imperatives of dominant social institutions like religion, economics, race, politics and sexuality.

While Durkheim as a liberal of sorts did not favor suicide, he wanted to affirm a world in which suicide is not an existential choice but merely a reflex of our various cultural and institutional affiliations and conditioning. The role of an ameliorating but positivist sociology was to *reduce* social problems like suicide by fine-tuning an otherwise intractable social structure. In this way, Durkheim's version of the socio(onto)logical reinforces the power of the social, notably through his notion of social facts, which has become canonical in sociology. Durkheim *assumed* that people are subject to causality and thus he radically foreshortened the horizon of social reform to minor individual-level reforms and a modicum of state intervention in the polity. While well-intentioned (compared, for example, to Herbert

Spencer's macabre Social Darwinism that would have welcomed suicide as population control), this ameliorating liberalism fails on metaphysical as well as political grounds to address *the role texts themselves play in reproducing a world that they would have us believe is basically impervious to our efforts to change it.* The minor adjustments of a surface liberalism occur only at the margins. Instead of providing a haven in a heartless world (Lasch, 1977), sociology reproduces heartlessness by depicting our social existence as generically subordinate. Durkheim crucially fails to understand suicide as a mediated existential choice and not the mechanical reflex of abject powerlessness that he takes it to be, thus heterotextually reinforcing the power of the social. After all, the person who chooses against suicide might be tomorrow's author (see Marcuse, 1955: pp. 211–16, on the utopian rethinking of Freud's death instinct as the impulse to avoid pain — domination).

I want to turn to the question of how contemporary sociology writes (off) an indeterminate, open world as metaphysical and political illusion. The issue here is how sociology scripts obedience through its representational text which depicts social laws and hence social conformity as inescapable. At least four things happen in the text fatefully to reproduce its topic in reality. First, science restricts writers and readers merely to the task of interpretation, proceeding from an original canonical literature including the texts of Comte, Durkheim and Weber. To be disciplinarily valid, it has been decided that sociological writing requires the imprint of Durkheim's notion of the generic power of the social, distinguishing sociology from nonsociology and science from nonscience. Nonsociology calls Durkheim's assumption of the generic power of the social over individuals into question; for example, Marx's version of the social suggests historicity as the possibility of *overturning* postulated social laws in a society beyond domination. In consolidating itself as a discipline, subsequent sociological texts only reproduce his original literature reified into a canon. So not only do positivist texts represent the social world uncritically, they also represent an originary canonical literature uncritically, reproducing its deeply freighted assumptions about the generic power of the social in the everyday research and writing that sociologists do.

In the case of sociology, a division of labor emerges between those who would tend the canon faithfully (theorists) and those who busily document the patterns of heteronomy exemplified by Durkheim's study of suicide. This sort of disciplinary boundary-maintenance is inherently stultifying in the way it valorizes, and deepens, the overall social, economic and intellectual differentiation that disqualifies a concept of the social totality. The differentiation of academic disciplines reinforces discipline in general by preventing people from comprehending the complexly interrelated social totality in any but partial terms. This reinforces conformity by making it seem impossible for people to break through the patterns holding them in the grip of what Weber called the iron cage of capitalist industrialization.

Talk about sociology's imbedded ontology of adaptation to reflected social laws of heteronomy is suppressed methodically. Legitimate sociology is invariantly the study of social causality and thus to dissent is shamefully not to be a sociologist at all. To talk and write nonscience is to traffic in nonsense (see Horkheimer and Adorno, 1972: p. 9 for a discussion of this issue). Sociology's right to exist as a separate discipline is suppressed as a sociological topic itself once we accept Durkheim's socio(onto)logizing aegis over the subsequent discipline. To be a sociologist is to represent the intractable social-factual, which conflates all possible historicity with the historical reality of domination today and yesterday. Thus the future is closed off from new texts and lives that refuse the postulate of binding social laws and hence individual obedience to hierarchy. Sociology thwarts disciplinary self-reflection in order to occlude the appearance of its own ontological posturing, inculcating the love of fate under the rubric of positive science.

Second, science relegates all traces of authorial presence in the text to the text's margins (preface, notes, dedication, bibliography etc.). This deauthorizes its version of an immutable world available to a community of disciplined scientists. Authorial traces of implicit and explicit advocacy, such as the play between text and its underlying desire, are removed in bald imitation of what sociology mistakenly takes to be the essence of the natural sciences (see Knorr-Cetina, 1981). Sociology mathematizes its prose as a further constraint on authorial perspective, thus reducing reading to little more than a competence in the analysis of tables, graphs, charts and statistics. Reading is thought not to require the mediations of thought, whether the interpretive work of hermeneutic analysis, the analysis of reader response or, outrageously, a deconstructive dialectic whereby reading itself becomes a new text, a strong writing in no sense inferior or derivative. Sociology's scientific texts invite a disengaged, representational reading, the implied reader being a mere receptacle for the piecemeal, supposedly unconstructed information that the text accumulates toward its ultimate synthesis of all differences, western philosophy's positive knowledge. The text's indubitability hinges on its neutralization of the authorial energy threatening to burst out of the confines of the social-factual. Science's author is concealed lest science appear to be the fiction it really is.

Third, science reduces theory to a tool for provoking researchable hypotheses, thus keeping everyday scientists busy. The text of science averages truth (reduced to correlation coefficients) out of a multitude of voices, but not because it is really ecumenical or epistemologically neutral — neutrality, of course, being the deepest value commitment of all. This epistemological ecumenism coopts what is really threatening about renegade writings that deny positivist science altogether and oppose the world that science reflects lawfully and would reproduce politically. It also crushes the speculative project of theory, which is now integrated into the research apparatus of science and denied any meta-theoretical purchase as a forum for asking science the question of its answers (as I am doing here). Theory's pragmatic value lies in its ability to summarize and organize middle-range research results. Its interrogation of deeper assumptions is closed off in the interest of disciplinary advancement. Intellectual imagination is thus routinized as theory-construction or theory-building, directly abetting empirical re- searchers who, it is said, 'use' one theory or another in order to 'explain' one social fact or another. Explanation is only the accounting for statistical variance in dependent variables (e.g., religious affiliation supposedly explaining some percentage of the variation in suicide rates). Truth is whittled down into purely technical operations of methodology, which attempts to replace concepts with number and figure. But, unbeknownst to positivists, the text of methodology can be read as the secret metaphysical argumentation it really is (see Agger, 1989b).

Sociology averages competing versions of the world in fostering an impression of its own busy productivism, relegating political pas- sion and perspective to the domain of nonscience. Yet this middling of theoretical perspectives, seemingly recouping something of value from every theory in an orgy of epistemological pluralism if not democracy, fails to arrive at a truly heterogeneous, decentering synth- esis but disciplines defiant viewpoints, further disqualifying them as illegitimate. American sociology has girded its center by integrating a whole host of theories that are thought usefully to supplement and complement the dominant positivist-functionalist mainstream, drawing phenomenology, ethnomethodology and even Marxism and feminism into the disciplinary fold as partners in the enterprise of descriptive empirical sociology. *But the center holds* as the dominant positivism reduces its opposition merely into versions of Durkheim's model of social causality, suppressing not only their political inten- tions but indeed their very opposition to a social science modeled on physics in the first place.

Finally, as I elaborate further in chapter 5, the sociological text splits marginal, political versions like Marxism and feminism into good and bad versions of themselves, disciplining the one and disqual- ifying the other as an unruly practice (see Fraser, 1989). Disciplinary Marxism becomes a legitimate version of sociology, giving social phenomena under investigation the imprimatur of lawful necessity — Marxism ironically enlisted to explain (away) the seeming inexorabil- ity of conflict among groups once transmogrified into Weberian conflict theory. Renegade Marxism is portrayed as the Gulag, laid at Marx's own feet as a supposedly inevitable outcome of *The Communist Manifesto* and *Capital*. For its part, feminism is divided into a domesti- cated liberalism, on the one hand, according to which women seek bourgeois family plus paid work alongside companionate men (whose own problems are understood empathetically), and, on the other, an incorrigibly antifamily, antimale, lesbian separatism. Familied feminism is then further reduced to a dispassionate version of male conflict theory, a Weberianized Marxism for which some degree of conflict between the sexes is inevitable, if manageable. Thus, appropriate women are to modulate gender conflict by attempting to 'balance' family and career in ways that are not threatening to men. Hence, patriarchy is reproduced through the deceptive heterotextuality of positivist sociology that convinces women to reproduce everyone but themselves.

### Reading as a Rewriting: Toward a Left–Feminist Deconstructive Method

Let me turn deconstructively to two brief passages from recent sociology textbooks that would reproduce the world in their image. Readings of these two passages help demonstrate the ideology- and ontology-critical possibilities of a left-feminist deconstructive method developed out of a synthesis of critical theory, poststructuralism, postmodernism and feminist theory.

> Indeed, far from being dead, marriage and parenthood continue to be important goals for all Americans (Hess, Markson and Stein, 1985: p. 266).

What is happening here? Even in its own terms, sociology fails to reflect the extant world, muddling what it calls facts, for all sorts of people eschew the married state. Fewer than one-seventh of Americans today live in the definitional nuclear family. *If* the concept of 'family' is meant to include people who may fall outside traditional patriarchal marriage, but who nonetheless share an enduring intimacy, *then* the text has the responsibility to make this clear. It could, for instance, explicitly broaden the concept of family for political reasons, notably in order to legitimize modes of intimacy that break the mold of the heterosexual dyad, plus children. But the text does not extend family in this way, although it admits cultural variations within heterosexual universality. Instead, it uses the term 'family' in the narrower sense, connoting requirements such as legal marriage, common domicile, economic union and, not least, heterosexuality — exactly the notion of family called up by the New Right today in its regression behind the sins of feminism, promiscuity, abortion and homosexuality that imperil what it means by traditional values.

 Why, then, does sociology in its own terms of adequate representation seemingly bend the 'facts' about the universality of family in this sense? Although its surface text is avowedly liberal, even liberal-feminist, advocating a better world for all humanity and, in this context particularly, more flexibility in sex roles and greater sensitivity of men to women and vice versa — *sexism reduced to heartlessness* — its subtext is deeply suppressed. The subtext here issues in a generic heterotextuality: the claim that 'all Americans want to get married' sustains what still exists of the reality of patriarchal family in order to inculcate student-readers with a sense of their normalcy if they choose to follow the traditional habits of dating, courtship, betrothal and finally marriage. Indeed, even divorce is routinized by the text, not as the end of family but as an even more desperate yearning for what is socio(onto)logically essential, namely *re*marriage. The subtext here intends that the 'fact' of family's universality would be enacted by readers reinforced to want family, although not the broad notion of family as any sustaining intimacy but family as legal heterosexual marriage *within* patriarchal capitalism.

Ironically, sociology itself shows that marriage almost inevitably works to the disadvantage of women. Women bear an unequal share of housework, childcare and nurturance; they are embattled and undercompensated in the realm of work; and they are sexually victimized. The liberal, even liberal-feminist, surface text describes the bourgeois nuclear family as universal in order to provoke its enactment as a way of validating its own distorted, counterfactual writing. (Of course, the 'family' valorized by sociological liberal-feminists is the companionate family of Betty Friedan's [1981] book, *The Second Stage*, and not the overtly male-dominated family of prior heartlessness.) Thus, a text that in 1984 may err by exaggerating family's supposed universality will by 1994 be corrected by new facts engendered by the text itself. Ironically, the claim that most Americans want to get married would eventually issue in its truth.

Since the Enlightenment, science has not simply frozen the world into laws by declaring the metaphysical impossibility of social change without also promising the powerless a future in which their powerlessness would be somewhat redeemed, if not in a revolutionary way. The goods society has been offered tantalizingly as an alternative to the Good, thus inducing readers/citizens to do their public and private 'duties' scripted for them by the text of social laws. Sociology as a liberal text sweetens deprivation by offering the enticements of the redistributive welfare state and heartful family, including upward mobility, occupational and status prestige, job satisfaction, spiritual plenitude and companionship. These are offered in return for a work and home life given over to the enactment of certain obligations, albeit somewhat different ones for women and men. Liberal social science rails against so-called social problems of industrial society like poverty, racism, sexism and environmental degradation while defending a universal subordination to the iron-clad imperatives of industrialization, Durkheim's generic power of the social.

The present is to be born out of conviction that the future will be different, science palliating subjugation with developmental optimism about an eventual postindustrial society (Bell, 1973, 1976) in which technology conquers the realm of necessity altogether, precisely the text of modernization theory. Sociology projects human betterment as an unalterable teleological outcome, so-called modernization moving us ever closer to the end of toil, politics, ideology; the text of science plugs the gaps of societal dissonance and defiance. Sociology presages a last-text inscribing social laws that obviates its own reproductive posture by successfully reproducing a world in its own seamless image. The mediation of socio(onto)logy will no longer be necessary in a world that reproduces itself automatically, beyond the need of books (see Agger, 1989a, for the development of this theory of 'fast capitalism').

Thus, in the passage quoted just below, the text announces the accompaniment of industrialization by progress, including shrinking power and income gaps between blacks and whites and women and men. Progress is preordained in the text of social laws and it is read in the small examples of social betterment today, which are inflated into the metaphysic of Progress writ large.

> There are small but definite causes for optimism...Full sexual equality will not be achieved in this century, but milestones in that direction will be detectable each day, month and year. The signs are unmistakable; progress, though slow, is inevitable...The glass is half full, not half empty (Doob, 1985: p. 302).

The text ends on a high note by promising women and blacks future reprieve from present inequality, describing mathematically a supposedly shrinking gap between black/white and female/male annual incomes — again, arguably a serious distortion in its own representational terms. Poverty has been feminized and black and brown unemployment continues to rise in the deindustrializing US. As well, it is spurious to assess overall wealth only with reference to reported income. Just as family is a universal, so, it is said, is the sweeping democratization, via technological advance, that resolves social problems conceptualized largely in economistic terms as unequal attainment of goods and services. This monetarization of social problems implies incrementalist welfare-state solutions which, like President Johnson's War on Poverty in the 1960s, end up being no solution at all. The text describes the easing of extant social problems both as fact and as fate, given society's modernizing logic. Not only are we to believe that subordination is unalterable but so, ironically, is the eventual technological transcendence of subordination in a promised postindustrial future, a notion designed to make the bad seem better in the meantime — the glass half full, not half empty, Ronald Reagan's optimistic metaphor.

It is difficult to resist, let alone deconstruct, the massive empirical chronicles of both fact and fate offered by a technical social science highly adapt at the depiction of the seemingly inert. After all, social scientists reliably chronicle birth rates, crime, social correlates of drug use, the political economy of welfare. Their technical acuity undermines the deconstructive critique of the ungrounded validity claims embedded at the core of statistical social analysis. It is tempting to relinquish the field of the empirical altogether to those who claim monopoly of epistemological authority simply because they have succeeded in mathematizing language and thus driving out thought. This is only to exchange one fetish for another — anti-empiricism for positivism. Yet there can be other addresses to the empirical world, albeit discourses that do not pretend authorial mindlessness as a methodological first principle (see Stockman, 1984, for a comprehensive discussion of developments in the post-positivist philosophy of science. Also see the debate in Adorno *et al.*, 1976).

## Writing as a Rereading: The Textual Politics of a Feminist Postmodern Critical Theory

The possible redemption of science hinges on the differentiation between non-positivist and positivist versions of knowledge and textuality. The crude caricature of positivist natural science embraced by many social scientists is untrue to natural science's own self-understanding. Einstein and Heisenberg first claimed that the natural universe is a non-reductionist force field of concatenating signifiers and signifieds. But to make good my notion of a new science I must ground it in the possibility of new ways to write science, which I draw from my fertilization of critical theory with resources from poststructuralism, postmodernism and feminism. This notion of a new science suggests a whole textual-political critical theory, with which I close this chapter.

Let me begin this section by discussing an example of positivist journalism from the mid-1980s. It was announced that 69 per cent of Americans supported the US attack on Libya for its supposed support of terrorist actions against Americans. I am not concerned with representational validity per se (i.e., whether 69 per cent was a correct number at the time, although that could have been a relevant issue for methodologists). Rather I address the ground of the validity claims being made by the journalist in question, notably his suppression of his own literary involvement in the text of his reportage. There is no simple datum reflecting 'support of the US attack on Libya' (or any other sociological validity claim) that can be assessed apart from the literary context in which we define and use our terms and conduct our surveys. Here, we are not told what protocol was followed in generating what the journalist claims to be knowledge. Were people asked 'Do you support President Reagan's strategic policy in this case?', 'Do you support the dropping of bombs on Tripoli?', or 'Do you support the killing of Libyans, including children?' The account in question did not disclose the basis of its own validity claims, the idea that the very term 'to support' is a construction that could have been varied to produce very different results — for example, the number 22 per cent if, alternatively, Americans were asked whether they supported killing Libyan civilians. The hypothetical number 22 is no truer than the number 69. Yet the reporter reading this news did not publicly stipulate the conditions of validity when he suggested that Americans supported the President.

Even more important, the science in question did not *argue for* one construction of validity over another, showing the political interest behind attempts to deconstruct the generic notion of support in certain protocol statements. Good science here would not only understand its own version of the term 'support the President' as a construction; Thomas Kuhn (1970) told us that much. Instead, it would argue for that construction in a committed way, that is, with the intention to persuade, to provoke empathy, to change the world, science no less than *King Lear* or *The Communist Manifesto*. So the problem with the Libyan question as science is both that we do not know what the percentages of support signify, nor do we hear the argument for that signification in terms of authorial desire — that is, in light of political aims. Good science would both exhume its own construction of the word *support* — in other words, here, what question the sample was asked — and then it would defend that construction in terms of its impact on the text itself. Science is a fiction in the sense that it listens to itself write and makes this echo of subtext directly a textual topic, hence opening science to public discourse and dialogue, and thus to democracy. In the case of news reportage of the Libyan issue, deconstructive rewriting would probably conclude that many Americans wanted to *drop* bombs over Libya as retribution for Libyan support of terrorists but, contradictorily, they did not want those bombs to kill arbitrarily.

The concept of a dialogical science open to its own assumptions, interwoven into its own argumentation, implies a concept of a dialogical politics. Deconstruction strengthened with critical theory as well as feminism suggests that the best world is optimally heterogeneous, nonlogocentric, decentered and open to the pleasure of the text, displaying the text's inherence in a subtext of indomitable desire that writing makes a topic in the back-and-forth of its own reflection and self-reflection. Where the positivist model of textuality wants only to communicate information, a one-way process of production and reception, a deconstructive version of science's text builds community out of discourses self-understood as necessarily incomplete, decentering and undecidable, modeling an intertextual politics that does not short-circuit the dialectic of product and process — a humane society and at once the route taken in order to achieve it.

For his part, Adorno (1973: p. 406) suggested that the only credible textual politics in an era in which language has been almost totally divested of its power to refuse, to negate, works through the world's contradictions 'from within', undoing the secret affinity of text with a world to which it would unhesitatingly attach itself as its source of meaning. Such a notion of negation contrasts with Lenin's claim that the early twentieth-century Russian proletariat required texts 'from without', from a vanguard. This sealed the subsequent history of state socialism as a dictatorship over the proletariat buttressed by a Marxist-Leninist scientism — faith in dialectic — no less disempowering than the scientism of capitalist countries. This version of Adorno suggests a more explicitly political deconstruction that reads the objectivist texts of science and culture against their grain as the real fictions they are, hence opening them to public discourse and democratic consensus formation of the Habermasian kind.

In this sense, fiction does not connote falsehood but, alternatively, writing's openness to its own desire as the foundation of a dialogical community of many writers, what Habermas calls the ideal speech situation. Science subordinates fiction to itself as escapist illusion, affording spiritual uplift in an otherwise implosive bourgeois society. Yet deconstruction shows the untruth of a science that represses its own purposeful construction of a signified world and, as such, is a political strategy of sorts, if a somewhat rarefied one. In the fashion of Derrida, where he declares that the margins are really at the center, I would add that fiction is not adequate science *per se* but is rather an example of generic discourse, whereas science is a particular discursive version unprivileged with respect to other discourses. This helps us address the timeworn problem of educating the educator that I raised in my introduction. The very construction of a science/fiction contrast is science's way of gaining primacy over the merely conversational, commonsense, everyday and literary, basing political authority on epistemological privilege that derives from the derogation of non-science.

This allows me to return to my earlier critique of Marx's (Marx and Engels, 1947) social-physics notion of ideology as a camera obscura, false consciousness simply inverting the world in order to sustain it. What might a different conception of science's ideology mean for a canonical Marxism still haunted by the Soviet experience of the vanguard party sustained by a heritage of mechanism and scientism? In rethinking ideology as a textual practice integrating writer and reader in an embryonic political community, I go beyond the notion of ideology simply as a representational inversion of reality to be turned rightside up in a future social order. Instead, ideology is writing that in concealing its own literariness, its own creative artifice, reproduces a readership that lives out its own unfreedom freely, as it were, ever the irony of oppression. (In chapter 3, I radicalize and historicize the practice of hermeneutics as a way of dealing with this problem of ideology's detextualization.)

Sartre (1976) said that Marxism is the thought of our time in the sense that human practice cannot be understood without some reference to the immensity of the capitalist practico-inert, the material world that capital so inexorably colonizes. But most Marxisms continue to fixate on the male proletariat, the supposed necessity of a dialectic of nature as an adequate model of history, and a quite reductive understanding of relations between so-called base and superstructure or world and text. Like other masculinist, mechanist social scientists, most Marxists continue to fetishize the productive realm of wage labor, ignoring the allegedly unproductive as a concern of merely superstructural analysis, whether women's studies, cultural studies or literary criticism. They thereby entrench the productivist subordination of reproduction to male wage labor and scientism.

A more adequate understanding of ideology as a disempowering writer-reader relationship is achieved not through this positivist Marxism but rather in a deconstructive and feminist version that thematizes the relationship between production and reproduction as the central problematic of the age, addressing how and why people continue to accept their own victimization. Texts, like housework, seemingly belong to the realm of the apolitical, which has been millennially reserved for women. Productivist Marxists too often perpetuate this denigration of domesticity, culture and science as merely superstructural, hence perpetuating the devalorization of reproductive activity in the world at large. Feminism, thus, is not simply 'about' women, except as women have had historic responsibility for child-rearing and housework. More globally, this deconstructive version of feminism, joined with the concerns of critical theory, addresses the domination of reproduction by production, private by public, fiction by science, women by men and unpaid by paid labor. If feminism is understood as a critique of all reproductive relations, then a critical theory of the text is a feminist topic, even if the text in question is not ostensibly about or by women.

As I argue throughout this book, it is increasingly obvious that Marxism cannot be split apart from feminism, each comprehending the fractured halves of a world torn between outside and inside. This fracturing is the epochal theme of western dualism that the Frankfurt School contends is the deepest subtext of oppression. Yet like mainstream social-scientific positivism, Marxism continues to deepen the subordination of reproduction — women, texts, the unwaged — by treating their subordination as somehow derivative from labor's domination by capital, a notion that is both wrong and politically arrogant. Through its scientistic representation, this duality concealing a deeper hierarchy becomes a self-reproducing prophecy. This is not to say that all contradictions have been displaced from the economic to cultural and sexual spheres — as if the more fundamental contradictions were ever solely economic in nature. Rather, *any* distinction between production and reproduction, world and text, science and culture, and work and household inevitably redounds to the advantages of production, the world, science and work, respectively. The oldest and most axial form of domination is the split between center and margin, the useful and useless, that is only further amplified in the subsequent dualities of capital/labor, man/woman and colored/white. Deconstruction crucially suggests a politics blurring the reproduction/ production contrast, margin always center and vice versa, each equally worthy.

Risking programmatism, and thus offending doctrinal deconstructionists who think they can avoid construction altogether, we need a version of textuality and public discourse that resists its own subordination to the supposedly more significant practice of production. This Marxist and feminist version of deconstruction argues that the essential voice of humanity is not the tool but the text. The critique of sexual politics is subsumed under a more global critique of textual politics, of *heterotextuality*. This helps us understand the various genres of social reproduction, from television to textbooks, that tie us to our alleged fate, declaimed in sociology as a generic subordination to the power of the social — capitalism and sexism.

It is no longer adequate, and probably never was, to combat bourgeois scientism with left scientism. This only perpetuates people's self-subordination to deauthored expert texts that appear to require no literary intervention by the reader, no hermeneutic of liberation freeing one from the bondage of texts' representational imageries. To the extent to which Marxism has become another lifeless canon over against the effort to rewrite it in the permanent revisionism of a deconstructive ethic, it is no less oppressive than the bourgeois scientism it dismisses simply as a world upside down, to be put right by politically correct left-wing scientists. Like all reproduction, writing will become worthy — an archetype of a free society — only when practice is not sundered into the productive and the subordinately reproductive, the useful and useless, a choice that is the essence of politics today. Perhaps this is only to say that it is virtually impossible today to distinguish between the text reflecting an upside down world and the world itself; it is no longer possible to separate the discourses that hem us in and the world to which they would bind us in a thoughtless enactment of what they purport to freeze into ontological cement.

The text as an archetype of human activity does not simply replace labor, or for that matter sex or race, as a new postmodernist fetish (see Lyotard, 1984), each 'age' embracing its own supposedly unique logos. The notion of text as generic discourse only acknowledges the thoroughgoing overdetermination of oppression by the discourses that disqualify our possible authorship. Whatever space remains open for self-emancipation in an incredibly administered world must be nurtured and thereby enlarged first in writing, since our lifeworlds are already saturated with the enmeshing signifiers of family, politics, science, religion and entertainment. Today's texts, like yesterday's ideologies, defy their ready demystification by a critical hermeneutic that defines texts' falseness with reference to unambiguous standards of evidence. (I develop this hermeneutic in the next chapter.) It is incredibly difficult to debunk the Baudrillardian simulations of fast capitalism (Baudrillard, 1983; Agger, 1989a) when they conceal their own literary artifice and hence blur the boundary between text and world. As I discuss in my concluding chapter, postmodernity is the name frequently given to a society in which the real texts inspiring social behavior are the ones that look least like books, confounding the development of a public discourse of social criticism and reform.

While the deconstruction of positivist social science is not a mighty contribution to overall emancipation, one of the insights of a decentering Marxist feminism written under the sign of poststructuralism and postmodernism is that every contribution addressing local problems is as valid and necessary as every other; people are dying and suffering everywhere. As Merleau-Ponty once remarked, socialism cannot afford to let even one person die for it. At the same time, as Fanon indicates, obliviousness to routinized daily violence is a kind of violence in its own right. I do not mean to concoct a new master text — a new social science, new Marxism, new feminism, new poststructuralism — that measures up to the logocentric standards of closure and iterability 'better than' science does itself. That is precisely how Marxism got itself into trouble in the first place, conceiving itself as what Marx called a natural science of history. Indeed, the deconstruction of deconstruction and critical theory too frequently reveals a self-indulgent Nietzschean relativism that rejects the prospect of the negation of the negation as yet another mythic version of the gullibly, cheerfully positive — an advertising slogan promising a whole new world, a whole new text, thus only subordinating readers anew under an incontrovertible code that quickly becomes cant.

The notion of a negation-of-negation, the Hegelian-Marxist ideal (see Jay, 1984b), need not augur a brave new world as oppressive as it is unlikely. It can simply offer a glimpse of the *non-negative*, the promise of all radical social change. This is an appropriate imagery of utopia in a world in which politics is so often terror and thought a mindless iteration of conventional wisdom conveyed conventionally, whether in the clichés of popular culture or through an intellectual productivism measuring thought in dollar signs and citations. Deconstruction is always a new construction in its allegiance to the marginal, the non-negative, on whose behalf it struggles to prise meaning out of the suppressed subtexts of political construction. In this sense, deconstruction, armed with Marxist and feminist insights, endorses a world that does not close or totalize. It embraces non-identity (Adorno, 1973) as a substantive political theory, a way of preventing tyranny and working toward substantive democracy captured in the imagery of the ideal speech situation or simply public discourse.

An exceedingly minimalist political agenda would urge that writing hold out against what Sartre called its own institutionalization, its own reduction to method. This way, thought retains at least a modicum of autonomy with which it can deconstruct claims of all sorts, including those of positivist social science. Accordingly, Marxists, feminists, postmodernists and poststructuralists will need to take up the pen against those who, by calling themselves Marxist, feminist, postmodernist and poststructuralist, thereby entrench a new canon whose implacability precludes dialogue, hence democracy. Whether art or science, writing is inadequate politics. Yet we must interrogate the notion of adequacy as part of the political process lest the texts that inspire us become our tombstones.

In this chapter I have developed the outlines of a feminist critical theory informed by postmodernism and poststructuralism. A critical theory of the text helps us read ideology for its suppressed authorial gestures that reveal larger assumptions about the nature of the world. In particular, the feminist focus on reproduction enables me to link positivist reproduction (as in representation) with socio-sexual reproduction (as in the reproduction of capital, human capital and labor power). This analysis demonstrates how vital reproduction is for late capitalism. It also helps decode the ways in which we write, read and live the hierarchies of production over reproduction manifested in inequalities of class, gender and race. In the next chapter, I continue my analysis of rhetorical and discursive issues in critical theory. I develop a model of critical theory as radical hermeneutics, arguing that theory is an interpretive practice that not only decodes texts but exemplifies critical imagination and builds democratic community. I argue that reading is not simply a passive process of reception but an active deconstructive engagement with texts. In this sense, I pursue my focus on the politics of reproduction, raised explicitly in this chapter. Reading is not only reproduction or reflection but production and construction. I defend the notion that critical theory is an engagement with texts that exemplifies the power of reproduction — here, reading — hence helping us reverse the hierarchization of production over reproduction, including writing over reading. This next chapter will extend my argument for a certain mode of critical theory heavily influenced by poststructuralism, postmodernism and feminist theory. This version of critical theory makes the textual and sexual politics of discourse its central concern, recognizing how important the cultural and socio-sexual production process has become at a time when discipline is a discursive accomplishment, reproducing hegemony as well as human beings. This next chapter on reading and writing will better help me address the literary production of discipline in the university and in academic discourse in chapters 4 and 5.

*Chapter 3*

# Reading/Writing Otherwise: Radical Hermeneutics as Critical Theory

In this chapter I address the project of critical theory as a mode of utopian imagination as well as a vehicle for building democratic community. I consider the discourse of theory itself as politically constitutive, notably in the ways it orients itself to texts, traditions and readers. Through poststructuralism and feminism in particular, I empower theory to read and write strongly and against the grain. Theory has both negative and positive functions here; it criticizes ideologies encoded in science and culture, unburying their concealed authorial desires; it also portrays the writer-reader relationship as a democratically dialogical one, thus auguring a new polity founded on principles of what Habermas calls ideal speech (an issue to which I return specifically in chapter 8). Critical theory is a political factor in its own right, entering public discourse both as demystification and as imagination.

This version of critical theory is indebted to the combined influences of poststructuralism, postmodernism and feminism in the sense that they suggest a politics of discourse, including the discourse of theory itself. In the preceding chapters I have discussed these cross-fertilizations as they have helped critical theory enter its third generation, beyond Adorno, Horkheimer and Habermas. Critical theory has tended to neglect the politics of its own discourse in its otherwise valuable attempt to theorize domination and the culture industry (see Horkheimer and Adorno, 1972). Discourse has become a crucial political factor in two senses: ideologies are now dispersed densely into the built and figural environments, no longer susceptible to ready decoding and debunking. As such, critical theory becomes a hermeneutics that must read through ideologies to their constituting authorial cores, opening textbooks, science and popular culture to close scrutiny. Second, discourse is a medium in which public talk can be revivified, opening itself to non-experts who use their communicative competence in order to participate effectively in public debates. In the second part of this book, I examine concretely how public discourse has 'declined', thus exacerbating other social problems that result from the disempowering of laypeople. Here I introduce the politics of discourse as an issue that affects theory itself. In this chapter I ask, how can critical theory use its understandings of the structures of domination in public life to intervene as a mode of counterhegemonic discourse in its own right? My answer has to do with the textual politics opened up for critical theory by the combined influences of poststructuralism, postmodernism and feminist theory. Together, these strains of thought help me develop what I call a radical hermeneutics of critical theory, not only criticizing public life as we know it but actively engaging in social change through reformulations of reading and writing as public activities.

## Reading and Writing in Fast Capitalism

The only way to address the degrading forces turning our prose into pieces of nature provoking their reenactment is in a different literary practice, revealing authorial artifice where before only figure had been. This is the literary practice of critical theory itself, which not only understands the social world complexly and critically but *understands itself understanding*, hence gaining vital self-consciousness as well as self-confidence. Disclosing narrative wherever we find it narrates anew; thus it is political practice — in particular, a politics of discourse. We must trace the palimpsest of versions of the world that have become the world itself. Another name for these versions is ideology. First, we can reveal them to be corrigibly literary products that could have been written differently; then we must reformulate them in politically different terms. Actually, these twin projects of authorial excavation and reformulation belong together in the generic practice of deconstructive reading, prefiguring a whole new order in which reproduction is revalorized as a form of creative activity itself. One might call this interpretive strategy a radicalized hermeneutics (see Misgeld, 1976; also see Gadamer, 1975) if one understands that understanding is directly a mode of political reconstruction and not an ancillary activity somehow less important than economic production. Interpretation constructs, suggesting new versions of old texts degraded into nature-like obtrusions in the built and figural environments whose unmediated reading engenders unmediated behavior. Radical hermeneutics is more radical than hermeneutic. It emphasizes that reading is writing itself, thus politics.

I do not ignore power by suggesting an interpretive political strategy. Reading stimulates imagination *and* prefigures nucleic forms of public life joining writers in gentle correction and literary community, what certain deconstructors call intertextuality. Interpretation is not all politics, even though it is political. Marxists (e.g., Lukács, 1971) have had this problem with Marx's critique of ideology from the beginning. Diverse structural thinkers resist the concept of ideology because it seems to imply spontaneist and idealist approaches to social change. 'To be a Marxist' appears to require the assumption that the motor of history is the clash of large-scale social and economic structures. But Marx also suggested that there has to be an electric moment when people realize they have only their chains to lose. At that instant, the preponderant weight of social structure would begin to lessen as people replace historians as the authors of history. As members of a dualist civilization, many Marxists view structure and consciousness as disjunctive alternatives. This is a mistake especially where we understand the material nature of consciousness as well as the textuality of structures.

In the meantime, power endures, silencing some and privileging others. Critical theory does not ignore this; it suggests a view of power refusing simple mechanism. Power is both imposed and self-imposed. To the extent of its self-imposition, it can be undone, especially (Marcuse, 1955) in an advanced industrial society close to eliminating what Marx called necessary labor time, including reproduction. The preponderance of the capitalist totality is not invariant, as left structuralists imply. Indeed, it cannot be undone without theorizing it as an historical artifice, even a 'text' compelling adjustment in its seeming deauthored ontological permanence. In any case, social change can only be fashioned through the literary practices of changing minds and organizing. Nothing guarantees a good end, even for Marx. *Capital* plots the likely crisis points of an unfettered economic order. The expropriation of the expropriators always depended on the tenacity and organizational skills of revolutionaries. That is, at some level socialism depends on *texts*, be they *The Communist Manifesto* or other modes of radical invigoration and critique. This does not dissolve history into consciousness, as if given a choice; it merely recognizes that narrative is a kind of power in its own right. Foucault said that power is everywhere; Marx said that power is nowhere but on Wall Street. Both are correct.

Critical theory prefigures a utopian order addressed differently in Habermas' image of an ideal speech situation (Habermas, 1970b, 1971, 1973, 1979, 1984, 1987b) in which the process of discussion among equal dialogue partners is also the product; socialism in Marx's original terms is not simply a library of canonical texts but a literary intersubjectivity in which writing solicits its gentle correction by other versions. In this chapter I consider how to slow down the degradation of signification in a way that hears its own critique at once as a mode of new construction, prefiguring and actually beginning to create a new order of democratic public discourse. The model for this kind of work remains Marx's critique of bourgeois political economy; he simultaneously demystified by historicizing the nature-like patterns of the bourgeois marketplace and augured a new economic order in which capital and labor would cease to be opposing terms of value (see Cleaver, 1979).

Yet the critique of ideology in its more traditional formulation is insufficient to address ideologizing texts dispersed deeply into social nature itself. It is no longer clear at all what is ideological and what is not. Opposition is too readily coopted in affirmative ways. By the same token, ideology does not self-consciously programmatize a certain state of affairs, refusing baldly to exhort or admonish. Rather, ideology — the mystification of the possible — is concealed in nature's seeming reflection in versions provoking themselves, ever the aim of social ontologies engendering our plight as fate. We must trace ideological claims into the degraded significances that they have become in order to undo their compelling hold on thought. Imagination is stimulated by a critique addressing ontology dispersed into things themselves, even if these things appear not to be texts narrated with a transformative intent.

Fast capitalism, a stage of capitalism beyond what the Frankfurt School called late capitalism, speeds up mind so much that imagination takes too long. Fast capitalism is distinguished by the way in which the line between the textual and the material is blurred to the point of indistinguishability, hence making it very difficult to decipher the texts of ideology enmeshing us in their thoughtless repetition. This foreshortens the radical agenda in this way by limiting it to local causes — the usual reformist agendas of interest-group politics. Thus, the goal of a radical hermeneutics conceived as a mode of writing and reading is to *historicize* textuality in a way that shows the temporality of its conception as a process of authorial artifice, hence of possible social change. Marx historicized the categories of bourgeois political economy by showing the historicity of the bourgeois world it conveyed. Similarly, critique would defuse and delay the instantaneity of dispersed texts that do not admit of meditative or mediating readings because they pulsate with the concealed authoriality of social nature. Reading would slow the degradation of signification so that things were not allowed to become identical with the signifiers covering them with names and senses. Instead, language would reclaim for itself the right to speculate, meditate, mediate — and thus reconstruct.

The historicity of texts opens up the possibility of their reformulation among communities of coequal speakers. This reformulation would follow a deconstructive critique showing author where before only figure had been. This is what the critique of ideology becomes for a feminist postmodern critical theory. The built, textual and figural environment must be reauthorized where texts have dispersed into things that provoke their own stupefied readings in a positivist world. Buildings, books and number can be read narratively once they are narrated deconstructively as the driven fictions they really are. The excavation of writing's historical character shows the act of authorial artifice that made self-conscious choices about design and discourse. In this sense, reauthorizing readings would allow us to glimpse the possibility of reformulation as both literary and political work. Texts need not script our lives where we recognize that texts themselves are forms of life (Wittgenstein, 1953).

This narration of dispersed but effective texts recoups their self-alienation into an exterior world. It takes back text from things where it restores the methodically suppressed traces of authorial signification from its identity with its topics. This critical strategy helps turns texts, concealed in the deauthored gestures of their public display, into public discourse, making them available to be interrogated and re-formulated. Deconstructive reading is not enough, however, in order to undo the disciplining effects of texts that conceal their own drive to identify with the given order. A positivist world read narratively still dominates. A radical hermeneutics must also engage the reauthorized version in dispute about social possibilities, refusing the ontologizing accounts congealed in sociology, cities and sentience that then repro-duce those accounts in actual states of affairs. Power is ever at issue in the effort to overcome texts' self-alienation in things; the dominant order defies versions of writing opening science and technology to radical self-management via public discourse; Habermas' ideal speech situation opposes positivist social being by assuming that everyone can join debates about the public uses of knowledge.

## Deconstructing Fast Capitalism

Thus, an interpretive approach to fast capitalism not only traces the palimpsest of authorial significance but also opens authoriality to a general community of equal speakers. This is what I mean by dis-course. A problem in western civilization is that writing remains an élite activity, restricting constitution and communication to those competent to draw blueprints, write prose, compose criticism and do mathematics. This is a tiny fraction of the world's people, but it need not remain so. Freire's (1970) pedagogy of the oppressed that teaches literacy as a tool of political liberation inspires a pedagogy of expertise empowering people to use heretofore esoteric languages of planning, the professions and science (see O'Neill, 1976).

These élite argots must not only be opened to outsiders; they must also be reformulated in ways admitting their own literary corri-gibility, thus soliciting gentle correction by other versions. Public writing (hence democracy) requires public debate, which, in the best case, is solicited by writing itself. Self-confident expression goes hand in hand with the equally vigorous desire to start arguments and invite rejoinders. New science and technology (Marcuse, 1969; Agger, 1976b) prefigure a good political community in the openness of talk to its own correction, another way of suggesting Habermas' communicative ethic as a political methodology of socialism. It is not enough to learn positivist languages of administration but to reformulate these languages reflexively so that their unabashed narrativeness humbles their efforts to control nature and other people. In any case, radical hermeneutics, the name I am giving this strategy of opening concealed texts of power to genuine public discourse, cannot simply dent the élite monopoly of text while accepting its positivist intentionality without losing its own mind. Positivist writing drives toward its own dispersal into social nature and thus positivist codes, especially science, must be rewritten, not simply learned and used democratically. The democratization of what Habermas calls dialogue chances is an insufficient radical agenda. We must also reformulate the discourse of positivist representationality itself, which is precisely the contribution of poststructuralism to third-generation critical theory.

Domination not only resists its authorization turning it into arguable public discourse but it also defies other versions of it. Finding the author in concealed texts of power does not require that discovered authors concede dialogue chances to other versions of their texts, challenging their ontologized worlds with the possibility of other, different ones. Dialogue silences where monologue overwhelms. Thus, the politics of interpretation, like every other politics, depends on persuasion, coercion, coalition and mobilization. Positivism will not concede science to other versions defying a positivist account of frozen social nature. The purpose of authorization is not to convert those who perpetuate and profit from domination's eternity but to lay bare our own authorial possibilities where heretofore they were occluded. Radical hermeneutics raises consciousness to the level at which it can recognize its own non-identity to the world engulfing it.

From that point, people who propose different, non-representational versions of the world can only prefigure a better world in the hurly-burly of power and persuasion. Positivism will not be undone in its own terms, nor will the built environment suddenly melt into air (M. Berman, 1982) upon deconstructive critique. Reading radicalizes but must also be relived as the possibility of new community. An authorized world remains the same unless we all talk and live it differently — the agenda of any political movement that wants to win converts and thus redistribute power. A politics of textuality must move outside itself in reconfiguring the whole material world of which textuality is only a part, albeit a pivotal one.

Radical hermeneutics suggests, indeed embodies, transformative lives in all sorts of public and private realms. Critique addresses many dominations, not simply those of dispersed textuality — of intellection, ideation, so-called superstructure. Critical theory written under the auspices of Adorno and a political version of deconstruction (see Ryan, 1982) refuses axial reductions to a single master narrative replacing labor with text as an archetype of generic human activity and thus domination. Critique decenters itself while keeping analytic principles of domination and liberation firmly in mind. Although my critique of fast capitalism suggests some overall tendencies, it does not apply itself ruthlessly to local contexts in which my analysis of textual dispersal and concealment may be less than apt. Radical hermeneutics reads the author back into narrativeless texts, rewrites them as public discourse, persuades others of the possibility of different discourses about the social world, and then interrogates itself in asking itself the question of its answer. Only thus does radicalism check its own tendency to become cant and canon, imposed on others from above.

In this way, we resist being swallowed by our own slogans — surplus value, organic composition of capital, reification, total administration, ideal speech, fast capitalism, dispersed textuality, authorization. As slogans, these cease to do any analytic and thus political work, a crucial weakness checked only by what Communist cells call self-criticism. Critique flattens into affirmation and thus apologia where it uses concepts to do the work of mediation and negation. The irony of a dialectical materialism is that we must use concepts to understand the degradation of these concepts into things, swallowing the attempt to criticize them. Word play does not do all of the analytic work available, and yet it cannot be avoided in favor of a Derridean relativism sticking so close to the world's names for itself that it refuses to think new practices for fear of being harmlessly constructive, thus irrelevant.

Fast capitalism degrades every concept quickly, celebrating its novelty and then dispersing it to name things that live as a parody of what their concept was initially meant to criticize. Freedom becomes freedom to buy, park, borrow. Justice embodies in police, army, prison, missile silo. Criticism becomes interpretation and explication, accepting its subordination by master texts. Repressive tolerance (Marcuse et al., 1965) goes farther than that, turning critique into its opposite in naming and thus reproducing practices it initially opposed. As I develop in chapter 5, Marxism 'is' the Soviet Union and democracy 'is' capitalism. This does not tolerate any number of Marxist versions but singles out the one that will do the most system-serving work, disqualifying the left by Sovietizing it.

In this sense, deconstructive critique must resist its own deauthorization into lazy concepts substituting for thought. Critical theory is not a body of received truths but a literary strategy, a way of reading and writing. Opposition to texts' degradation takes the temporal form of slowing down the signifying process, halting the proliferation of names and labels bound to dissolve into their own othernesses. Calling domination something else only degrades yet another word, but language cannot transcend constitution and still communicate the energy of transformation driving it. Indeed, critique strives less to be science than to create community out of mutually provocative and respectful versions, refusing definitive interpretation as a conceit of Promethean mind — how Marxism got into trouble in the first place. This does not mean that we have to abandon rigor, especially if rigor's opposite is the mushy method of humanist subjectivism, a problem for feminist theorists and methodologists who eschew abstraction as male projection. Opponents of positivism do not have to renounce any language of figure, especially where we can reauthorize mathematics as a literature in its own right and thus use it to comprehend the mathematizing forces of fast-capitalist administration turning us all into number.

A powerful political force in its own right, reading must be revalorized by those under the sway of a mechanistic version of the relation between ideal and material. Textuality materially intervenes in history where texts as matter provoke or compel certain enactments of its version of metaphysical possibility. In fast capitalism this literary process of provocation both accelerates under the imperative of capital reproduction and takes nondiscursive forms where writing no longer enjoys its previous distance from the world it addresses and thus can no longer be easily read, and hence criticized. A version of hermeneutic reading indebted to both critical theory and poststructuralism slows down and reauthorizes text acts as a mode of political resistance and reconfiguration; we need not apologize for this. The region of the political is both smaller and bigger than it once was — smaller in that nothing much of importance seems to take place in the sphere of formal public debate, bigger in that politics disperses itself into the disguised texts of the quotidian that provoke their own reception and thus reproduction.

A radical hermeneutics politicizes what appears to be only nature (but is really text — argument for a certain social condition). My critique of disciplinary sociology (Agger, 1989c) models a critique of all disciplining, blending Habermas and Foucault through a postmodern-feminist appreciation of Adorno's negative dialectics. These names matter only as autobibliographical signs of my own engagements. As such, if taken too literally as pedigrees, they risk the inertia of all names given to things that are then swallowed in the names themselves. The sign must possess some distance from the reality it addresses lest it take on a concealed reality of its own and thus substitute for the thought thinking it in the first place. I avoid the congealing tendencies of my own thought without pretending an originary intellect that, in the fashion of Madison Avenue, promises wholly 'new and different' products — this time, social theory. By inscribing the names Adorno, Foucault and Habermas to describe some of my textual beginnings, I suggest a version of them that elucidates all of us — me through my reading of them, them through the invitation to read them on route to understanding me. This is precisely what is meant by the hermeneutic circle in which all textual interventions are undecidably enclosed.

Radical hermeneutics reads discipline in terms of a politics of signification's degradation. When names dispersed into nature as pre-given objects do our constitutive work for us, we need new names to give to things. Before that, though, we need to read social nature as an authorial achievement concealed in the reifications of a positivist culture. Sociology as a positivist discipline was important to me only because it represents a generalized fact-fetishism dulling historical imagination (see Horkheimer and Adorno's collection of essays published under the general editorship of the Institute for Social Research, 1972). Sociology's names — family, institution, role, stratification — swallow the realities they originally meant to describe, in particular rendering oppressions ontological as a generic social nature (see Piccone, 1971; O'Neill, 1972c; Paci, 1972; Agger, 1989c). In turn, science's text reproduces the contingent family, institution, role and stratification named by sociology to be invariant features in its discourse of the power of the social — that further empowers the social. It does this by copying them into its pages, ironically proving itself by reading inequality off social nature once it has provoked it as fate.

Now I recognize that sociology does not count for much. Yet it helps me model a critique of discipline; I unearth this critique from the way academics let names work as the essence of disciplinary advancement, today the apology for texts' forced identity with the world they address. In chapter 2, I read sociology as a modal positivism, concealing its own political agendas written into its presuppositionless representation and hence reproduction of the present social order. Description is more than ontology; it risks beoming a world when published as a definitive account. Critical theory reads discipline in the texts enforced as discipline on disempowered readers. Thus, critical theory aims to turn readers into writers. As a story, methodology can have a different ending.

Any text disciplining imagination by appearing not to be writing at all — the essence of fast capitalism — requires narration; it narrates itself storylessly. Domination has been regionalized in order to avoid being traced to a single axial principle that can be opposed as such. Discipline happens in numerous local settings and must be opposed there. Domination can be reduced neither to a regime, country or conspiracy nor to what some call dominant structure (Althusser, 1969). Instead, powerlessness corrupts heterogeneously, requiring de-disciplining readings and rewritings with nuanced tones and textures. Although feminist postmodern critical theorists regard the nature of discipline today as history concealed in secret writing, disciplining proceeds locally according to local requirements of rational administration.

Deconstructive reading with a political intent theorizes by authorizing disciplines suppressing not only theory but all thought. It suggests a better world in a communicative ethic of many speakers. Critical reading, by authorizing dispersed texts, not only opens up the possibility of other versions; it also refuses to canonize a single defini-

tive version, ever the corruption of apodictic knowledge. Deconstructive reading goes still further. Not only does it narrate social nature
and then open it to possible reformulations. It also refuses to play off
these reformulations in an epistemological or moral marketplace, preferring *to criticize as a political way of being human*; strong reading
addresses disciplining monologue in the voice it recommends. Critique and construction blend where authorization purposely provokes
other versions prefiguratively as a form of community itself.

Deconstructive reading sharply demystifies by showing author
where before only figure had been. At the same time, it gently
provokes other versions as a way of implanting intertextuality in a
living community of literary mutuality. The critic must balance negative and positive passions here, vigorously opposing versions that hide
themselves behind the appearance of social nature while at the same
time challenging concealed discourse to voice itself in a dialogical
way. Concealing its authorship in order to monopolize authorial authority, positivist text contains within it the possibility of its own
reformulation. In any case, we must believe that closed versions can
be opened and made part of dialogue itself lest we arrogate naming,
hence power, to ourselves. The left's right is no less wrong than the
right itself (Breines, 1985).

Is this adequate politics? This depends on how we intend adequacy as well as politics. It is adequate if we read politics in places
where it is not usually sought, notably in signs and codes dispersed
into nature as its own reproduction. Debunking slogans is today
political work. A positivist culture transvalues the political into virtual
ontology, albeit found in cultural products and processes and not in
abstracted metaphysical tomes. Positivism exists precisely to replace
the speculative metaphysical construction of the Greeks that at least
preserved a distance between itself and the world. Positivism disqualifies utopia on grounds that it cannot be perceived, measured, oper-
ationalized. Method in replacing metaphysics becomes metaphysics.
Critique reads the metaphysics hidden in scientism's allegedly onto-
logyless account of the given world as a version that can be opposed.
Critique then engages with science in inviting it to be different from
the world it surreptitiously narrates. Ontology *itself* prefigures good
community; nothing is better than the conversation about what
'better' ought to mean — theory's literary praxis.

By finding politics encoded in dispersed codes we begin to live a
new politics and hence create a new polity. Positivists temporally
separate theory and practice in order to postpone theory's practice
indefinitely. In the meantime, scientific fetishism precludes deeper
speculation about the good. And now in fast capitalism fetishes become texts in their own right, especially with regard to the mathematics that has virtually replaced speculative construction in the
human studies. Number is the ultimate dispersal of sense into a sentient
world, defying its other versions by seeming not to signify at all. I can

think of few more effective political strategies today than to replace math with metaphysics especially where we read math as the secret metaphysic that it is and would become — absolute fungibility made a principle of social organization.

I do not simply propose a better metaphysic than sheer representation; metaphysical construction itself is good because it cannot avoid inviting its own correction, thus joining community. Plato's good defies other versions to best it even if Plato would reject those versions as inadequate. At least he gets us talking, reading and writing in the interplay of versions tolerant of each other — indeed, needing each other as reciprocal audiences. Greek truth is the time and trouble it takes to get there, not simply truth objects found pregiven to philosophy's lens. Dialectic thus connoted dialogue for Plato; ironically, his apodictic sketch of the good life in *Republic*, the original perpetualization of domination, belied his implication that the good life was the time spent together arguing it. A left-postmodern version of Plato would use Plato's own dialectic and especially its simultaneity of theory and practice to undo the explicit Plato of *Republic*.

But this is neither a Platonist treatise nor against Plato. For better or worse, Greek metaphysics at least augurs a depiction of utopia resisting the degradations of positivist culture, where non-science is dismissed literally as nonsense. But critique today does not have the luxury of *de novo* construction of Plato's type; the weight of positivist writing is nearly preponderant. We must reverse the direction of the textual so as to prise the mind free to think a different world. Politics is ontological construction where today ontology resides in building, culture and figure, thus precluding other versions both of it and the world it provokes. Where Plato meant for people to live the *Republic* directly, the positivist banishment of constitutive metaphysics is no less metaphysical for all that. The extirpation of ontology is itself a political agenda — adaptation, acquiescence, adjustment. We oppose it by revealing it as agenda, now so deeply buried as to be virtually invisible in the things into which it has been dispersed (see Institute for Social Research, 1972: pp. 202–3).

Hermeneutics is a way of life where all reading is a version of writing. Derrida's poststructuralism makes us think differently about the activity of reading, dehierarchizing the traditional positivist relationship between authorial construction and a subordinate interpretiveness. Deconstructive critique constructs where it reveals the narrativeness of versions not heard as stories. By insisting on the world's textuality, reading offers new versions. Critique refuses its subordination to the weight of the given by 'giving' it differently. The world's textuality is political because, after all, the world is present to us as the untranscendable horizon of human possibilities. Existentialism continues to illuminate where it compels us to embrace the worldliness of metaphysical questioning; historicity is not flattened with the aid of method but celebrated as the occasion of new histories (see Adorno, 1973; O'Neill, 1972c).

Fast capitalism replaces knowledge constitution with positivist representation now projected into technique itself. The mirror supposedly reflecting the world becomes a world itself, producing behavior it supposedly only records phenomenally. Where German idealists questioned the possibilities of all knowledge and history, today critique is reduced to commentary, explication of text, a narrow interpretive accounting. Even deconstruction becomes methodology. The denigration of reading as derivative and dependent reflects the overall domination of reproduction. This does not mean that we can suddenly empower critique as if its denigration did not occur, writing marginally, epigrammatically and playfully in the way Derrida does. To be critical, reading must address its marginality while insisting on its centrality — a process of becoming in which reproduction struggles to produce, not simply buttress. In this sense, critique expands the sense of available constitutive work.

As I discussed in chapter 2, the critic acts politically when he or she refuses the dominating western order of value — production over reproduction, capital over labor, men over women, text over commentary. As Marx indicated, value is the real battleground of the political. Indeed, the transformation of use value into exchange value is one of the best examples of textual dispersal in fast capitalism, a process accelerated since the mid-nineteenth century. Commodities conceal the social relations that make them valuable by becoming enmeshed in the cash nexus assigning them significance only to the extent of their cost and self-reproduction as exchange value. Marxism criticizes the degradation of use value's significance in a money economy, arguing not for the abolition of money itself but for the social relations concealed in transforming use value into exchange value. Marx was for utility and against the dispersal of utility into its money representation, especially where that dispersal empowers some and immiserates others (see Marx, 1961: pp. 136–41).

> That which is hidden for me through the medium of *money* — that for which I can pay (i.e., which money can buy) — that am *I*, the possessor of the money. The extent of the power of money is the extent of my power. Money's properties are my properties and essential powers — the properties and powers of its possessors. Thus, what I *am* and *am capable* of is by no means determined by my individuality (Marx, 1961: p. 138).

In capitalism money encodes the hierarchical social relations that brought money about in the first place. By concealing its own textuality in this sense, money is accepted immediately as a legitimate standard of value and thus reproduced in monied practices. Money mathematizes domination once read as a text concealing its own textuality — historicity. Marx did no more than read money in *Capital* (n.d.: pp. 97–144); here I am trying to read readings that money would provoke, thus to rewrite money as an example of our oppression by the books we write and then forget how to read. Today it seems that everybody writes but nobody reads. In reading money Marx explicitly challenged the nature-like account of money offered by British political economy; in reading positivist culture, I challenge the accounts of the mathematizing social sciences like sociology.

Not only is my account more fundamental than Marx's because I try to generalize his own particular reading; I could not read writing not meant to be read without Marx having already read money as a dispersed and thus self-reproducing text. In this sense, I call my account Marxist. In a similar sense I call myself feminist because my version presupposes the feminist reading of sexuality as a text of gender (see Beauvoir, 1953). I read Marx's politics as an urge to reprivilege use value over its money transformation, thus suggesting all sorts of institutional changes across the economic system and polity — and, feminism would add, the realm of intimacy. Marx suggested more than that, too, where he implies that money is the most fundamental form of domination in capitalism. I do not disagree, although the strategic priority is not to assign priority to one or another level of domination but to figure out how to read domination not meant to be read at all. In this I look to Marx for guidance. But it is impossible in the late twentieth century to endorse Marx's own unexamined hierarchy of productive over reproductive activity in the way of most economisms (e.g., the implication that only commodities bear use value, not also children, sexuality, intimacy). For me, Marx's reading of money is among his most fundamental contributions to an enduring critical theory.

In reading money for the world it both represents and reproduces, we reduce its fetish character. In fast capitalism significance is lost as text becomes thing; reading recoups it and at the same time learns from it. Marx in reading money opened a whole social theory around which money pivoted both as text and thing. In reading sociology as a modal form of positivist science in chapter 2 I continued that reading. Here I want to understand better what Marx's reading of money and my reading of positivist culture have in common beyond a certain political intent. *They both pursue sign into the things that signify today.* As such, they learn from the texts dispersed and concealed in the exterior environment and also refuse their accounts of an unalterable social nature.

Indeed, a deconstructive reading strategy goes one step further. In authorizing hidden texts as they have become compelling things, reading's account models a different world. By refusing bourgeois political economy's non-semiotic understanding of money, Marx suggested a world in which money's phony equivalences do not rule human behavior. By refusing positivism's world, I suggest a world in which meaning does not have to erode into things that take over the monopolistic and monologic process of constitution. And by reversing the erosion of signification, I open signification to a democratic community of writers, a powerful political strategy in its own right.

In presupposing the incorrigibility and infinity of interpretation, radical hermeneutics forestalls its own methodologization. Utopia oppresses where it only inverts the old; Marxist positivism is still positivism, just as left and right oligarchies subordinate. Critique must check its tendency to install a new absolute and thus short-circuit the spiral of writing and reading guaranteeing the identity of epistemological and political democracy (see Marcuse's Second Preface to *Reason and Revolution*, 1960). Although domination is wrong absolutely, dissent is not for that reason absolutely correct. By resisting versions disqualifying all contest, critique must facilitate its reading as another corrigible version lest it canonize into another inert order of being.

This is not a plea for tolerance; tolerance today only tolerates the horrible (Marcuse *et al.*, 1965). By authorizing hidden texts, deconstructive reading wants to vanquish their accounts in order to change the world. Yet a dialectical spin must be put on a different version of versions refusing to arrogate all moral authority to itself. My version of critical theory will doubtless provoke alternative formulations, as it should. The point here is that the good society, whether named socialism or ideal speech situation, is *the talk it takes to resolve the babel of tongues* — realizing that we cannot achieve a definitive resolution. It is one thing to beat back counterrevolutionary versions, as we must attempt to do. It is another to refuse all talk that challenges and corrects. The good is in getting there, even if 'there' always eludes us. Or if the good does not materialize *en route*, at least we can avoid the bad by institutionalizing communicative democracy.

## Critique as Text

Deconstructive critique recognizes that it will be criticized itself. It should be defensive only where it realizes that criticism is not meant to open the world to many versions but would establish itself as an enduring version. It should be open to criticism where critique is playfully and dialogically intended — where the point of criticism is to start or refresh human relationships and not simply to scold or punish (see Ackerman, 1980 as well as my discussion of him in chapter 8). Positivist habits of mind run so deep that we can barely refrain from turning our defensiveness on those who need it least — our comrades. The left competes with itself in a self-destructive way because its scientism frequently gets the better of its transformative desire, freezing utopia into a hellish hierarchical nightmare. Too many Marxists forget Marx's passionate opposition to capitalist being; instead, by doing their own positivist version of writing, they ironically reinforce positivism's hegemony. This has been said often, but it must be said again: Marxist validity is not theory but practice, better, a practice that theorizes itself in the process of its own becoming. To put this in literary terms, Marxists avoid tyranny by imagining how their writing will be read, hence lived.

Radical hermeneutics reads the world against itself, exposing its verities as corrigible literary products. Where things authorized to be read as texts seem to defy utopia, reading historicizes and thus reformulates history. Smith and Ricardo, Davis and Moore, Parsons and Bales are thus read to express ironic dialectical truth. They depict a frozen world, including their accounts as buttress. The world, in its need to be written, reveals its own deficit of obedience. Thus, critique takes advantage of the world's openness as an opportunity to write and live differently, what Foucault called thinking otherwise. There is no more profound political agenda than to reformulate formulation's own role in reproducing the given — thus revealing the 'given' to be only one among a number of narrative possibilities suppressed by methodology.

Thus, critique utopianizes even where it avoids construction. In resisting ontology, the critique of ontology suggests a different order of being to which it contributes its own example. Unlike positivism, though, it accounts for its own role in bringing being into being. Critique's utopia lies in the norm of democratic speech it exemplifies in its ability to be simultaneously self-confident and tentative. It drives to change the world, and it recognizes its historicity as a mortal account requiring other versions to complete its humanity. But left critique fears challenges where it recognizes that the world too frequently crushes negation. It must get beyond this, however, if its utopian norm is really to become a constitutive principle of social order. Irony and radicalism belong together if radicalism is to avoid its own eclipse.

Few Marxists or feminists admit irony where any sign of weakness could be exploited by the dominant discourse. It is easy to understand left fascism as a response, albeit totally inadequate, to the liberal fascism of money and science. In this sense, the Frankfurt School understood the tendency of Marxism to degenerate into a repetition of dominant categories of value. Marxist economism only repeats the economism of the world at large; it fails to think itself contributing to the problem it addresses with the perverse passion of the canonical. For its part, mainstream feminism rejects the politics of production because Marxism traditionally missed the importance of reproduction as a region of important human experience. In this way, left feminism fades into a liberal version economizing women's public exploitation and familizing gender relations.

Opposition epochally finds itself at a disadvantage where it opposes an order that would control the meaning of value. Critique must simultaneously address mystification in its own terms and yet rise above it by insisting on a new order of being. Language must both refuse old meaning and yet engage old meaning in terms clarifying its deceptions. Marx read money not because he wanted money himself but because he opposed the way money encodes and thus reproduces value in capitalism. By the same token, feminism reads pornography as a sign of what happens to women under patriarchy and thus risks giving women's objectification an undue ontological significance — as if pornography, like money for Marxists, were here to stay.

Critical theory must struggle toward a new language in which to reorder and thus reflect a new order of being. Western language split between subject and predicate conceals hierarchy under what appears mere differentiation. Language authorizes domination, and then it is dispersed into things that talk to us and compel us to enact their fateful codes. Thus, we need a new version of language in which to convey and contribute to a new order of being — one alive to the aporias of language and yet willing for all that to dwell within talk's circularity in gentle and reciprocal dialogue (Wittgenstein, 1953). Deconstruction suggests that language uses us; yet it can also augur a mode of being in which language's structuring tendencies are checked deconstructively — by thought, reason, imagination. A radical hermeneutics traces the oppressions of language in order to undo them. In this sense, 'new' language will trade on past meanings and yet in so doing will say something else, thus allowing lives to be lived differently through it.

A future society, dispensing with money's concealment and thus the reproduction of skewed exchange relations, will require symbolic media of exchange. Money can still represent, if not falsely. In reading money, Marx opens the possibility of a world in which money tells its own story unproblematically and in which people acquire sufficient amounts of it. Similarly, a feminist society need not dispense with imageries of sexuality, especially where sexuality has been freed from its representation as the violence men do to women. It is difficult to foretell the future language games of a free society without knowing exactly how present ones structure thought and life into unacceptably confined possibilities. The only way out of bad talk is through more talk, trading on but transcending past meaning.

Critical theory translated into a reading strategy via deconstruction undoes language repeating self-destructive behaviors by recognizing that language itself is a form of behavior. Meaning cannot subsist beyond language, and thus the Marxist search for apodicticity is as futile as the Enlightenment's pursuit of eternal laws of social motion. We can only live within systems of meaning structuring the pregiven grammars of rhetoric. Yet by opening closed texts to authorizing readings we necessarily change meaning. Money encodes and thus reproduces an order of value peculiar to exchange economies. By reading money Marx suggests an alternative order of value in which money does not stand for and thus deepen the theft of surplus value; Marx thinks money otherwise by reading it for what it tells us about social order. Critical theory at once stays within the circle of meaning already established and then suggests different meanings, playing off the sense of the old. Marx's 'value' is certainly not the same as capitalist value, and yet to suggest its possibilities he must read capitalist value for its aporias.

This version of deconstructive reading constructs by thinking text otherwise. It makes deception reveal itself and thus bespeaks a social order in which deception facilitates domination. My concern with domination's text is materialist and not purely aesthetic. I do not want to read literature for its insight (although as a pastime that is certainly work many already do) but to read science, money, edifice and figure as literary artifices that conceal their narrative nature and thus provoke worlds of which they pretend to be disinterested accounts. Where Marxist aestheticians read literature for its class truths and feminist critics read for gender truths, they do not realize that their own sciences are fictions concealing authorial commitment to new versions of those texts. Hiding its literary auspices in this way, deconstructive reading pretends an indubitable account that in turn deauthorizes into the cant of political correctness, thus risking its own hierarchy over other accounts. Although hierarchy over the false is certainly an acceptable political goal, critique inattentive to its own literariness risks oppressing companion versions, thus turning itself into yet another arrogant architecture that effaces the traces of its own conception.

Otherwise, critique thinks falsehood not to establish an eternity of truth but to turn truth into a corrigible accomplishment of many speakers, precisely what we ought to mean by socialism. Not only do dispersed texts of science, money, edifice and figure misrepresent; they seem not to represent at all and thus they only reproduce the world encoded in them as ontologically unalterable. Hence, reading is difficult in fast capitalism. We do not know exactly what is text and what is thing; better, it is hard to discern where text's thinghood conceals its authorial artifice in a way that it could have been written differently. Yet there seem to be many books out there, especially works intending critique and transformation. They are almost inevitably swallowed in the maw of administration; their textuality fails to become a thing having a prominent place in the public world. Instead, the real texts today defy easy reading, dispersed into things compelling 'readings' of adjustment, adaptation, acquiescence. These are the damaged lives most of us live.

Books do not look like texts and texts are things in fast capitalism. In this situation critical theory risks obscurity by standing apart.

Yet there is no real alternative lest critique reduce itself to dominant discourse as method. It is said that the critical theory of the Frankfurt School, indeed Marxism generally, has had translation problems in the New World, where the original thinkers presupposed sophisticated knowledge of European philosophy and high culture (see Hughes, 1975: p. 169). True, but translation in the sense of popularization would not have helped. Adorno is not a television show, popular magazine or board game anymore than he can be 'mainstreamed' as a sociological theorist once reduced to simple English. *Negative Dialectics* (Adorno, 1973a) opposes commonsense with the irony of dialectical allusion; today clarity obfuscates. Thought must labor to think the categories of German idealism differently, deconstructively. Adorno did not write straightforward social theory, whatever that is, because administration defies straightforwardness to understand its complexities (see Hughes, 1975: p. 170).

Positivist academic disciplines want simplicity in order to divert thought from comprehending its complex object, the totality of domination in which discipline itself plays a part. Critique must wrestle with the mystifications of ordinary and disciplinary language in order to wrest language from its straitjacket in the straightforward. This requires Promethean deconstructive work, especially where authorial figure has been virtually erased from the text of science and must be interpolatively replaced as if it had been there all along. Critical theory cannot simply read and rebut books because it must instead read money, science, edifice and figure as the real texts of the time. Adorno's *Negative Dialectics*, like this work, struggles to become a thing when things are books and books nonentities. Adorno wants to be read for his reading of other discourses concealing domination; I want to be read for my reading of text/things compelling adjustment. Yet I realize that even within academic fields this sort of implosive reading strategy goes largely unheard because it does little recognizable disciplinary work.

I do not produce hypotheses, contribute to a literature, or suggest ways of 'applying' my version to the world in remediating it. It is far too late for that. A critical theory of public life must be relentlessly negative, piercing the illusions of the dominant quotidian. And if academics themselves do not read books appearing to do little disciplinary work — that are undisciplined — how can we expect anyone else to read and think? But writing cannot account for its reception, and thus it ought not try to ensure its comprehensibility to readers it thinks it knows. Writing relying too much on a sense of its audience only reiterates. I do not counsel a studied obscurantism, courting preciousness. I simply think the dilemma of writing about and against administration in an overly administered world. We risk the same fate as everyone else. Writing's auspices must be sought elsewhere; for me, they exist in a notion of critique that radically plumbs writing for echoes of thought methodically concealed so as not to invite its rejoinder. Popularity is not a measure of truth but, today, of unconsciousness.

The standard criticism of critical theorists is that they write obscurely in order not to *have* to enter the fray, exhibiting the intellectual's usual disdain for the people (e.g., see Slater, 1977). But what is the virtue of being sucked in and thus under, apart from having done one's political duty? Critical theory distances itself in order to be as direct as possible about the way ideation entwines us materially, subverting even the words we use to express our rage and then formulate alternative living arrangements. Obscurity educates and liberates where it resists banalization, reduction to platitude, and thus affirmation. Positivist culture degrades signification by denying imagination the ability to think beyond the categories covering the present in ontological amber. Deconstructive reading addresses this evisceration of imagination as a way of understanding how all sorts of marginality are disciplined.

Deconstructive reading politicizes interpretation where it recognizes how books that become things defy interrogative responses and thus new social arrangements. This reading strategy insists on its right to interpret texts littering the exterior landscape with their dispersed and thus suppressed significances, opening them to reformulating readings as a way of taking back the word. This is how specialist writing is amplified into public discourse through the latent critical tendencies of poststructuralist literary strategies. Recognizing that many books have become things and are thus unreadable as the acts of authorial mediation and constitution they originally were, real books insist on their distance from things. This is a way of being direct, not evasive, in spite of doctrinaire caricatures to the contrary. Today it is not at all clear what is political, allowing for all sorts of sectarian disputes about strategy. I view politics as the region in which the least political things provoke the most political behavior — the area in which money, science, edifice and figure compel their own readings as nucleic forms of public life. Critical theory insists on the right to name the political, especially where politics hides behind the label of ontology, mere representation of what 'must' be. Politics and ontology are separated by history, although in fast capitalism politics uses ontology well as a way of concealing its own historicity and hence susceptibility to reformulation.

Radical hermeneutics, another name for a deconstructive reading strategy, politicizes by opening texts to narration. This is inadequate strategy where not all public things encode an ontology of adjustment and affirmation. Yet it is a beginning; it is unavoidable where we no longer know what it means to read or even *what* to read in the way of arguments constructed by apparent authors. The world seems to argue for itself without the seeming need of ideological buttress. But this is false. Falsehood must still insist on itself with the aid of versions of what must be. Critique in penetrating falsehood imagines the possibility of different worlds and thereby helps them come to be.

The name radical hermeneutics is a problem, as are all slogans announcing their political sufficiency. 'Radical' recognizes that hermeneutics is typically conservative. But why do it, then, if its disengagement requires politicization from the outside? Although labels are risky for what they claim for themselves — always too much, for example historical materialism or communication theory — we cannot strategize without them. Perhaps I should simply say that I am doing, and propose, critical reading and writing. But critique intends things I do not mean as well. It might connote a foundationlessness forever avoiding the work of positive architecture. And hermeneutics suggests reading strategy, which becomes political strategy when I add the adjective radical.

We do different sorts of work in opposing domination. All the things we do are material because they matter and are matter. Cultural criticism, another self-limiting slogan, is my version of politics today, and thus I politicize reading where I believe empirically and politically that reading and writing are at stake in fast capitalism. The problem is not only that there is no public anymore for whom one can write but also that there are no more books to be written that can stand outside the world they address and thus oppose. This is politically serious, given a certain perspective on how capitalism complexly administers mind and thus inhibits resistance. We feel that we must apologize for 'merely' reading where orthodox Marxism makes us feel guilty about not doing ostensibly more political things like organizing workers, women, the Third World. Not to apologize is a good political beginning in its own right for it says something about how we must revalue public and private activities. That economics matters does not require us to be economistic — thus dualist, sexist, stupid.

Radical reading not only undoes secret ideology, appearing not to be, but in doing so helps us think differently about the possibilities of public discourse. Critique, if successful in authorizing dispersed texts of money, science, edifice and figure, recreates a public world in which people read and write together as a dialogical norm of community. If that is to happen, critique must think about the way it wants to relate itself to other versions and to readers and incorporate that desire into its critical approach to texts and things. The rhetoric of negation bears within it a glimpse of the possible. Thus, difficult writing imagines a historical situation in which it becomes clear — and understands its own responsibility for narrating that history. Perhaps this is only to say that negation is not enough; I offer this caution to textual fetishists who conflate the material and textual worlds so thoroughly that text seems to have no outside, thus losing the specificity of a critique of ideology addressing discourse as a medium of domination.

The lament that no one reads or writes — that there is no viable public sphere — must recognize that *in saying that* it already models a better public world. Critique suggests itself as a norm where it understands its opposition as the implication of a possible positive to which it contributes through its own version. Critical theory builds community by understanding how positivist culture vitiates community, making texts things and things texts. In thinking the complex totality, critical theory thinks it otherwise, measuring it against a standard of historical possibility giving sense to its angry opposition. The challenge for criticism is to understand this about itself. Reading presupposes a standard of otherness grounding anger in the possibility of happiness. It needs to articulate the imagery of this otherness in order to provoke negation toward new construction. If it does not, it tends to be swallowed, domesticated, academicized, professionalized, precisely the fate of much thought today.

Viewed as a deconstructive reading strategy that makes private texts public, critical theory is not method but historical intervention prising imagination free from the exterior world, enmeshing it in the tautology of itself.

> The only Theory able to raise, if not to pose, the essential question of the status of these disciplines, to criticize ideology in all its guises, including the disguises of technical practice as sciences, is the Theory of theoretical practice (as distinct from ideological practice): the materialist dialectic or dialectical materialism, the conception of the Marxist dialectic in its *specificity*. (Althusser, 1969: pp. 171–2).

Once critique develops into an interpretive rule, it disciplines attempts to use it differently, passionately, wildly. Yet without some discipline critique peters out in the endless play of signifiers — whatever that might mean politically. The challenge is to theorize without being ruled by theoretical abstraction. Without theory, critique fails to think the structural properties of its topic and thus goes nowhere politically. Too much obedience to the rule of concepts in architectonic rigor stills the passion of politics; critique becomes another academic specialty to be applied anywhere and everywhere. Deconstruction suffers both fates, neither developing a social theory within which we can understand and thus oppose language's structuring domination of mind nor resisting its own methodologization in English departments. It is telling that 'critical theory' in the American university describes both a version of Marxism of the kind I am developing here *and* an approach to literary interpretation — again, the problem of two cultures.

Who can we read to find out how to criticize while remaining alert to the way critique intends itself as a norm of a better society? Who 'thinks otherwise' without being idealist or irrelevant? The list is probably very short. People on this list resist the reduction of their writing and reading into method even if some have been unsuccessful, notably Marx. We are never fully responsible for how we are read. Readers write texts, even — no, especially — where they imagine the texts to be perfect copies of nature. Yet we have some control over our reception the more we are clear about the implications of our mode of talk for a new society. That way we resist becoming either high theorists (Habermas) or cherished celebrities (Derrida, Foucault). In any case, precious few examples of good readers and writers exist. After all, academia disciplines. Thus, we ought not look there for many examples of public intellectuality. And the world of letters confines thought by fashion in refusing politics as dirty work unsuited to people who would live the life of the mind.

A prominent critical theorist once told me that we need heroes, not only people whose work we explicate but people to whom to appeal for moral energy. At the time I thought he was justifying idolatry. Having thought more about it, I am now convinced that he was right. We need heroes to help us imagine the audience to whom we write, to sustain us as dialogue partners. Without heroes we are too isolated and thus too frequently beaten down when things go wrong — we cannot get published, obtain decent work, enjoy hospitable colleagues, sustain imagination. Our heroes need not oppress us if we can avoid reading them methodologically but only as people who complete our speech by gently correcting it. Political community must start somewhere, even between two or three people who nucleically create the example of public discourse and thus a decent public life. The point is to begin.

It is by now a truism among those who teach writing that getting started is the hardest thing (see Becker, 1986). Theoretical readers read, read, read, believing that writing cannot begin until all the interpretive bases have been covered. Reading disciplined by the rule of method reads too much for fear that the community of scholarship will reject the argument as unstudied. This is especially rampant on the left where scientism and professionalism prevail like never before. Critical theory in going public refuses to be ruled by authority structures, which proliferate specialist discourses in order to keep outsiders out. In the process, our theory will be corrected in a way prefiguratively modeling a good polity. If anything, writing today risks being overeducated, so obedient to tradition that it loses its voice. This will not be resolved by scrapping some of the accoutrements of scholarship like footnotes, bibliographies and third-person voice, although none of these is essential. Instead, writing must self-confidently risk criticism, disapprobation, even oblivion. Those who truculently chastise critical theory for its political aloofness are less courageous. They frequently do not even write but spend endless hours studying *Capital* or other modern masters of left scholarship. Hermeneutics done by radicals is no less conservative than Bible study. Neither reinvigorates public discourse.

As I have suggested in this chapter, a critical theory of public life needs a way of reading specialist texts that encode powerful ideological recommendations for conformity and quiescence. By reading deconstructively against the grain of these dispersed texts of popular culture, architecture and science, we can engage these secret discourses in argument. As well, in the very act of dialogical engagement, we model a better polity in which dialogue chances, as Habermas calls them, are roughly equal and in which communication exhibits generous qualities of temperateness and reciprocity. Only in these ways can discourse help to create a more open public sphere, especially that special discourse which emerges from one's engagement with persuasive texts. In the next two chapters, I look closely at the specialized discourses of academic disciplines both organizationally (chapter 4) and textually (chapter 5). This will prepare the way for arguments made in subsequent chapters for a more public intellectual practice that emerges dialectically in counterpoint to the organization and rhetoric of positivism.

*Chapter 4*

# Aporias of Academic Production*

In this chapter, I extend my analysis of the politics of discourse, introduced in the first three chapters of this book, to a focused analysis of the politics of disciplinary knowledge and discourse. The feminist postmodern critical theory that I developed in my opening chapters is applied specifically to the textual politics of the academy and of academic writing. This helps me round out my analysis of the literary production of discipline, which I extend to an analysis of textbooks in the following chapter. In this chapter, I describe the institutional context within which disciplinary knowledge and discourse are situated. In the following chapter, I examine ways in which textbook writing in American sociology reinforces a hegemonic view of the social world rooted in the powerfully deauthorizing rhetoric of positivism, according to which sociological writing reflects society presuppositionlessly. This suggests a non-positivist version of social-science methodology that acknowledges and even celebrates the author-iality of science, thus opening science to informed public discourse (see Agger, 1989b), a theme to which I return in the second half of this book.

## The State Management of Knowledge

The dominant view of American academia is characterized by the metaphor of an open market of competing ideas, paralleling the liberal metaphor of a market economy. In this chapter I suggest that the activity within American universities is more analogous to a state-guided Keynesian economy. In turn, this helps me develop a notion of literary political economy that accompanies my left-feminist-postmodern theory of the politics of textuality. Replacing the metaphor of Adam Smith's free-market economy with that of an economy directed by the state will help me better understand the current contradictions of academic production in public and private

* with Allan Rachlin

research universities and then to suggest new ways of viewing and carrying out oppositional intellectual work, both in research and teaching. This analysis follows from the theoretical foundation-setting carried out in the opening three chapters in the sense that it derives from the overall perspective of a critical theory that is highly alert to the relationship among textuality, ideology and institutions. Many left-wing intellectuals confront a dilemma by virtue of their precarious and somewhat self-contradictory role in the university (see Norton and Ollman, 1978). The replacement of metaphors with which to understand the production of knowledge — open market by state management — will enable me to understand this dilemma of intellectuals who are at once privileged state or corporate employees and radical critics. This analysis further suggests a way to overcome the non-identity of theory and practice, which is characteristic of public life in late capitalism, including the public lives of leftist intellectuals (more generally, see Kann, 1982). I return to this theme of socially critical intellectuality in my two concluding chapters.

The state management of knowledge can be understood via a theory of the state that includes not only government and its economic steering functions but also higher education as well as religion and other aspects of culture and entertainment (see Miliband, 1973: pp. 38–41, 215–18). The state management of knowledge involves, among other things, the increasing pressure for state-employed academics to do work within the defined limits of empiricist scholarship and to publish their work in mainstream (i.e., ideologically and methodologically vouchsafed) journals. These requirements, in turn, help shape the educational environment that students encounter as they pursue their university studies. Academics attempting to establish and maintain careers within the confines imposed by the academic profession will perpetuate the limiting worldviews within which they are themselves constrained. By so restricting the definition of legitimate scholarship, as well as its literary organization, corresponding constraints are imposed upon students who are denied exposure to ideas that challenge conventional wisdom.

An increasing degree of the state management of knowledge in late capitalism almost exactly duplicates the increasing degree of state intervention in the economy and polity, beginning with Roosevelt's implementation of Keynes' macro-economic theories in the 1930s, which largely replaced the neoclassical open-market assumptions of Smith and later bourgeois economists. Why is the state management of knowledge as well as its public hegemony increasing, particularly in the managed academic production of the social sciences? The answer relies in large measure on the Frankfurt School's interpretation, also developed in the 1930s, of the increasing state manipulation of popular culture and entertainment in late capitalism. What is happening in the university parallels larger developments in culture and society as a whole. According to this neo-Frankfurt perspective, the university is not a world apart, an ivory tower (see Lewis, 1975), and never was.

The Frankfurt theorists like Marcuse (1964) explained this 'one-dimensionalization' of all thought, experience and discourse in terms of capitalism's heightened need for greater individual conformity and adherence to duty in the realms of work, consumption and cultural reproduction. Marcuse's (1955) *Eros and Civilization* provides as good an interpretation as any of this psycho-erotic 'introjection' of political-economic alienation, a theme to which I return in chapter 7 in a different context. He suggests that an expanding technological surplus in post-World War II capitalism requires tightening the noose of self-imposed social control lest workers taste a palpable alternative to capitalist everyday life (see Marcuse, 1964, for this argument about the systemic necessity of false needs). What in the 1955 book he terms 'surplus repression' (akin to Foucault's notion of discipline) is self-repression and self-domestication beyond the basic limits required in any mature industrial civilization. And an aspect of surplus repression in Marcuse's terms is clearly the growing inability of people to develop theoretical understandings of the social world. Instead, people achieve only microscopic understandings of their lifeworlds — a kind of positivism of the quotidian that accepts given appearances for what they are. In my opening three chapters, I attempted to understand the scripts of the quotidian in literary terms, borrowing from critical theory, postmodernism and feminism. It is my contention that ideology needs to be understood as a textual production which helps the social system reproduce itself through readers who fail to understand that these scripts of obedience have actual authors and could be written differently.

The Frankfurt School's critique of positivism extends these other insights into the growing systemic need for state-managed knowledge and the manipulation of consciousness and desire (see Habermas, 1970a; Horkheimer and Adorno, 1972; Agger, 1976b). In this climate, the total administration of academic scholarship is merely an instance of the general reduction of critical thought and writing to operational definitions, where social science is transformed into mere data gathering and statistical manipulation. Thus, the 'mainstream' in the social sciences is almost by definition grounded in a methodological protocol of piecemeal data gathering and secondary data analysis using the techniques of a mathematical positivism.

The resulting intellectual homogeneity and hegemony, with their exclusion of alternative epistemologies and methodologies, weaken the open-market metaphor. Managed knowledge, regulated by a standard of scholarly legitimacy that prohibits competitive challenges, necessarily violates the liberal ideals of Mill's original notion of the 'marketplace of ideas'. The metaphor of an open market of ideas no longer bears much relationship to the practices of academic production and hegemony except as ideological self-justification. The left is particularly caught in the crucible of this outdated metaphor. Refereed scholarship, in spite of its self-advertisement as ideologically neutral, is in reality governed by norms and practices that defy Mill's liberal idealization of an open market in which the strongest, most meritorious argument will emerge victorious. What really happens in social-science production clearly defies Mill's idealization of a market unconstrained by value assumptions and the like (see O'Neill, 1981). Refereed journals are aimed at communities or subcultures of knowledge that are relatively homogeneous. To this extent, work that falls outside the putative mainstream is inherently disadvantaged with respect to its likelihood of acceptance and publication. Either such work is sent back by an editor or editorial committee without having been reviewed (perhaps deemed 'unsuitable' for the journal or publisher in question) or else reviewers chosen by the editor evaluate the work's validity and worthiness unfavorably.

The absence of non-positivist work in mainstream social-science journals cannot be explained only by the reluctance of radical authors to submit their work to these outlets. It is instead because such work either does not get reviewed at all — dismissed as 'unsuitable' — or else it is processed through the referee system and found wanting with reference to mainstream-positivist criteria of validity. This is the way in which discipline has become a literary production. According to a recent editor of the leading American sociology journal, fully 25 per cent of the manuscripts received under his editorship were returned to authors without even being reviewed, clearly demonstrating an aspect of the state management of knowledge at the level of academic editorial gatekeeping (see Stryker, 1983; see Agger, 1990, for a general discussion of academic writing as real estate).

This creates a further dilemma for radical scholars who aspire to survive and even thrive in bourgeois academia. Tenure and promotion decisions are increasingly made on the basis of one's academic productivity measured by the appearance of one's articles in refereed academic journals. With departments and administrators under pressure to ensure that tenure decisions are made on a 'rigorous' basis, deviant cases — whether involving women, minorities or non-positivists of all stripes — come under ever tighter scrutiny. A central criterion in tenuring is whether a scholar has achieved national prominence in his or her discipline. The common measure of such national standing is whether that person has published in the 'leading' positivist journals and whether such published work has received citations by other scholars. Thus, about the only way for left and non-positivist academics to legitimize their own intellectual integrity is to publish in journals that appear to avoid ideological sectarianism and thus have at least some credibility as vehicles of legitimate scholarship. But in times of academic retrenchment, it is increasingly rare for social-science academics to survive by going this route, especially where colleagues and administrators disqualify such journals either as non-refereed or as insufficiently prestigious.

Mainstream refereed journals constitute vital media of state production inasmuch as they represent and reinforce a certain acceptable work style and mode of academic presentation. The state management of knowledge proceeds through a referee process that is deeply ideological and methodologically narrow, facilitating discipline by deflecting scholars' critical intelligence as well as by leading them to do narrow 'applied' research directly benefiting both the state and capital. Social science research is robbed of a potentially ideology-critical role in late capitalism inasmuch as it strengthens the linkage between the technical requirement of economic steering and the production of knowledge in the policy sciences (see Diesing, 1982). The more that academic social scientists produce machine-readable data susceptible to exotic technical and statistical manipulation, the greater will be their potential access to decision-makers at the upper levels of state steering. This is particularly reflected in the alleged urgency for academics to engage in applied or funded research, notably on grounds that this will help ameliorate public universities' crisis of underfunding. Business interests and research scholarship thus become more closely linked, contextualizing the literary production of discipline.

### Illusion of Individual Autonomy

The deflection of critical intelligence that is a byproduct of refereed scholarship is most important in terms of an ideological analysis of the increasingly tight bond between what Marx originally called the base and superstructure of capitalism. Higher education, along with culture and entertainment, has been firmly implanted with the economic imperative of managed consumerism in order to guard against underconsumption. A still more central object of the state management of knowledge is the rerouting of critical intelligence into the nitpicking descriptive positivism of social-science empiricism. This stifles the left as thoroughly in late capitalism as did McCarthyism formerly (see Lewis, 1988). Centrally administered social control becomes virtually unnecessary with the self-administration of the academic production process.

It is more effective for academics to police themselves through proscriptive editorial practices than it would be for academic administrators to exact academic disciplining externally. Self-censorship, Foucault's discipline and Marcuse's surplus repression, operates at the level of editing as well as in the hiring and tenuring processes. Such self-governance for the most part precludes the need for overt administrative control of scholarship. This is especially pernicious in the star system of social science in American universities, which is governed by a virtual 'ratings' or 'rankings' of the 'best' (i.e., most prestigious) departments (see The Conference Board of Associated Research Councils, 1982). Reputational surveys borrow social scientists' own problematic methodological techniques in showing that the 'best' departments are those that are the most quantitatively and methodologically oriented.

The illusion of academic self-management is just true enough to deflect the charge that academic production is not at all governed by rules and norms of an open marketplace but really rests on deeply centralist definitions of academic legitimacy. As long as editors and department chairs can point to the apparently entrepreneurial nature of academic work, then the pernicious management of acceptable knowledge can proceed apace. Domination is fortified by covering it in the illusions of individual writers' autonomy, a central feature of ideological occlusion in late capitalism. By supposing that every piece of submitted work will get a fair reading, the ideological metaphor of an intellectual open market is maintained; in reality, little of the kind prevails. The academic production process is managed by ideologically- and methodologically-bound editors and editorial boards. In turn, *their* authority is constituted by professional associations and boards of trustees which appoint or elect them to edit major journals and university presses, and by department heads and administrators who sanctify their publication outlets as the only legitimate media for publication.

## Revising the Metaphor:
## From Mill to Keynes and Beyond

It would be simplistic to suppose that American social science journals mechanically weed out leftist, feminist and postmodern work and reject it out of hand. In fact, the process of ideological mediation between authors and readers is much more subtle, and for that reason usually more effective. Admittedly, the management of knowledge is not seamless. Counterhegemonic work does, on occasion, get published. Jürgen Habermas, for example, in spite of his obvious affiliation to the Hegelian-Marxist tradition, has enjoyed some visibility in mainstream social science (see Rule, 1978: pp. 123–39). State management of knowledge, despite a few exceptions notable mainly due to their scarcity, usually operates to restrict the symbolic codes of leading social-science journals by disqualifying work that does not rely heavily on quantitative methodology. A quantitative Marxism has arisen that borrows quite directly from the positivism dominating mainstream social-science research (see Wright, 1976, 1978; Wright *et al.*, 1982).

The publication of such work, less threatening because it accepts the research apparatus (surveys, computers, grants) and epistemological assumptions of the reigning positivism, facilitates the impression of journals' openness and reinforces the hegemony of positivist quantitative methods, making it that much harder to publish genuinely heterodox work of a kind that seriously challenges the literary production of discipline. Although one can domesticate a certain version of Marxism for publication in the leading sociology journals, it is virtually impossible to 'mainstream' critical theory, poststructuralism or postmodernism where these traditions challenge the discursive norms of positivist literary disciplining. Derrida and Foucault radically challenge positivist notions of reading and writing, making them highly threatening to the statist literary production process in contemporary academic life.

Contrary to this impression of ideological impartiality, ideology-critical manuscripts are usually rejected out of hand precisely because they defy the implicit criteria of state-managed knowledge, notably a combination of a work's pragmatic relevance to technocratic system maintenance (e.g., in the so-called policy sciences) and a work's participation in the ethos of quantitative method, survey research and statistical analysis. Philosophically-oriented manuscripts which eschew either pragmatic relevance or quantitative methodology are rejected; or, if not rejected outright, they are put through elaborate processes of revision that domesticate the work's outrageous argument and prod its convergence with mainstream positivism. Journal editors often respond to such papers by saying that they need to acknowledge the existence of other viewpoints, suggesting a cumulative model of scientific progress that has already been discredited by historians of science (see Kuhn, 1970).

But not only ideologically heterodox work is rejected by these mainstream statist publication outlets. Work that refuses to conform to positivist literary strictures regarding a linear comprehensibility, the citation of accumulated literature and the embellishing use of figures is also disqualified. The literary production of discipline depends heavily on screening procedures that filter out not only ideologically-driven scholarship but all modes of textuality that challenge conventional understandings of the relationship among texts, politics and academic life. For this reason, Derridean deconstruction is especially eschewed by the positivist social sciences, which model themselves after the natural sciences in their self-image as authorless practices. Derrida challenges positivist textuality to disclose the sweaty, passionate, perspectival work of authoriality that underlies every literary endeavor, science no less than poetry or philosophy.

Of course the policy- and method-driven nature of universities and academic publication outlets is not likely to change without overall social changes. But a modest proposal is in order here, one that at least acknowledges internal contradictions in the dominant metaphor of productive activity in the academic social sciences. It is too obviously untrue that there is an open market of ideas — Kuhn's normal science — for Mill's original liberal market metaphor to survive unscathed. This metaphor shift — open market to state management — could have the positive effect of bringing ideology and authoriality out into the open, once journal editors and scholars disabuse themselves of the pretense to impartiality, deauthorization and meritocracy (for a discussion of the illusion of academic meritocracy see Lewis, 1975). Bourgeois scholarship needs to catch up with the structural changes in capitalism by modifying its own self-understanding in order to suit the organizational practice of managed academic capitalism as well as the strong literary practices of writing and reading.

The very notion that a manuscript can be objectively reviewed through the referee system is an outcome of the objectivism holding sway in both American social science and capitalist society at large (where phenomena are thought to be identical to their reflected appearances and to have no deeper dialectical depth or capacity for self-transformation). Knowledge cannot be constituted merely through the mechanisms of an institutionalized intersubjectivity, especially when, as Hegel reminded, the truth is dialectical. Marx added that 'readers' are often subject to distorting false consciousness. Derrida argued that every reading is a version of writing, strongly reshaping the text in question. The referee process presupposes Popper's principle of falsifiability endorsed by positivists. Dialecticians oppose this consensus theory on the grounds that it fails to account for false consciousness; after all, the lonely defiant may see more clearly than the many alleged authorities lined up in support of conventional wisdom. Derrideans oppose consensus theory on grounds that consensuses are inherently flimsy, subject to deconstructive implosion from within their own language games.

The open marketplace of ideas, embodied in an objective system of refereed scholarship, is a virtually useless idealization of scientific progress. Readers read manuscripts in terms of their own epistemological and substantive interests. As poststructuralists tell us, reading itself is a deeply constitutional process whereby the author of a manuscript and its reader might as well be on different planets. If we assume that truth is dialectical and not cumulative, then we must reject the positivist tenet that neutral observers (readers) can arrive at a correct consensus about objective truth. Nor can writers simply copy the truth from a pregiven cosmos that unresistingly yields its secrets to transparent language. Instead, knowledge is inherently implicated in the dialectic of theory and practice; truth is as much a result of practice (including the practices of reading and writing) as its cause.

How might scholarship and the academic production process instead be organized? While this is a complicated structural problem involving the whole political economy of capitalism as well as its literary economy, notably the role of scientific-technical knowledge in the logic of capital, one could at least observe that radical intellectuals can best legitimate their own work as an alternative to the state-managed knowledge of positivist literary conventions. Radical intellectuals would thus attempt to demonstrate the legitimacy of their own literary styles and publication outlets as alternatives to mainstream discourse and journals. By overturning the market metaphor, radical scholars will show that *all* published knowledge is subject to one or another set of interests or 'biases', with state-managed knowledge being no more valid than counterhegemonic knowledge. This self-legitimation process would belong to a struggle within the academic institution to abolish the distinction between refereed and non-refereed publication outlets as well as between mainstream and marginal outlets.

This would salvage the valuable notion that some ideas are truer than others, preventing an utter epistemological relativism, while insisting that the marketplace of ideas does not produce truth simply by subjecting manuscripts to anonymous readings, which are always strongly constitutional in their own right (leading to deconstructive infinite regress). All publication outlets are in a sense refereed; no outlet is impartial in its standard for publication. Every manuscript is read by someone, including the writer, before it is published. Is there, then, a valid way to judge the 'quality' of various journals, a central concern of hiring and promotion committees? Once we accept the premise that all published knowledge is managed (viz. Habermas' sense of the intimate bond between what he calls knowledge and interest) — whether for purposes of system maintenance or radical criticism and social change — then we must accept the inherent incommensurability of subcultures and literary modes of knowledge that proliferate in the social sciences today. Journals, thus, cannot be compared as to their degree of objectivity or impartiality but only in terms of their stature *within* their own subculture, language game or paradigm. And that sort of comparison, if it is to avoid the circularity of reputational surveys, must be made simply on the basis of the *readings* that scholars and committees make of the articles, journals and presses in question. There is no royal road to truth apart from the corrigible literary practices of reading and writing (which are themselves dialectically inseparable, as Derrida indicates).

## Radical Scholarship and/as Radical Pedagogy

Reading, writing and teaching are inextricably bound together. They are all ways to constitute meaning; none of them is privileged epistemologically. The ideology-critique of refereed scholarship is one form of counterhegemony within departments and universities. As the false universalism of the refereed marketplace is revealed, people may come to recognize that there are all sorts of legitimate, if ideologically heterogeneous, modes of academic production, including reading, teaching and community organizing. The critique of ideology serves the concerns of both job security and critical pedagogy, eventually leading to a broader and more democratic public sphere in which knowledge is dialogically constituted and not filtered through the mediations of statist interest, an issue I rejoin in chapters 9 and 10 below.

Issues of pedagogy and the individual scholar's own efforts to achieve professional recognition must be understood to be parts of the same struggle. The narrow definition of legitimate social-science research and the limited exposure of students to diverse perspectives during their education are interrelated aspects of the state management of knowledge. The repressive character of an ideologically homogeneous faculty permits the nonproblematic socialization of students into a narrowly defined academic (hence necessarily political) world. A professoriate comprising academics with similarly narrow perspectives and modes of literary presentation as well as interpretation reinforces the superficial understanding of everyday life imposed on students throughout their academic experience. Such a professoriate further entrenches students in the quotidian, Gramsci's hegemony, that disqualifies radical social change as hopelessly utopian. Future generations are thus effectively taught to be self-administering.

If this understanding of the activity of academic radicals is sound, the patent Marxist depiction of the agitational role of left-wing scholarship needs to be transformed considerably. Academic leftists can be agitational in the sense that they criticize, both in their pedagogy and in their writing, the increasingly pervasive ideology of positivism and technocratic élitism that by its own definition rejects defiant societal alternatives and literary versions out of hand. Journals that publish only positivist work are paralleled, and constituted, by a social order that rewards literary and economic productivism. The academic left has to fight tenaciously for *the legitimation of a non-instrumental rationality* that defies the productivist categorical imperative which makes production and consumption the only measures of human integrity (see Horkheimer, 1974a, 1974b), an issue raised earlier in chapter 2. Thus, concern with a person's 'output' (measured in numbers of publications in mainstream academic journals or in dollars of sponsored research) ought to be replaced by concern with the quality and integrity of work done within the paradigm, language game or subculture within which that work is situated.

Radical intellectuals can teach students and colleagues that this sort of instrumentalism and productivism are deeply destructive of the human sensibility and lead to frozen relations among people (where the scholar 'becomes' her or his curriculum vitae). They can struggle to resist the instrumentalization of academic decision-making, just as they can help students resist the ceaseless mathematization and rationalization of university curricula in the name of a specious occupational relevance. They can try to build a qualitative curriculum that does not succumb to the ethos and mythos of high technology, along with its banishment of the non-quantitative and non-productive. In this sense, an ideology-critique designed to legitimate a non-instrumental or qualitative rationality is really, in institutional terms, a struggle-from-within against the technocratic university in late capitalism.

In this effort, teaching must be upgraded as a relevant academic and political role. Large public universities must resist their definition as solely research oriented; instead, it must be stressed that research and teaching are integral (and integrated) activities. If students are lost to the ethos of pragmatism and productivism, the proving ground is lost also to translate critical theory into relevant terms of contemporary experience and struggle — exactly the sort of accessible critical theory of public life that I am trying to develop here. We cannot recreate the public sphere without transforming the ways in which we produce 'human capital', the credentialed experts of the next generation who flow out of our universities and professional schools in vast numbers. Students' postmodern imperviousness and cynicism are only social products of a disenchanted popular culture and can be challenged by mind-opening, enlivening pedagogy that shows students that they are the potential authors of their own fates.

As I said in my introduction, when I talked about the educating-the-educator problem, this sort of consciousness raising will not take the didactic and authoritarian form of Lenin's vanguard knowledge ('rural idiocy') but instead will acknowledge the *dialogical grounds of socialism* conveyed in a variety of socialist metaphors all the way from Gramsci's counterhegemony to Habermas' ideal speech situation (see chapter 8, below, for a fuller discussion of the relevance of Habermas' critical theory of communication to my critical theory of public life). This dialogic structure of socialism guarantees that élite-mass relations will be optimally democratic. Within such dialogue, citizens teach intellectuals about their own phenomenological experience of alienation — the generative themes of their own quotidian subordination — while intellectuals reconstruct that knowledge theoretically and return it to the people in the form of a structural analysis of the linchpins of their alienation and possible liberation. Such knowledge, conveyed in accessible public texts and teaching, forms the basis of a scenario of radical social change as well as a substantive imagery of a public life in which the discursive privilege of expertise is democratized deconstructively.

Radical pedagogy and radical scholarship must be joined dialectically lest academic Marxism become too rarefied, untested by the dialogical challenges confronting the rehabilitation of consciousness. The classroom is a laboratory; there, teachers can thematize alienation in a way that relates quotidian experience to the large, invisible structures producing it. Young minds can be confronted with the institutional nature of what might otherwise appear to be banalized social issues to be solved merely through statist fine-tuning, the typical reformist strategies of the welfare state. Social problems of poverty, alienation, racism and sexism can be understood in systemic terms; their solutions will be portrayed not in piecemeal incrementalist ways but rather as components of an overall strategy of socialist and feminist transformation. Likewise, the problems of domesticity that every student experiences — unemployment, broken relationships, sexism, racism — can be addressed in terms of a neo-Marxian and feminist analysis that carefully links the personal and political, suggesting counterhegemonic activities that make sense to people on the level of their own struggle to live decent, democratic lives. This stress on the politics of the personal comes directly from the feminist component of a feminist postmodern critical theory, outlined in the first three chapters of this book.

As Korsch (1970) warned in 1923, the dictatorship of the proletariat too quickly becomes a dictatorship over the proletariat if we are not vigilant in preserving the fragile dialectic between experts and citizens in the transformative process. Radicalism remains subversive in postmodern capitalism only where it is able to address lifeworld themes of alienation and domination relevant to people in the here and now. Marxisms that require literal knowledge of *Capital*, as well as of latter-day expositions of it, are at too great a remove from the anxieties and possibilities of the quotidian in the late twentieth century (Adorno, 1974a).

> The *ethical* unity of Marxist knowledge remains, however, a programmatic ideal unless it is brought to the level of *pedagogic practice*. Here we encounter the problem of the role of Marxist knowledge in the relation between the party and the proletariat. In simple terms, communicative competence is likely to remain the one-sided talent of party theorists and organizers obliged to work with a silent and obstinate proletariat with little experience of the world of ideas, debate, and free consensus. The danger is that people may be herded together in the interests of their political leaders who have community on their lips or in their plans but not in their hearts (O'Neill, 1976: p. 8).

A socialist-feminist epistemology thus grows out of our pedagogic experience with victims of the logics of capital and male supremacy. We can construct a critical phenomenology and textuality of everyday life in late capitalism that are relevant to the concerns of students and citizens (see O'Neill, 1972c and Paci, 1972 for the development of a phenomenological Marxism). We will discover in our teaching not simply the robotized instrumentalism captured in Lasch's (1979) notion of a culture of narcissism nor in Marcuse's (1964) concept of false needs but also an incipient social progressivism that has no coherent theoretical or political voice. There is certainly a good deal of administered apathy and possessive individualism in American culture, as Tocqueville first described in *Democracy in America* (1961). But there is also a visceral awareness of the distorted political-economic structures of American capitalism, sexism and racism. Students in my own urban northeastern university understand the desperation and degradation of unemployment, which they view not as an unfortunate accident of fate that happens to unlucky individuals but as a systemic outcome (even if they do not yet name this system capitalism). They largely view these systemic outcomes fatalistically, not realizing that ideology produces discourses of fate (like sociology) that fatalize surreptitiously. Deconstructive political work can unlock these fatalizing discourses as the authorial artifices they really are, laying open to students the possibility of a transformative imagination with which they can begin to deal with their own sense of outrage.

They do not yet speak of their lives in these terms. Our role as critical educators is to give them, quite non-directively, a discourse with which to *name* what they already perceive but cannot theorize and hence change. This naming accompanies a radical imagination that points beyond itself toward a new order of things. As soon as we work through the structural causes of local deindustrialization and the fraudulence of Atari capitalism as a solution, as I do in chapter 6, students can begin to glimpse a new social order not premised on severe renunciation and imperative coordination, in which, with 1844 Marx, work and leisure begin to blur under the sway of democratic self-management and workers' control (see Agger, 1979a: pp. 316–39). For this act of imagination to take place, however, we must be sensitive to the *populist and popular* grounds of a possible American radicalism. Most students simply do not understand that socialism, Marxism and feminism are not exhausted by the realities of command economies and separatist cults. They react to plant closings, violence against women and environmental degradation with a pretheoretical mistrust of vast centralism rather than a clear structural understanding of patriarchal political economy. So the task of a critical theory of public life is to teach students a discourse through which they can articulate their own critique of what is happening to them and others, creating exactly the sort of democratic social movements that militate against Korsch's dictatorship over the proletariat (see Boggs, 1986).

Accordingly, metaphors of frontier democracy and grassroots social organization are more inspiring than the metaphor of the Paris Commune, which probably connotes hippies on the Left Bank to students today! The challenge for American radicals is to nurture this incipient radical populism in a socialist and feminist direction by giving students new names for their own intuitive notions of grass-roots democracy. The original Students for a Democratic Society in their 1962 Port Huron statement attempted to blend American populism with a more explicitly leftist agenda, showing the way for this kind of work. (They were ultimately unsuccessful because their work was not theoretical enough, which is why I address the problems of public life not from the vantage of C. Wright Mills, who heavily influenced the American student movement, but via the Frankfurt School, feminism and postmodernism.) The feminist postmodern critical theory that reconstructs and extends Marx's dialectical method is appropriate to this Americanization of radical themes in that it, too, depends on the reappropriation of radicalism conceptualized not as delivered truths but as a fluid discourse readily adaptable to circumstances. The challenge for the feminist postmodern critical theorist in the classroom is to show the convergence of populism and non-authoritarian socialist feminism in a way that lets students make their own choices and participate actively in the dialogical process of formulating their own critical and theoretical categories. As any leftist teacher knows, this is easier said than done, given the enormous momentum of hegemonic ideology encoded in popular culture, family values and education itself.

Research and teaching are reciprocal; the reinterpretation of a postmodern feminist Marxism as an enduring analytical method accompanies students' dialogical confrontation with their own lived experience and incipient radical imagination. A living Marxism, informed by feminism and postmodernism, answers the questions asked by our students, refusing to impart a stale protocol of crabbed economic analysis and canonical textual interpretation (although at some point that tough-minded intellectual work is necessary, too). Discussion in 'social problems' classes of the nature of surplus value must be shown to be relevant to students' understandings of local plant closings and labor struggle as well as sexual and racial politics, just as elaboration of the Frankfurt School's concept of total administration must be made relevant to the popular culture of television, movies and music that defines the discourse of the quotidian for many young people.

## Political Intellectuality in Postmodern Capitalism

An American Marxist-feminist academic can operate effectively in a political sense only if he or she acknowledges the limited nature of the twofold task at hand: we must reinterpret and creatively adapt dialectical categories, pointing toward new and ongoing strategies of radical social change including 'new social movements'; we must also participate in a socially critical pedagogy that treats students as valued dialogue partners and imparts to them not finished truths but a mode of imagination and articulation — public discourse — that helps them relate their personal alienation and anxiety to larger structural issues and thus to work beyond their seemingly intractable horizon of possibilities. In this dialogical process, educators are themselves educated.

The greatest challenge for academic radicals influenced by feminist postmodern critical theory is to make sense of the vast gap between the personal and political both in one's own life and in the lives of students and colleagues. Radical scholarship must be bent to the task of *translating* personal experience into public issues, hence politicizing them, precisely the desideratum of C. Wright Mills' 'sociological imagination' (see Mills, 1959: pp. 3–24) as well as socialist feminism (see Fraser, 1989; although, as I have said, Mills' version of the personal-political relationship is insufficiently structural).

> Socialist education cannot succeed except where people *love* the world and the society of people. The pedagogy of the oppressed therefore cannot be one-sided or manipulative nor can it be fostered by people who lack *humility* and are arrogant and domineering. Socialist humility in turn has no place where a few people set themselves up and are unwilling to bend in the service of the people because they lack *faith* in the partnership of the oppressed. However, critical socialist pedagogy is more than a prescriptive ethic. As outlined by Paulo Freire, whose work I regard as a practical extension of Habermas' ideal of emancipatory communicative competence, the pedagogy of the oppressed involves an applied method of entry and organization of local communities whose critical tasks are opened up through the generative themes — slum, development, water, infant mortality — of daily life in the colonial world. It would be an important and relatively easy intellectual task — as easy in practice as it is dangerous — to extend Freire's methods of 'conscientization' to the education of the internal proletariat of industrial and urbanized societies where the challenge does not derive from absolute illiteracy but from the relative illiteracy that results from the increasing technical and professional practice of social change and reform (O'Neill, 1976: pp. 9–10).

In our research and university lives we ought to try to challenge the illusion of an open market of ideas and insist empirically that mainstream social science produces state-managed knowledge serving the interest of domination. We must challenge the positivist definition of scholarly legitimacy — surveys, computers, grants, value-freedom — and instead insist on the validity of non-instrumental, non-quantitative knowledge. We must argue that theory *matters*, even if it defies easy domestication in the prevailing academic division of labor, which sets up rigid boundaries among specialties.

This emerges in the political practice of struggle within the university to have knowledge evaluated within its own paradigmatic

frame of reference — the norms of its speech community or subculture — and not in terms of its contribution to the cumulative advancement of objective knowledge as well as state functioning. This is the
only way that radical intellectuals can ever hope to have their products
appraised in their own terms. We must insist that our work be *read*
and that our 'merits' somehow be assessed in terms of the emerging
totality of our whole sensibilities and lives and not just in terms of our
lifeless curriculum vitae, which, like all texts, can be read in any
number of ways. This process of reading (and not simply counting or
summing) may actually open up dialogues and start constructive arguments, prefiguring a discursive polity in its own dialogical example.
We must use the ethics of liberal tolerance against the betrayed liberalism of the state-managed academic marketplace, which resembles a
monopoly both intellectually and methodologically.

Non-instrumental, non-productivist intellectuals must also insist
on their own role in preparing students for responsible and critical
citizenship, just as they reserve the right to engage in probing speculation about ultimate social purposes and values. This is important even
if such speculation appears devoid of present utility and does not lead
to funded research or other pragmatic applications. Students must be
introduced to a vocabulary that will enable them to name and comprehend their own experiences in a dog-eat-dog world as cynicism is
transcended by dialectical imagination.

These tasks of writing, reading and teaching are neither separate
nor sequential. They are instead complementary responsibilities that
must occupy radical academics if they are to survive in bourgeois
academia and to begin to link theory and practice counterhegemoni-
cally. What is the 'product' of these interrelated critical activities? That
is the wrong sort of question. Elsewhere (Agger, 1977a, 1977b) I have
suggested that the product of radical intellectual praxis is not simply
works, readings or lectures but a genuinely 'dialectical sensibility', on
the part of both teacher and students, that joins the theoretical imagination of a different, better world with its prefigurative practice as
dominant discourse in the here and now. This image of a dialectical
sensibility which begins to live social change in the immediate present
has a number of inspirations, including the Freudian Marxism of
Marcuse (see Marcuse, 1955, 1969; Agger, 1982) and phenomenological Marxism (see Piccone, 1971). As I elaborate in chapter 6, I am
particularly indebted to the formulation of the possibility of 'organic
negativity' by Paul Piccone, who draws on Gramsci's counterhegemony as well as on a critical reconstruction of phenomenological
themes (see Piccone, 1976, 1978; Antonio, 1983).

Piccone argues that the system produces 'artificial negativity' that
inculcates risk-taking and innovative behavior while releasing pent-up
surplus repression or self-alienation. Marxism itself is fairly easily
domesticated as it is accorded a legitimate, if marginal, niche in the
academic division of labor, as I discuss in the following chapter where

I examine textbook discourse. Instead, radical intellectuals must seek a genuine negativity that transcends both the bourgeois order and its subtle loosening of the constraints of self-alienation. It is not enough that radicals teach courses on Marxism, feminism and the Frankfurt School (although that is a useful beginning). They must, in the totality of their lives, *portray and exemplify* the possibility of a qualitatively different dialectical rationality that informs their reading, writing and teaching.

That would be a progressive contribution to new social movements in late capitalist countries inasmuch as the statist university is the training ground of credentialed human capital. While our role in new social movements like environmentalism, the women's movement and antinuclearism may not be enormous, in the absence of an organized socialist tradition in the US critical intellectuals can begin to reduce the dominant cultural and ideological hegemony both in our writing and our teaching. We must resist a monolithic academic capitalism that turns the life of the mind into a business, degrading the professoriate into fungible quanta of labor power. In our struggle for self-legitimation as well as public discourse in the bourgeois university, we take a first halting step toward a way of life beyond the imperatives of an assembly-line mentality.

I continue this line of analysis in the next chapter, where I consider sociology textbooks as powerful exemplars of positivist, capitalist and sexist knowledge. (I return to my more positive agenda of a postmodern intellectual life in chapter 9.) I argue that critical scholars must attend to these textbooks as political language games that need to be challenged for what they suggest about the intractability of the present social order. This attempt to undermine what I call disciplinary hegemony is part of the critical agenda that I have sketched out in this chapter. It is readily apparent that the state management of knowledge includes not only a valorization of applied and funded research that directly contributes to the maintenance of the welfare state as well as global capital; it also involves the composition of substantive knowledge, often encoded in textbooks, that help form 'human capital'.

# Chapter 5

# Do Books Write Authors?: Textbooks and Disciplinary Hegemony

Where in the last chapter I described the institutional context within which disciplinary knowledge is produced, in this chapter I suggest some of the implications of the state-management of academic knowledge for disciplinary discourse. I focus my discussion on sociology textbooks, which in many respects resemble other standard textbooks in both social-science and natural-science disciplines in the senses that they contain encyclopedic information about current disciplinary knowledge, they address lower-division college students and they are remarkably similar within disciplines (reflecting a certain common stock of disciplinary knowledge that they then iteratively reproduce).

Sociology textbooks are prisms through which to 'read' the mainstream discipline of sociology, which in its own exemplary way contributes to the state management of knowledge and ideological hegemony, as I suggested in chapter 2. Read deconstructively, the textbooks disclose all sorts of positivist assumptions about the social world, epitomizing the concealed ideology in fast capitalism. Although there is a growing literature on sociology textbooks (Wells, 1979; Herrick, 1980; Maslow, 1981; Perrucci, 1980; Papp, 1981; Porter, 1981–82; Morgan, 1983; McCarthy and Das, 1985; Agger, 1989c), it is rare for faculty and editors to engage directly with issues of pedagogic and disciplinary substance. Many read sociology textbooks merely as compendia of conventional sociological wisdom governed by publishers' market concerns, and thus we ignore their contribution to the general discourse of the discipline. In my study of textbook ideology (Agger, 1989b), I evaluated current sociology textbooks both in commercial terms and for what they tell us about the deep assumptions that sociologists make about the social world (but rarely articulate in their journal and monograph writing). Indeed, as a deconstructively-oriented critical theorist, I believe that critical readings of sociology textbooks help to refract the central problems of social-science positivism generally, shedding further light on the literary practice of disciplinary hegemony.

Simply to focus on the commodity-like nature of college sociology textbooks is to ignore how their assumptions about the nature of the social world influence present and future sociologists. Many critics of sociology textbooks dislike these books simply because they *are* commodities; in their homogeneity and banal quality they fail to reflect what these critics contend is the real heterogeneity and depth of our discipline. Although the fact that textbooks are written to make money is important in itself, especially insofar as it constrains innovation, the introductory sociology textbooks revealingly disclose what Erich Goode (1984: pp. 22–3) calls 'standard American sociology', the discursive state of the art. In fact, most current textbooks include vast bibliographies containing citations from the current journal and monograph literature. Although textbooks are pitched at the high-school reading level of our underprepared college students, they aim to report current research and theory. Major publishers simply will not acquire textbooks that dispense with this scholarly buttressing, nor will faculty adopt them. Thus, sociology textbooks are not merely empty forms (e.g., Tischler, 1988) if read attentively or deconstructively (Culler, 1982).

## The Illusion of Sociological Heterogeneity

I disagree with those who contend that the textbooks are substantively different from one another — indeed, that authors who choose to write textbooks can give ample expression to their intellectual creativity (e.g., Hess, 1988; Kammeyer, 1988; Lamanna, 1988; Persell, 1988). The sameness of the introductory sociology texts indicates not only the commodification of textbooks but also the intellectual hegemony that they both reflect and reproduce. In this case, the Gramscian term 'hegemony' indicates the monolith of core assumptions about good sociology; it is manifested in the fact that books write authors, not authors books — hence the texts' remarkable similarities.

The homogeneous nature of sociology textbooks is reflected in four interrelated ways: 1) their basic approach to epistemology or the philosophy of science (I call this approach positivism); 2) their misleading theoretical ecumenism; 3) their treatment of Marxism; and 4) their treatment of feminism. I contend that the similarity of American sociology books is not simply a market reflex, dictated by prevailing adopters' taste, but reflects the homogeneity of the discipline as a whole. The mainstream consensus about what constitutes good sociology — involving assumptions about the nature of science and society — is readily apparent in the introductory textbooks. They 'repeat' each other not only because to do otherwise would imperil sales but also because most sociologists who write and teach from textbooks accept the core of sociology as elaborated encyclopedically in the many texts.

Introductory sociology books socialize not only students but also the faculty members who teach from them. Indeed, many graduate students and junior faculty members are acculturated to our common disciplinary assumptions by teaching through the chapters of the introductory books. In this sense pedagogy merges with academic professionalization, underlining the disciplinarily constitutive nature of the textbooks. The books not only reflect the discipline; they also help to reproduce it in the way in which they expose graduate students and faculty to the consensus underlying the dominant approach to epistemology, methodology and theory.

### Positivism

The textbooks participate in a certain view of the social world characterized by positivism, a mirror-like theory of knowledge discussed in chapter 2. Although most textbooks acknowledge that sociologists' perspectives or values may slightly cloud their research, this is only a qualified value-freedom, a nuanced positivism, and not a substantial equivocation about the possibility of reflecting the world 'out there' in the text of science. Discussed in chapter 1, the recent convergence of certain European intellectual developments, including poststructuralism, phenomenology, critical theory, neo-Marxism, and feminist theory, challenges the adequacy of the positivist reconstruction of the logic of social-scientific inquiry (Held, 1980; Culler, 1982; Ryan, 1982; Eagleton, 1983). Yet American sociology clings to an outmoded positivism as elaborated in Weber's (1968) strictures on objectivity in social research and in Durkheim's (1950) *Rules of Sociological Method*, in which Durkheim demarcates sociology from psychology as the study of the inevitable social constraints on human behavior — 'social facts'.

Virtually every introductory sociology textbook opens with a section on theory and method which proclaims the resemblance of sociology to the natural sciences in its pursuit of laws and hence of prediction. This version of sociology suggests certain invariant social, sexual and economic patterns including capitalism, patriarchy, division of labor, hierarchy and the domination of nature. Although authors of nearly every textbook implicitly or explicitly oppose 'social problems', these problems are portrayed as inevitable products of societal modernization. They can be addressed problem by problem or simply accepted fatalistically. If Weber's iron cage and Durkheim's anomie are unavoidable, as the textbooks imply in their static science-like descriptions, people may either become yuppies or commit suicide.

Standard American sociologists first describe these inflexible social patterns and then they propose remedies for the unfortunate social problems stemming from them. Analysis and advocacy are sundered. Few textbooks reject Durkheim's and Weber's vocal opposition to

Marxism's link between theory and practice. Students and faculty are taught that the social world can be mirrored on the science page, that the world is governed by laws or inflexible patterns (correlations, if not causes), and that the purpose of sociology is merely to describe these patterned 'social facts'. All of this might be tolerable if sociology did not completely coopt radical alternatives which derive from the eleventh thesis on Feuerbach, in which Marx and Engels say that the point of science is not only to understand the world but also to change it.

### Theoretical Ecumenism

Nearly every introductory textbook claims that sociological theory is ancillary to the empirical research enterprise, a prosthetic arm of science; as such, theory is to provoke testable hypotheses, not, alternatively, to be a sweeping source of what the Frankfurt School considered speculative reason and hence autonomous social criticism. The major textbooks suggest that each official sociological theory has its strengths and its weaknesses, and they aim at a fruitful synthesis or balance. Finally, the books canonize three (and only three) theories: functionalism, symbolic interactionism and conflict theory. The problems with this approach are fourfold: first, much nitty-gritty *American Sociological Review*-level positivism is not theory-driven at all; second, when people actually use theory to frame their empirical research, they use a wider variety of sociological theories than the three mentioned above; third, symbolic interactionism is not a theory at all but a research strategy belonging to the genre of microsociological constructivism that includes ethnomethodology and social phenomenology; finally, as I will discuss next, conflict theory is not Marxism, as the textbooks claim.

### The Mainstreaming of Marxism

Textbook Marxism is really Weberianism — conflict theory, as the texts call it, citing Dahrendorf, Lenski and occasionally Giddens. The distance between Weber and Marx is shortened in order to vitiate Marxism politically; the textbook Marx proclaims the ubiquity and eternity of 'conflict' as an unavoidable fact of social and economic life. Marx, however, foretold an *end* to conflict; it was Weber who countered Marx and Marxism by eternalizing conflict. Indeed, mainstream sociology assimilates Marxism to Weberian conflict theory (e.g., Collins, 1975). But Marx and Weber in different ways answered the most fundamental question of all: is structured inequality inevitable? In addition, the textbook Marx mouths Weber's announcement of the eternity of social conflict, thus disqualifying conflict-free social orders such as socialism. The textbooks coopt Marx by anointing him a 'father' or 'founder' of conflict theory, thus obscuring the crucial political difference between Marx and Weber.

Oppositional movements and voices, such as Marxism and feminism, are bifurcated into a demonic, radical, wild rump and a safe, respectable mainstream. Sociology's Marxism is 'good' conflict theory, whereas the 'other' Marxism is held responsible for the Gulag Archipelago. Generally, safe Marxism is unfolded in the early theory chapter, where Marx reposes along with Durkheim and Weber in the pantheon of Grand Theorists. Rebel Marxism — the bloody streets of St Petersburg, the KGB, and the Cultural Revolution in China — is presented in the later chapters on stratification, social change and social movements. The books suggest that Marx advocated violence, thus ensuring his disrepute among American readers.

Finally, Marxism *qua* conflict theory suggests that 'social problems' of poverty, unemployment, uneven development and the like can be solved piecemeal — without changing the whole system. Sociology's Marx ironically becomes a proponent of the capitalist welfare state.

## The Mainstreaming of Feminism

Whereas a Boy Scout Marxism resides in the theory chapter, a Girl Scout feminism is found in the chapter(s) on gender, family and sex roles. Whereas bad Marxism is Siberia and good Marxism merely 'conflict theory', bad feminism is a man- and child-hating lesbian separatism, while good feminism is the corporate feminism of *Ms.* magazine, the National Organization of Women, and sit-coms like *Kate and Allie*. Women are supposed to work 'with men' to sort out their mutual problems of lovelessness, alienation and who will do the dishes. Sociology is subtly homophobic; the liberal textbooks support gay rights but not the radical- and socialist-feminist politicization of personal life — sexuality, family, housework.

One textbook suggests that radical feminists are unruly at meetings; another assures us that only 5 per cent of the population are gay; another defends prostitution on functional grounds; another (written by two women!) argues that all Americans want to get married and have children; another suggests that male impotence (a social problem!) is caused by women's liberation; yet another suggests that the 'traditional' woman's role included benefits as well as costs. The text's feminism is domesticated, familied, nonstrident. Difficulties between the sexes are conceptualized as just that: faulty negotiations between spouses. Men are victims, too. Predictably, the treatment of women in the major introductory books is restricted to the 'women' chapters on family, gender and sex roles. Some textbooks even assimilate feminism to the very conflict theory to which they have reduced Marxism.

## Rewriting Textbooks or Rethinking Sociology?

Anticipating the charge that textbooks reflect little more than the profit motive, I also examined mainstream sociological journal writing (Agger, 1989b). My deconstructive reading of the 'Big Three' journals in American sociology suggests that there is no more heterogeneity in the leading journals than in the textbooks. They all participate in the narrow universe of what one might euphemistically call midwestern (and sunbelt) empiricism — positivist, technical, atheoretical, narrowly framed. Although these journals publish the occasional 'theoretical' or 'qualitative' article, such articles must employ many of the figural devices of quantitative sociology — save for survey data manipulated statistically (Agger, 1989b: pp. 179–209).

It is much easier to read the mainstream textbooks for their concealed ontological and ideological content than to extract hidden assumptions from densely methodological mainstream journals. It is precisely the prosefulness, the discursiveness and the 'reading level' of the textbooks that grant access to these buried assumptions about the social world. It is harder, although not impossible, to crack the dense technical codes of the journal articles. One might observe that science disciplines, like 'standard American sociology', purposely conceal their large assumptions about the world. At least, they do not reflect on them in a sustained way.

In any case, the commodification of sociology textbooks ensures that the mold will not be broken by heroic authors who want to reformulate the discipline in non-positivist and more radical terms. Although the biggest college publishing houses boast an array of specialized 'niche' books, along with their eclectic four-color bestsellers, these are few and far between. The best known is Stanley Eitzen's (1985) *In Conflict and Order*. And this is by no means a Marxist book, merely a comparison of conflict and functionalist paradigms. Interestingly, Eitzen (1988) is one of the only analysts of textbooks to address the 'asymmetries of power' between author and publisher, implying that heroic authors can do little to change business as usual in college textbook publishing.

Publishers crow with self-satisfaction about the alleged pluralism of the textbooks they publish. Successful textbook authors view themselves as creative participants in a collegial process. Most American sociology instructors continue to adopt the standard product in their own teaching; a few do not. So be it. Courageous textbook writers are no more likely to make a difference than gutsy article or monograph writers; they will not get published. The real problem is the common core of assumptions animating mainstream American sociology. In the last analysis, whether 'we' can change these assumptions, and hence the whole discipline, depends on how many of 'us' — critics of the mainstream — there really are. Without 'different' faculty, there will be no 'different' books or articles, nor, ultimately, a different world.

My analysis of sociology textbooks suggests some methodical ways to read disciplinary discourses for their telling but concealed assumptions. Sociology is not simply a compendium of facts and theories but a style of argumentation which is epitomized by the representational depiction of 'society' (presumably all societies, past, present and future). Student-readers are expected to gobble up these facts and theories as if they perfectly reflect the world out there. A critical hermeneutic, rooted in critical theory and deconstruction, suggests, alternatively, that disciplinary discourses represented in textbooks create the world in their own image as much as reflect it passively. Where sociology conveys a certain essentialized view of class, gender and science, it deftly reproduces the current orders of class, gender and science by draining history from them. This is an enormously subtle and powerful form of ideology — powerful because subtle. Few student-readers recognize the ideologized nature of the reality presented to them via these representationally positivist textbooks. Instead, they quickly come to believe that the social world requires the inequalities and hierarchies reflected in the textbooks as a frozen social nature.

### Texting Teachers or Teaching Textbooks: An Agenda of Socially Critical Pedagogy

My discussion of the textbook ideology and ontology encoded in a positivist discipline like sociology helps practically exemplify what I have called the literary production of discipline. My main concern in the first half of this book, the literary production of discipline is the topic addressed by my synthesis of feminist postmodern critical theory. The texting of sociology's world can be deconstructed by reading the textbooks against themselves, the critical model of which is provided by a politicized version of Derridean deconstruction (as outlined in chapters 2 and 3). I have demonstrated some of the outcomes of this deconstructive reading in this chapter. Although it is important to treat the textbooks in their own terms, it is also crucial to demonstrate the possibility of readings that go against the grain of the given text. In certain respects, the most interesting readings of positivist writings are those that are discouraged by the texts themselves. In pursuing these readings-against-the-grain, a deconstructive analysis of textbooks shows the aporias, omissions, lapses and suppressions inhabiting the texts in question.

By opening texts to the possibility of their own political undoing, showing their treatment of Marxism and feminism as distinctive strategies of disciplining, we suggest the possibility of new texts — new versions of society and thus new ways of inhabiting the social world. I believe that textbooks are crucial because they exemplify the concrete ways in which academic disciplines educate both the faculty who teach from these books and the students who ingest these books in introductory-level courses as foundations for their further curricular formation. *Textbooks substitute for teachers just as their own authoriality has been suppressed.* The people who teach (from) textbooks are neutralized, confronted with the Promethean task of 'delivering' the many-hundred pages of factual description and citation about which students are periodically tested in order to evaluate their progress over the course of a semester or academic year. The textbooks are written to be self-sufficient, requiring no particular pedagogic verve or imagination to 'deliver' them — simply an ability to keep a week or two ahead of one's students in one's reading! Similarly, as I have argued in this chapter, the textbooks' authoriality has been effaced; one can barely find traces of the busy work that went into scripting these mammoth tomes — perhaps on the acknowledgments pages, where colleagues, secretaries, editors and loved ones are thanked for assistance offered over the years required to see these books through 'production'.

The deauthorization of textbooks goes hand in hand with the death of the teacher — of pedagogy generally. Some of the concerns that I raised in my previous chapter about the conjuncture of research, writing, publishing and teaching emerge here in the context of my discussion about textbooks' effect on pedagogy. Textbooks are 'product' churned out by publishers in order to make profit. They are 'adopted' by teachers and departments in order to standardize curricula as well as boost the apparent scientificity of disciplines in which textbooks summarize the scope and method of the discipline. (This is especially important in social-science disciplines, where textbooks exist partly to convince people that sociology and economics are as scientific as biology and chemistry.) Textbooks are 'delivered' by teachers who have no other role than to organize students' readings, repeat the gist of the readings in lectures, show movies and organize testing and grading.

Of course, textbooks do not kill the teacher. S/he lives to fight another day. Deconstruction demonstrates convincingly that there is no simple 'delivery' of textbook material in a teacher's lectures (which inevitably 'rewrite' the material in question), nor is it impossible for teachers to resist the text's imprimatur by contradicting or going beyond it. Teachers are not absolutely captive of the literary organizations of their disciplines any more than Foucault's self-administering prison inmates are eternally doomed to their bondage. One can teach against the grain of textbooks both by helping students discover the silenced author of textbooks (in much the way I have done in this chapter) and by provoking students to imagine different worlds from the ones frozen into science by these books.

This is precisely the challenge of socially critical pedagogy. Textbooks, like all books, can be opened, shown to be silent writing which could have been done differently. Textbooks can be problematized and read to reveal the assumptions of whole disciplines, not simply the 'factual' findings encoded in them encyclopedically. This is the challenge of critical pedagogy, showing students that they can read strongly against the grain of texts and even become writers themselves. Here is where some of the institutional constraints discussed in the previous chapter loom large. It is extremely difficult in the large introductory-level classes taught at many public universities to assign term papers and actually read them closely and critically. Instead, faculty fall back on machine-readable examinations that lend themselves well to a transmission model of education. Only with herculean effort can faculty break through the monologic and passive language game of these textbooks, inventing ways for students to engage strongly with the sense and sentience of textbooks. One of my colleagues, an intellectual renegade, requires his students to write a 'book', as he tellingly calls it, working through and beyond the textbook material. Of course, the instructor devotes a great many hours to reading and helping students revise their 'books', which disclose their own lives told sociologically with the aid of concepts found in traditional textbooks. Their lives become books by authorizing the lifeless textbooks typically used in such classes.

This is an excellent example of critical pedagogy formulated along the lines of poststructural and postmodern reading strategies, strongly preparing students for further engagement with disciplinary writings and for doing their own professional writing. Predictably, some of my colleague's students resist — even hate — his requirement that they write a book. The average American 18-year-old university student has been thoroughly disempowered in face of textuality; few read, let alone write, by the time they get to college. Where most major college textbooks are written purposely at the high-school reading level, it is no surprise that students do not believe that they can (or should) become authors themselves. By the end of the semester, some of my colleague's students have been empowered by becoming writers after having learned to read and rethink strongly. Others remain deadened before textuality, expressing hostility or simply ennui about what they have undergone in the course. I am not suggesting this classroom experience as a formulaic way of engaging in empowering critical pedagogy but simply trying to point out the powerful connection between the texting of the social sciences, on the one hand, and the literary disabling of our students (and hence our whole culture), on the other. Nevertheless, as this example shows, it is possible to confront textbooks deconstructively, hence politically, by opening them to authorization and reauthorization.

The only way that books will cease to write authors and readers is for teachers to teach the next generation of students that the world opens from texts outward — that life is a text in which all of us play roles (Derrideanizing Shakespeare!). In face of the nearly intractable political present, this is as good a radicalizing strategy as any other. Domination has become a text in fast capitalism, as I argued in chapters 2 and 3. People must be taught how to read, and then rewrite, these texts of domination. They can do this in college class-rooms, where textbook education holds sway, by learning to read against the grain — the central textual-critical strategy of Derrideans. In fact, I believe that this is ultimately a better strategy than for writers to compose 'different' textbooks, whatever that is supposed to mean. To be sure, as I have argued earlier in this chapter, we must change the 'content' of textbooks, making them less sexist, classist and racist. But a poststructural reading of textbooks indicates that the very idea of textbookishness is problematic — the notion that we can encapsulate a discipline in large, glossy tomes written in the passive voice, with the definitive ring of self-confident scientific exposition. Surely Derrida would insist that textbookishness contradicts the inhe-rent playfulness and political openness of writing and reading, instead imposing discipline on writers, readers and teachers. Although it is possible to read through textbooks critically, as I have done and as I argue that teachers must teach how to do, this is less an argument for new versions of the old textbooks than a deconstruction of the literary practices dominating academic production today, both in journal science and in textbook publishing. Although radicals can and should write 'new' textbooks, in doing so they risk contributing to the disempowering of teachers who 'deliver' these books to students through lectures and of student-readers who ingest these tomes in order to reproduce them in objective examinations.

One could expand endlessly on critical curricula, work that is important and already well underway. But this work tends to focus on the *what* of reading lists and not on the *how* of writing, reading and teaching, where I understand teaching to be a way of showing how reading (and, ultimately, writing) gets done. The most important task is for us to retheorize pedagogy as a literary practice in its own right, work that I and others (e.g., A. Luke, 1988) have begun to do. Teaching demonstrates how language can interrogate, and eventually become, text, a strategy of dealing with what Derrida calls logo-centrism. The problem with textbooks is that they disempower writers, readers and teachers equally. In appearing to have no authors as well as to be susceptible to simple transmission, textbooks entice us into the chilly, deadly, world of the falsely frozen present, ever the literary strategy of positivism (which has become the dominant ideology of late capitalism). Rethinking textbooks involves reteaching textuality, which remains the single most vital task of political pedagogy today.

In the next section of this book, I turn from a theoretically-inspired critique of disciplinary knowledge, which has led to these reflections on the politics of textuality in this chapter, to focused discussions of social problems of modernity and postmodernity. Using the theoretical insights gained so far, I discuss crises of social and economic reproduction and suggest ways in which these crises can be exploited in order to rebuild the public sphere. In the next set of chapters, I am particularly concerned with the decline of public discourse as a generic feature of late-capitalist societies in an age of decline. Clearly, the literary production of discipline is a component of the decline of discourse, just as the deconstructive democratization of the university and of academic writing helps reverse discourse's decline. The themes developed in these opening chapters return more concretely in the remaining five chapters.

# PART 2
# Critical Theory and The Social Problems of Modernity

# Chapter 6

# The Dialectic of Deindustrialization

In this section of the book, I address various important crises of social and economic reproduction in late capitalism as *social problems of modernity and postmodernity*. These are social problems that imperil the smooth functioning of capitalist public life, flowing, as Marx recognized, from various structural contradictions at the heart of capitalism (and, feminists correctly add, at the heart of patriarchy). Using the theoretical framework developed in the opening five chapters, I probe these crises of social and economic reproduction for the opportunities they create for radical social change. In this and the following four chapters, I discuss issues of deindustrialization, the production and reproduction of socio-sexual otherness, the collapse of democratic civil society and its legitimation mechanisms, the decline of public discourse and postmodernity as a social problem. All of these problems signal some fundamental fissures in the capitalist system; none can be resolved in isolation from the others. Thus, I do not propose simple solutions but instead suggest concrete ways in which a critical theory of public life can view issues portrayed discretely by the hegemonic media and statist social sciences. As much as anything, then, these five chapters can be read as contributions to the ideology-critique of positivist social science and journalism, which persistently refuse to understand apparently separate social problems as inter-related.

## On Modernity: From Marx to Habermas

In this chapter, I build on my analysis of critical theory in chapter 1 in order to trace the evolution within Marxism from the founding thought of Marx to the recent work of second-generation Frankfurt School thinkers like Jürgen Habermas who helps me to develop a critical perspective on advanced capitalism and, in particular, on the problem of its deindustrialization (see Bluestone and Harrison, 1982). I argue that neo-Marxists and feminists who seek to address the changing shape of high-technology capitalism must abandon significant empirical portions of Marx's original critique of capital while retaining his dialectical method, which vitally links theory and practice. First, the internal transformation of Marxian theory from Marx to Habermas is examined in order to extract what remains of a valid dialectical approach to capitalism. Second, I describe a dialectic of deindustrialization (see Habermas, 1970a; Agger, 1976b, 1979a, 1979b) that consists of simultaneous advances and retreats in the processes of class contradiction in this emerging era of high-technology capitalism. Finally, these developments within capitalism will be related to the possibilities of emancipatory practice, such as they exist.

Like the whole book, this chapter is conceived in the tradition of Marx, yet it calls on a reading of Marx's method that historicizes and revises his original critique of political economy. This is precisely the project of the feminist postmodern critical theory that I sketched in the first half of this book. It is possible to delineate a dialectical/deconstructive method that essentially separates Marx's immanent critique of the logic of contradiction between capital and labor (the notion that capitalism is torn between the economic progress of capital and the exploitation of labor) and an empirical theory of the emergence of crises in the real world (see Agger, 1983). Such a separation is necessary lest *Capital* be read not as an immanent critique of the logic of capital applicable to later eras but as a specific empirical theory valid once and for all. Against Althusser (1969; but also see O'Neill, 1982) *Capital* may be read as proposing a specific application of dialectical critique to 1860s capitalism in Europe and England and emphatically not as an invariant model of systemic breakdown and emancipatory overthrow. As Gramsci once remarked, the socialist revolution must be a revolution *against Capital* — that is, against all canonical texts and traditions.

Such a reading requires us to accept that capitalism is inherently self-contradictory, with 'progress' (profit) in one sector conditioning regress (alienation of labor) in another, auguring the system's eventual collapse. But this reading also delimits Marx's specific empirical sketch of crisis tendencies in volume 1 of *Capital* as relevant to the entrepreneurial stage of capitalist development in which the welfare state had not yet come to the aid of private capital. This is the baseline sense in which I define myself as a Marxist, allowing the contributions of critical theory, poststructuralism, postmodernism and feminist theory to extend and embellish the Marxian edifice, crucially adding to it a feminist politics of reproduction.

As I argued in chapter 1, theorists associated with the Frankfurt School have tried to understand new developments in advanced capitalism both to deflate the authoritarian certainties of the 'scientific' Marxists of the Second and Third Internationals and to identify possible agents of socialist transformation (see Marcuse, 1955; Korsch, 1970; Lukács, 1971; Horkheimer and Adorno, 1972; Antonio, 1983).

Adorno, Horkheimer and Marcuse sought individualized transformative agents, even as deep as the instinctual substratum, that keep alive the memory and dream of liberation, as I argue in the next chapter. They were largely successful in this, although their own politics of the personal unfortunately failed to link up with developments in feminist theory, which stressed many of the same themes.

Marcuse's Freudian Marxism is especially pertinent to this reconstruction of Marxist method (see Agger, 1982), an issue I develop further in the following chapter. In *Eros and Civilization* (1955) and *An Essay on Liberation* (1969) Marcuse charts the increasing penetration of surplus repression or domination into people's deep sensibilities in a technologically sophisticated corporate era. His argument is that the forces of both external and internal social control mount in this era when workers can otherwise taste the forbidden fruits of their liberation from the regime of scarcity yet are still harnessed to the capitalist division of labor (Marcuse, 1969). In his 1969 book, composed during the heyday of the US New Left and counterculture, Marcuse identified a new vehicle of socialist transformation in the 'new sensibilities' of individuals who refuse to separate socialist process and product, choosing instead to live qualitatively different lives in the here-and-now (also see Jaggar, 1983 and Fraser, 1989 for a feminist articulation of the same notion).

By 1972 Marcuse was castigating the New Left for both its rejection of structural theorizing and its spontaneist irrationalism and authoritarianism (see Marcuse, 1972). Yet his notion of initially individualized modes of rebellion that form a bridge of sorts between private consciousness and full-blown class struggle remains one of the most powerful modifications of Marx's original dialectical method. It is clear that Marcuse does not abandon the whole imagery of nonauthoritarian socialism but rather imbeds it in the daily struggles of people and groups who in diverse and eclectic ways are attempting to forge liberation in their immediate lifeworlds, perhaps initially oblivious to the solemnities of the *Manifesto* and *Capital* (see Marcuse, 1955: pp. 204–6). Habermas (1989b, 1984, 1987b) takes up the same theme in his 'new social movements' theory, which he grounds not in Marcuse's Freudianization of Marxism but in a communication-theoretic reinterpretation of historical materialism. (For a more fully Marcusean version of a feminist postmodern critical theory, see my *Beyond the End of Ideology*, 1991c.)

This recalls some of the sentiments expressed in Marx's 1844 manuscripts, where he described the blending of human nature and external nature through creative praxis as a socialist aim. The Frankfurt thinkers returned to early Marx in order to create a twentieth-century agenda of aesthetic politics that projects the possibility of simultaneously self-creative and productive work. Yet from within the Frankfurt tradition Jürgen Habermas in *Knowledge and Human Interests* (Habermas, 1971: pp. 32–3) challenged what he took to be the original Frankfurt School's indulgence in a vocabulary of liberation that he regards as excessively romantic. While certainly not a mechanical Marxist (and indeed an inspiration for my own discourse-theoretic version of critical theory here), Habermas suggests that Marcuse, Horkheimer and Adorno went too far in resurrecting the 1844 imagery of creative work, overreacting to the scientism and determinism of the Second International's brand of Marxism. I adjudicate the debate between Habermas and Marcuse, Adorno and Horkheimer more fully in chapter 8, where I extend Habermas' communicative reformulation of critical theory in the direction of feminist postmodern critical theory.

Habermas in effect reformulates the Marxist critique of ideology as a practical-pragmatic critique of all systematically distorted communications, including asymmetrical conversations and all social relations characterized by the élite monopoly of symbolic and system-steering codes. He argues in *The Theory of Communicative Action* (1984, 1987b) that capitalism can be shaken to its foundation only if the realm of language and communication is reconstructed so that citizens share more fully in the process of system guidance. Habermas uses the model of public discourse — argument governed not by control motives (such as brow-beating) but by the search for consensus — as his imagery of substantive socialism or what he calls 'rationality', which he anchors in people's everyday lifeworlds. He contends that ideal speech can inform all future social relations in the sense that it represents a process of undistorted speech and action in which every interlocutor shares roughly equal 'dialogue chances' (see chapter 8, below).

It is a misreading to suppose that Habermas restricts emancipatory projects to the realm of talk, regressing behind Marx to John Stuart Mill. In this sense, I believe that Habermas tries to avoid the reintroduction of logocentrism, which is anathema to Derrideans. He suggests, rather, that domination has to be reconceptualized as involving not only economic deprivation but other distortions of what Marx earlier called the relations of production — and, feminists like Chodorow (1978) and Fraser (1989) add, of reproduction. Habermas tries to reenergize the silenced proletariat by appealing to its innate (but currently distorted) competence in self-determining thought and action. Thus his communication theory of society implies counter-hegemonic strategies that attempt to uncover and organize our potential for mastering our productive infrastructure and the social relations that underpin it.

In this sense Habermas revises Marx's original critique of bourgeois political economy and transforms it into a critique of all distorted performances in language (which I call 'socially structured silence' in chapter 8). He broadens Marx's critique of political economy, based on Adam Smith and David Ricardo's original sketch of the laws of an open economic marketplace, into a critique of the technocratic guidance of a complex socio-economic system, based in large measure on the monopoly not only of capital but also of information, credentials, dialogue and discourse. In this way Habermas supplements the original critique of political economy with a critique of technocratic guidance, but he does not thereby abandon Marx's analysis of the self-contradictory logic of capital. His goal is still to liberate labor, conceived as distorted communicative competence, from domination.

This new formulation of historical materialism takes Marx's original critique of political economy as its point of departure. It goes beyond him, however, by suggesting that the monopoly of capital is now reinforced and occluded by the monopoly of information, credentials and discourse (see Mueller, 1973; T. Luke, 1989). Although the aim of the new Marxism from Lukács to Marcuse and Habermas is still to disalienate labor, utopian metaphors and images have significantly changed since Marx, especially under the influence of a postmodern feminism that fundamentally challenges the androcentric biases of the Marxist tradition. Marcuse's 'rationality of gratification' and Habermas's 'discourse' flesh out Marx's image of socialism in culturally and historically more relevant terms in order to project qualitative social change in meaningful, nonthreatening ways. This theoretical redevelopment, borrowing from feminism and postmodernism as well, allows us to address concrete problems of public life in theoretically and politically relevant terms.

## A High-Tech Capitalism?

The recent work of Habermas in particular underlies much of what is to follow in the way of a concrete discussion of the dilemmas of deindustrialization and its 'high-tech' solution. I draw from Habermas' (1975) analysis of legitimation crises an overall perspective on the displacement of contradictions from the realm of class struggle to new socio-ideological and cultural spheres. Habermas, more explicitly than any other neo-Marxist to date, has extended and deepened Marx's original critique of political economy by applying it to new topics unexamined by original Marxism (either because they were unforeseen or because they simply did not fit Marx's preoccupations with the particular manifestations of economic contradictions of market capitalism). Beginning in *Legitimation Crisis* (1975), Habermas suggests that bedrock contradictions of the logic of capital have been displaced from the economy pure and simple and now extend into every sphere of public and private life. (Harry Cleaver, 1979, would respond that Marx never meant that internal contradictions were restricted to the economy but were always inherently political-economic in nature.) In *The Theory of Communicative Action* Habermas characterizes this as the colonization of the lifeworld by the system.

He offers a systems-analytic Marxism that helps us bridge between the original political-economic concerns of Marx in *Capital*, on the one hand, and lifeworld concerns of dialogue and discourse. Habermas' perspective is important because he relates the systemic level of structural contradictions to the microscopic analysis of the lifeworld in a way that develops better images of the transformation of public life in initially prefigurative personal and interpersonal ways. Habermas' effort here parallels and fertilizes a politics of discourse that I theorize through a feminist postmodern version of critical theory.

Habermas (1970a) also offers an important critique of technology and science as ideology, a central component of my discussion of the contradictions of Atari capitalism. He suggests that the *laissez-faire* legitimation of earlier market capitalism has been largely replaced by the scientific-technocratic legitimation that cedes all system-steering authority to an élite of systems managers. Habermas contends that this Atari ideology of impenetrable high technology is even more impervious to radical critique than, earlier, religion and market economic theory because science and technology seem to banish the realm of political values and instead reduce all decision-making to pragmatic instrumentality. Habermas contends that this impervious scientific-technical worldview functions as ideology by illegitimately conflating the realms of substantive communication and self-reflection (the proper preserve of informed thought and talk about qualitative values), on the one hand, and the realm of technical action, on the other. This in effect ensures that system-serving behavior is perpetuated inasmuch as we lose our capacity to distinguish among ultimate social values, an exercise banished by positivists since Wittgenstein's (1981) *Tractatus Logico-Philosophicus* as nonsense.

This new Marxism, via Habermas as well as other strains of discourse theory including poststructuralism, postmodernism and feminism, may be turned to the tasks of analyzing the present problem of deindustrialization and then suggesting possible radical responses. In particular, the mythos of high technology can be challenged both within and outside of Marxism by suggesting a host of new contradictions that a high-tech capitalism will confront in the years ahead. The notion of deindustrialization has become prevalent in economic analysis, as well as in the media, pointing to a number of phenomena: the shift in population from northeastern US cities to the sunbelt states; massive US and UK unemployment in traditional heavy industries like automobiles and steel; increasing suburbanization, only partly counteracted by urban gentrification on the part of upper-middle-class young professionals; and the aging of the population, creating a heavy burden on the social security and welfare systems.

In this context, I will now examine the dominant technocratic response to deindustrialization and then suggest several contradictions that this response is likely to engender. This analysis will be conducted in the spirit of feminist postmodern critical theory in the sense that it will examine the shifting constellation of forces in both the base and superstructure that simultaneously hamper emancipatory projects and may trigger subterranean forces of resistance as well.

Three distinctive crises occur increasingly in an advanced capitalism pinched by energy shortage, ecological disruption and uneven regional development, both domestic and international. First, the paid work force is increasingly hierarchized and fragmented along the axes of skill, unionization and work style. Second, domination is explosively introjected and then externalized with rage as economic pressures and dissatisfactions colonize the realm of personality and household, seen in increasing violence against women, gays and minorities as well as cultural misogyny, heterosexism and racism (issues that I examine in the next chapter). Third, the mythos of scientism and technology deepens as the reins of power are increasingly handed over to technical élites, who we (must) trust to keep us off the shoals of economic crisis. Let me address these three emergent crises of late capitalism in turn.

The phenomenon of the dual labor market is often described in terms of a growing gap in skill, income, work style and occupational prestige between white- and blue-collar workers (Beck, Horan and Tolbert, 1978). The growth of a so-called new working class or new middle class is addressed by both Marxists and Weberian sociologists of work. The former identify a labor aristocracy (Engels' and Lenin's term for internal stratification of the proletariat); the latter speak about the increasing structuration and differentiation of the work force in advanced industrial society (Giddens, 1973). But an important new realm of labor comprises deskilled, low-income, nonunionized and status-poor female pink-collar workers largely found in the service sector of the economy (e.g., waitresses, maids, keypunch operators, bank tellers). As left feminists (e.g., Walby, 1986) argue, there is now a tripartite division in the work force along these dimensions of income, work style, unionization and status, showing the way in which class and gender lines have begun to blur. Neo-Marxists describe this division among paid workers in terms of occupational status differentiations: white collar denotes a largely male professional work force with high income and high status; blue collar denotes a largely male unionized manual work force with relatively high income but somewhat lower occupational prestige; and pink collar refers to the characteristics of largely female labor in the deskilled, low-income service sector unprotected by unionization.

This analysis of the increasing fragmentation and stratification of the proletariat in high-tech capitalism stems from Harry Braverman's *Labor and Monopoly Capital* (1974), although it also incorporates categories and concepts from socialist-feminist theory (see Eisenstein, 1979; Jaggar, 1983). Braverman updates Marx's categories of labor exploitation in a concrete analysis of the modern work force. He suggests that the seeming 'embourgeoisement' of the proletariat — the rise of a middle-class mass culture, with a relatively comfortable material standard of living in the urban United States — is largely a myth. He argues that certain sectors of the proletariat are more exploited than ever, notably in terms of technological deskilling, lack of unionization and unemployment. Braverman did not address directly enough the increasingly sexual-political and racial lines drawn between the male white- and blue-collar fractions of the working class, on the one hand, and the largely female and non-white pink-collar fraction, on the other. Braverman's analysis can be extended to show that the rise of a high-tech capitalism in response to the deindustrialization of traditional heavy industry is not likely to bring either the everlasting cornucopia of consumerism or the 'pacification' of labor as workers turn from the sweaty din of the industrial shop floor to the creative and antiseptic confines of the computer labs. Instead élite white male workers are likely to benefit disproportionately, while a whole new cadre of deskilled and undercompensated pink-collar manual and service workers picks up the slack.

High technology in itself will not upgrade paid labor in general but only those fractions of labor that stand to gain from the increasing subjugation, exploitation and deskilling of other larger fractions of labor. These lines are particularly drawn around the issues of gender and race, as socialist feminists point out. Thus, high-tech capitalism is likely to deepen extant divisions between sex classes as it increasingly fragments the proletariat and creates an almost quasi-managerial class of privileged and relatively powerful professional and technical workers.

It is a mistake to view the embourgeoisement and upgrading of the work force in a monolithic way. In capitalism there is always a trade-off of power and privilege with respect to class formations; some gain where others lose. And those who gain are always a small élite. The yuppie entrepreneurs who run computer companies are no less capitalist than the mill owners of Victorian England. It is false to suppose that the computerization of industry, to the extent that it is happening, is a positive augur of a benign postindustrialism, except in the dialectical sense that it brings with it new contradictions, such as sex and class struggle, that might one day sound the death-knell of capitalism. High-tech capitalism only sinks the contradictions deeper into the economic and emotional soil of the proletariat, women and people of color.

The second crisis of high-tech capitalism, involving the increasing introjection, personalization and domestication of domination, clearly stems from the growing fragmentation and stratification of the working class as well as from women's burden of unpaid household labor (see Shelton and Agger, 1991). To the extent that US women workers earn only about 60 per cent of male workers' earnings, tensions between the sexes rise. In a transition between traditional heavy industry and high technology, with all sorts of internal dislocations such as redundancy and technological unemployment, economic vicissitudes will increase the scapegoating of sexual-political minorities, particularly in the sphere of domesticity, where women have always borne the burden of culturally legitimate male supremacy. As blue-collar males are thrown out of work, they bring their resentment home with them and take it out on wives and children who symbolize for them a feared-because-desired sexual-political 'other', as I explore further in the next chapter. Women take the brunt of the quite literal beating as working-class and middle-class men who come upon hard times mistakenly blame the women's movement (and not transitional capitalism) for their own economic problems.

Women, gays and ethnic and racial minorities are increasingly scapegoated as men respond defensively to 'privileged' minorities boosted by affirmative action programs and entitlements. All this reflects the traditional displacement of rage onto even weaker Others, carefully documented in the authoritarian personality study by Adorno and his colleagues in their attempt to explain the dynamics of fascist resentment (see Adorno *et al.*, 1950). In capitalism, economic misfortunes among the largely male proletariat are worked through at the expense of even lower and less powerful groups, especially — and this is what is so contemporary as an explicit issue — in the realm of domesticity. Ku Klux Klan nightriding is now overshadowed by violence against women as a gesture of rage and desublimation.

This second crisis of high-tech capitalism is addressed in Habermas' (1984, 1987b) analysis of the colonization of the lifeworld, including his discussion of system-lifeworld relations and the various pathologies that result from them. He suggests that advanced capitalism founders to the extent that systemic imperatives of domination penetrate too deeply into the pretheoretical realm of lived experience. This is self-contradictory, ultimately blocking the system's own vitality and efficiency, in that the system requires a relatively unencumbered lifeworld as a source of personal creativity and innovation. Habermas parallels Derridean arguments about the undecidability of closed systems. He also follows Paul Piccone's (1976, 1978) important analysis of 'artificial negativity', which I discussed in chapter 4. Piccone suggests that the system requires a calculated loosening of the bonds of what Adorno earlier called 'total administration' and Marcuse 'one-dimensionality' in order to guarantee a supply of economic risk-taking and a safety valve for otherwise implosive deviance. Habermas suggests that it is ultimately irrational for the system to colonize the lifeworld if that colonization enforces a false (because impossible) identity between the system's functional requirements and lived experience. The system requires nonidentity — nonconformist socialization, escape valves for implosive deviance, innovation — so that capitalism's shell of bondage does not become intolerably confining and thus counterproductive.

In this sense, a Habermasian analysis of deindustrialization suggests that the frightening intensification of sexual and political violence is dysfunctional in the system's own terms because it allows systemic contradictions to be displaced into the realm of already threatened privacy (even if, as Fraser, 1989, notes, 'privacy' is not so private after all). If men and women cannot maintain a semblance of civil relations, drawing some succor either from the bourgeois nuclear family (Lasch's 1977 'haven in a heartless world') or from more progressive domestic forms, the already confining system will wear them down. Advanced capitalism, a Picconesque version of Habermas would suggest, requires artificial negativity in order to allow individuals some reprieve from an increasingly administered ('colonized') work existence, although not at the expense of women traditionally assigned domestic roles of nurturance.

Noted by both Marcuse and Habermas in the late 1960s, the third crisis of high-tech capitalism is the emergence of science and technology as ideology, leading to intellectual and political regression. Elites must legitimate their monopoly of system-administering privileges, notably through a theory of social-problem solving that cedes all conversational and symbolic rights to a technocratic minority. In mainstream sociology the classic Davis-Moore (1945) theory of the inevitability of stratification is one early example of this scientific-technical mythos, which has become even more pervasive in the meantime.

Habermas (1970a) in his writings on science and technology as ideology as well as in his more recent writings on communication theory (Habermas, 1984, 1987b) argues that the market-capitalist ideology of balanced supply and demand gradually gives way to laws of the technocratic monopoly of dialogue chances in crisis-prone late capitalism, an issue I develop in chapter 8. The system-steering prerogatives of élites have been legitimated since the origins of western sociology in Durkheim and Weber through the structural functionalism of Parsons (1951) in terms of the putative 'necessity' of technocratic management of social and economic complexity. This is to confuse the ubiquity of differentiation (all specialization, in Durkheim's sense of the division of labor) with the alleged necessity of stratification (in Weber's sense of the differential distribution of power, prestige and wealth). This confusion is at the heart of the ideology of modernity; it is rooted in the notion of the inevitability of technocratic expertise, unchallenged by the substantive rationality of what Habermas calls the lifeworld.

Habermas' communication theory thus extends Marx's critique of the alienation of labor toward an analysis of technocratic legitimation through unchallenged science and technical guidance. Science and technology function as ideological props of a social system that requires citizens to cede all system-steering rights to élites. Habermas suggests that domination in late capitalism occurs when the rationality of technique invades the domain of communicative action, replacing the motive of consensus formation, which he contends is the implicit intent of every speech act, with the motive of sheer control. As I develop further in chapter 8, Habermas in effect wants to secure an emancipatory impulse grounded in the structure of speech itself in order to replace the disappointed philosophy of history embraced initially by Horkheimer and Adorno in the 1940s, only to erode into a dismal 'negative dialectics' after World War II. He argues that communication theory helps simultaneously to explain the colonization of the lifeworld by systemic imperatives (notably via the media of money and power, the common currencies of abstraction and sheer control) and a guarded optimism about the inherent purpose of consensus formation contained in the structure of speech itself, suggesting a vital basis of counterhegemony that he argues critical theory has lacked since Lukács. In chapter 8, I assess the merits of his communication theory in terms of its implications for my critical theory of textuality.

High-tech capitalism is particularly likely to deepen the mythos of science and technology as specialists exude the mystical and esoteric talents of the initiated. Most people recognize that high technology requires a high science that is virtually impenetrable by the practical reasoning of everyday life. Science and technology achieve interface in the high-powered computer from which ordinary knowledge is excluded. As I argued in chapter 4, trends in higher education reflect this development. Computer literacy is quickly becoming as important as the old literacy of reading and writing and university administrators are retooling classical liberal arts education into curricula heavily weighted in favor of applied social science, computer science, economics and engineering. This shift in educational priorities at both secondary and university levels reinforces the overall faith in scientific and technical expertise. A more subtle effect is to rob curricula of the potentially critical and subversive insights of the humanities and social sciences. While much of this curriculum change is defended in the name of financial expediency (falling enrollments, a changing economy and the like), many teachers recognize that administrators and curriculum planners who favor the increasing scientization of education use economic short-fall as an excuse to rid the schools and universities of the radicals of the 1960s.

In this climate, including widespread industrial layoffs and economic stagnation, it is no wonder that the mythos of high technology has such a galvanizing appeal. The collapse of the industrial infrastructure of New York, Pennsylvania, Massachusetts, Michigan and Ohio is met with renewed optimism about the various silicon valleys mushrooming to take their place. In turn, this inherent faith in science and technology gives the mandarins of high technology even more system-steering power than the Enlightenment bestowed on the doyens of natural science in the seventeenth and eighteenth centuries.

Against both liberal and orthodox-Marxist appraisals of the Frankfurt School's critique of science — particularly as captured in Horkheimer and Adorno's (1972) *Dialectic of Enlightenment* — the critique of bourgeois scientism and technocracy is an urgent priority for a critical theory of public life.

The Frankfurt position, now as before, is that faith in science and technology reinforces passive acquiescence to a *status quo* that is experienced uncritically, without mediation by overarching categories of justice, truth and beauty. Trust in high technology reinforces the collapse of what Marcuse (1964) called the first and second dimensions of experience: the mundane level of Hegel's *Verstand* (everyday understanding, often governed by the technical interest in control) and the transcendent level of *Vernunft* (objective reason, capable of interrogating the nature of truth, justice, and beauty and unafraid to challenge the relativizing commonsense of a one-dimensional society; Hegel, 1966). Interestingly, Habermas reverses Marcuse's Hegelian differentiation of dulled everyday commonsense and transcendent reason, arguing that the decolonization of the lifeworld will produce substantive rationality grounded in normative consensus formation — democratic discourse.

High-tech capitalism rests on a further bifurcation of knowledge, with technical specialists at the upper echelons of corporations and the state usurping even more of the dialogue chances of citizens while giving them the illusion of technological and political-economic mastery by offering them home computers and other electronic entertainments. The computerization of education is likely to have the effect of further legitimating the unchallenged system-steering authority of a scientific and technical élite while it convinces the powerless that they, too, can have access to the tools and codes of power by using home computers and consuming mass-mediated electronic culture. This pseudo-democratization of advanced technology goes hand in hand with the pseudo-democracy of representative democracy (with periodic mass elections predicted and thus ensured before the polls close by survey researchers, replacing the direct democracy of the Athenian *polis* and New England town meeting).

In this sense the pseudo-democratization of computer skills and technology in late capitalism reinforces a one-dimensionality of thought and behavior, where in earlier capitalism people experienced a certain critical distance from the esoteric symbolic codes and practices of economic élites. As Adorno and Horkheimer argued in the 1940s, the superficial advances in enlightenment really betoken knowledge's regression where enlightenment is equivalent to scientific and technical advancement. The more we rely on canned computer knowledge and culture, the less we can think, speak and write critically about the social totality, an insight central to a postmodern version of critical theory. There may be an inverse relationship between privatized passive reliance on canned entertainment and knowledge and a critical literacy that allows us to transcend the pregiven categories of possible knowledge insinuating themselves into the discourses of bytes, text editing and software.

The high-tech solution to deindustrialization and uneven regional development in the United States will engender these three original types of class and gender contradiction, unforeseen by Marx. This analysis assumes that the stewards of state and corporate planning can successfully circumvent the increasingly obvious roadblocks littering the path of gradualist economic expansion. It is clear to most liberal and conservative economists that the neoconservative administrative strategies of Ronald Reagan and Margaret Thatcher only accelerated the tendencies toward serious class, gender and race confrontation. These strategies reversed the Robin Hood mechanisms of the Keynesian welfare state that are desperately required in a system rooted in the self-contradictory logic of capital producing unemployment and thus underconsumption (see Galbraith, 1967).

Reaganomics forgets the lessons taught by Keynes and implemented by every US president since Franklin Roosevelt. Reagan dismantled the safety nets of the US welfare state precisely when they were needed most in order to protect the economic system against both insurrection and underconsumption. The high-tech strategy of capitalist survival depends on the transcendence of the self-limiting short-term administrative strategies of Reagan and Thatcher; instead it substitutes a longer-term incrementalism designed to shore up the US economy's position in the world market (especially in relation to Japan and West Germany). High-tech capitalism transcends the desperation of Reagan and his ilk; it preserves his ultimate aim to save capitalism (the desideratum of all welfare state politicians since Roosevelt), yet it more fundamentally attacks the technological irrationalities underlying US industry, particularly in the urban northeast.

It may be optimistic, even from the point of view of welfare state liberalism, to suppose that the technocratic stewards of the US economy and polity will be able to reverse the inevitable backlash against Reaganomics among the poor and minorities. A reindustrializing high-tech capitalism will move forward only if the statist 'executive committee of the bourgeoisie' in the Bush era can temper its immediate class interest and instead recognize its longer-term interest in protecting global capitalism against its own excesses.

But high-tech capitalism brings a general diminution of collective intelligence as it reinforces state and cultural hegemony. It may also intensify struggles within the proletariat among class fractions, notably between ethnic and sexual-political minorities, on the one hand, and patriarchal males, on the other. In addition high-tech capitalism further links the realms of work and domesticity, giving us even less space in which to restore ourselves in non-sexist ways beyond the imperatives of a totally administered world. Yet at the same time a new critical theory inspired largely by Habermas allows us to suggest the emergence of new social movements responding to social problems of modernity and postmodernity. The intensification of sexual-political persecution, the further splitting of the working class into a dual labor market and the growing computerization of the economy, education and culture might have the unintended consequences of creating new avenues and agents of radical social change, notably (but not exclusively) from within the women's movement.

The most pertinent struggles in this emerging high-tech capitalism are taking place on three levels: pink-collar service work, the politics of domesticity and higher education. As women increasingly enter the paid labor force into menial, deskilled and underpaid jobs, the potential grows for socialist-feminist struggle within the ranks of organized labor as well as in the housework force on which capitalist patriarchy rests. Similarly, as sexual-political persecution grows in direct response to the transitional agonies of industrial-age capitalism, including widespread male unemployment, women increasingly struggle to take control of the social relations of reproduction and to overcome traditional gender roles in the family as well as in the paid workplace. Finally, the further integration of higher education into a state and corporate agenda might have the effect of prompting educators and students to reevaluate the demise of liberal arts curricula and perhaps even to resist the further linkage of academic production with the requirements of political economy and ideology. On this last front, the struggle by left-wing social scientists to resist the reduction of academic work into the system-serving terms of disciplined scholarship (where knowledge is evaluated only in terms of its instrumental relevance) is an example of this mounting resistance, as I explored in chapter 4.

In this sense the creation of new critical theory will be facilitated by the convergence of neo-Marxian political economy and its critique of ideology with the theoretical thrust of socialist feminism, alerting us to the emerging contradictions of pink-collar alienation, the dual labor market and sex-political persecution. Above all, socialist feminism links the personal and political in a way that allows us to understand the phenomena of deindustrialization and reindustrialization in concrete terms, notably in regard to the dialectical bond between what happens in (and in between) the realms of work and domesticity, production and reproduction. Orthodox Marxists retain Engels' analysis of the origins of patriarchy in capitalism. Socialist feminists address the important interchange between enduring productive contradictions and their displacement in the realm of reproduction, suggesting liberatory strategies located in both personal and public life. After all, as Adorno, like feminists, recognized, in capitalism there is no such thing as *private* life.

What socialist feminism ultimately lacks, and what my version of a feminist postmodern critical theory attempts to provide, is the dialectic of production and reproduction. Socialist feminism is too frequently a descriptive and moral account of the relationship between alienation 'out there' (in capitalist political economy and its social relations of production) and alienation 'in here' (the social relations of reproduction in patriarchal society). Western Marxism retrieves and extends socialist feminism's important vision of a reconstructed daily life in the context of its analysis of the structural vicissitudes of late capitalism in an age of technological advancement and contraction.

Habermas' recent version of Marxism is a powerful complementary source of dialectical vision in this analysis of deindustrialization, notably in the way Habermas has understood system-lifeworld penetration or what I have called the relationship between the public and personal or production and reproduction. Habermas points to the inherently self-limiting nature of the colonization and rationalization of the lifeworld in high-tech capitalism, a kind of impervious second dimension that resists complete cooptation and administration. Habermas locates this resistance to complete heteronomy in the nonidentity of system and lifeworld, indeed in the social system's requirement of innovative, risk-taking subjectivity formed through the dialogic relations of intimacy, school, and culture. The social system cannot dispense with this inviolate zone in which communicative action takes place lest it lose its dynamism, however irrational and self-contradictory in the long term. For example, the system cannot dispense with the human activity of computer programming, a thoroughly value-laden task that must be carried out according to a substantive rationality of deliberate decision-making. The social system in its own terms cannot be self-regenerating; human subjectivity must be vestigially free in order to make systemic on-course corrections (the fine-tuning measures of technocratic incrementalism). A society of robots does not serve the interests of capital, even though the logic of capital (and here all Marxists would agree) tends toward ever-increasing robotization (reification, alienation, domination, and so forth). This suggests inherent dialectical resistance contained in the very activity of dialogue itself, as Habermas has suggested and as I further develop in chapter 8. Short of the full eclipse of reason, our resistance to the artificial intelligence of canned programs is a liberatory act, as are attempts to protect our various lifeworlds (family, school, culture) from rationalization.

This suggests a research program for Habermas-generation critical theory that sheds the quietism of Adorno's pessimistic philosophy of history but refuses to repeat Marx in literal terms. Such research would attempt to locate the weakest links in computer capitalism as a way of amplifying the possibility and actuality of counterhegemonic activity. If Habermas is right, this counterhegemony will probably spring from attempts to resist the further colonization of lifeworlds in the struggle to secure and protect communicative rationality (as well as to correct the various asymmetries of our lifeworlds). This is very much the agenda of a feminist postmodern critical theory of the kind that I developed in the first half of this book, showing how the politicization of discourse can empower readers to become writers, hence citizens. In defiance of system-steering élites who infiltrate and manipulate the lifeworlds of cultural reproduction, education, and intimacy, people will attempt to articulate what has remained unspoken: the discursive nature of our institutions and thus their susceptibility to reformulation.

By tracing all institutional objectifications back to their pretheoretical grounds in the lifeworld, especially dialogue and textuality, we demonstrate the possibility of spontaneous resistances that can be mounted against the lifeworld's further colonization. In showing that people do try to create livable social spaces in which to escape systemic rationalization and colonization, we can buttress the original Marxian optimism about piercing bourgeois hegemony. A postmodern-Habermasian research program would attempt to document the instances where people initiate microscopic social change by writing the social texts of their own lives in defiance of the disciplinary imperative of high-tech capitalism. If in this era of despair such 'evidence' is scarce, then critical theory can at least confirm Adorno's notion that the 'whole is untrue' without utterly abandoning hope that one day the tide may turn.

In this chapter, I have tried to establish an institutional framework within which we can talk meaningfully about problems of public life in an age of decline. Deindustrialization, as I have argued, is an outcome of the basic logic of capital, as Marx understood it. But the logic of capital has taken surprising turns since the mid-nineteenth century, when Marx reasonably expected an apocalyptic capitalism to be replaced imminently by socialism. Although crisis tendencies have not disappeared (this being capitalism, after all), they have been managed and mediated by an interventionist state and culture industry that have checked economic crises and created new consumer needs as well as continued to depoliticize the realm of reproduction. These new crisis tendencies, like deindustrialization and the uneven development that it both causes and reflects, demand new concepts and strategies of social change. It is useful for me to think about social change in terms of local resistances to systemic crises, much as Habermas (1984, 1987b) has done in his analysis of system and lifeworld and much as feminists like Fraser (1989) do when correcting Habermas' sharp differentiation of public and private realms. In the following chapter, I move from an analysis of economic crisis tendencies in late capitalism to an analysis of psychic and cultural crisis tendencies. What I call the dialectic of deindustrialization is matched on the psychic and cultural levels by a dialectic of desire that is an important political factor in its own right.

# Chapter 7

# The Dialectic of Desire

## The Dialectic of Desire and the Telos of Capitalism

One of the central contributions of a feminist postmodern critical theory of public life is to recognize ways in which liberal capitalism embodies a secret fascism that can be undone by theory and practice committed to the preservation of marginality. Both postmodernism and feminism defend the micro against the macro, the personal against the political, margins against the center. In Adorno's terms, they defend non-identity and thus the possibility of liberation via critical intelligence and action. Adorno understood fascism to be the obliteration of otherness, of non-identity, under sway of the disciplinary tendencies of bureaucratic administration. He developed his critical theory precisely to give voice to the importance of non-identity, which he made the basis of his call to overcome the identitarian principles of capitalist administration and organization.

In this chapter, I continue my discussion in the preceding chapter about surprising ways in which capitalism undermines its own social and economic reproduction. Here, I focus on ways in which the effort to exterminate whole groups of people leads to a mode of solidarity with the dead in memory that serves to protect and nurture people's desires to be free. Public life today is characterized by the loss of memory; things happen so quickly that memory, like all thought, is degraded, thus robbing people of the anamnestic capacity to retrieve *le temps perdu*, whether the imagination of utopia or the recollection of nightmare. Memory is a crucial component of a feminist postmodern critical theory in the sense that it protects us against a fast capitalism endeavoring to destroy history by sealing off the eternal present from both past and future. Historicity — the experience of the possibility of social change — is crucial for liberation. Without a sense of where we have been and where we might be going, the present will be experienced falsely as a plenitude of possibility. Critical theory, now as before, insists that historicity is an essential element of the human condition, allowing us to redeem past and present suffering in the process of creating a society in which people suffer less. In this chapter, I discuss ways in which the destruction of memory is ironically inimical to a system that otherwise profits from an everyday life in which the past stands only for yesterday.

Most interpretations of the genesis of critical theory do not adequately address the relationship among the well-known Frankfurt analysis of domination in post-Depression capitalism, their understanding of fascism and their own identities as Marxist Jews. This is not to attempt a version of psychohistory. While that might be fruitful, it would be too much a device of bourgeois historiography; I am interested in the particular past, including intellectual biography, only as it might illuminate larger dialectical trends in social structure and open what few emancipatory avenues remain. Of course the Frankfurt theorists as Jews acutely felt their own estrangement from the dominant German social order that threatened their mortal existence. (Walter Benjamin committed suicide in 1940 just before he thought he was to be caught by the fascists.) But it is insufficient to reduce their revision of Marxism to this biographical contingency. Instead their identity as outsiders and potential victims was not simply a cause of their subsequent critical theory but a moment within the complex totality of biography and history that allowed them to see the unfolding social world in a new and innovative way. Their own estrangement as left-wing Jewish intellectuals was for them an example of universal estrangement, which they understood in Marxist terms. But rather than viewing their cultural formation as a reflex of their own class-position, their self-understanding as Marxist Jews became a mode of theoretical articulation in a world gone mad (see Horkheimer, 1974a: pp. 101–18). It is that mode of articulation which I want to bring to bear here as I discuss the meaning of the Holocaust for an emerging critical theory of public life.

The Frankfurt theorists even in the 1930s recognized in almost singular prescience that the perverse horrors of embryonic German fascism would not be erased by an Allied victory, seemingly the triumph of western reason over Aryan myth (Marcuse, 1968: pp. 3–42). Rather they suggested that there is a dialectic of victor and vanquished whereby, in Hegelian terms, the essential nature of the vanquished is *aufgehoben* — negated, preserved, transcended — by the victor. In this sense they offered a profound analysis of anti-Semitism that did not exaggerate its historical specificity but rather viewed it as a stage in the development of what Adorno was later to call 'totally administered' society. The eradication of Jewish 'otherness' by the fascists presaged the attempt to eradicate all deviant otherness in post-World War II capitalism, including sexual and racial minorities. Horkheimer, Adorno, Benjamin and Marcuse wrote a Judaic Marxism that, first, allows us to understand the Holocaust as a stage in the development of capitalism and, second, to speculate about the persistence and intensification of both introjected and projected aggression in late capitalism. In this chapter I explore the relevance of the Frankfurt analysis of fascism, and its subsequent *Aufhebung* in our era of one-dimensional capitalism, for a politics of resistance based, in the first instance, on the strategy of solidarity-with-the-dead. Memory can be mobilized against fast capitalism.

What is most innovative about the Frankfurt interpretation of German fascism is the idea that the capitalist 'authoritarian state' which vanquished fascism both preserved and streamlined fascist tendencies of absolute social control. The Frankfurt theorists suggest that the Holocaust, with its blend of factory-like barbarism and mythic belief in a master race, is really a metaphor for all class domination and particularly for the authoritarian state that fully emerged after World War II. Indeed much of the Frankfurt work in the 1930s was prophesy: they predicted what Franz Neumann (1942, 1957) called Behemoth — the militarily mobilized society of Nazi Germany as a dialectical stage in the evolution of Adorno's totally administered society. The kind of absolute integration represented by the concentration camps, where all subjective otherness is quite literally demolished under sway of the 'preponderance of the object', as Adorno called it, is nothing less than the *telos* of the entire Enlightenment, in which the Holocaust and monopoly capitalism are the two most recent stages, themselves dialectically intertwined.

Adorno and Horkheimer were later to systematize their thoughts about the dialectic of myth and enlightenment, suggesting that the aim of western Enlightenment is to destroy the delicate dialectic of subject and object that for Hegelian Marxists is the very nature of the human condition, as well as the promise of a future non-authoritarian society (Horkheimer and Adorno, 1972: pp. 3–42). They regard both fascism and capitalism as institutional embodiments of tyrannized subjectivity, where their respective purposes are not only to elevate the master race to its world-historical destiny or to increase profits but rather to exterminate all deviant opposition that resists absorption into the social totality. This was a highly original interpretation for it freed Marxism from a dogmatic reliance on strictly economic factors — the pitfall of economistic Marxism — and instead introduced a blend of Freudian depth-psychology and dialectical Marxism to explain the transmission belt between subjectivity and objective social structure. A feminist postmodern critical theory needs this psychodynamic grounding (avoiding its potentially essentialist overtones; see Jacoby, 1975, for a version of this 'negative psychoanalysis') in order to comprehend the ways in which discipline or domination is self-imposed as well as imposed from the outside.

It is in this vein that I want to suggest that the Frankfurt analysis of fascism, later to emerge in the empirical studies of 'authoritarian personality' in the late 1940s (Adorno *et al.*, 1950), offered a notion of the *dialectic of desire* that explains all sorts of vicissitudes and blockages in the subsequent development of advanced capitalism. Desire in this sense, in line with Marcuse's (1955: pp. 32–5) later more explicit writings on the possibility of a Freudian Marxism, to be discussed below, is both a subjective and objective process that links the individual to social structure. In its destructive form, desire seeks the total absorption of the surrounding object-world, virtually an infantile projection ('oceanic feeling' in Freud). As we shall see, desire is also potentially a utopian concept in that its destructive-aggressive tendencies can be seen not as a death instinct desiring the destruction of oneself and others but as an impulse that wants to overcome the pain of an alienated social condition. In this sense, critical theorists join postmodernists in attempting to energize revolt and resistance by capitalizing on what they both contend is the incontrovertible non-identity underlying the human condition and language. A feminist postmodern critical theory understands that fascism is the attempt to eradicate non-identity and marginality. Fortunately, desire, like deindustrialization (in the previous chapter) and dialogue (in the following chapter), is dialectical, presenting resistances to these attempts to subsume everything under the sign of identity and logos — the essence of the positivism undermined by Derrida as well as by Marcuse's version of Freudian Marxism, which are remarkably similar projects in this sense.

Fascism and the authoritarian state that sublated it — only streamlining its destructiveness — are never unequivocally successful in completing the postulated mission of the death instinct. Desire is inherently dialectical, as Marcuse's Freud suggests, because it contains both gratificatory and destructive components. As such, while desire clearly has the capacity for destroying itself and others (and now the whole world), it also possesses, according to this dialectical interpretation, an ineradicable inner core that resists both external and internal domination, what I have called an inner second dimension (or dimension of transcendence). So a dialectical view of fascism would suggest, as I will later, that the 'absolute integration' of subject and object in the death camps was never complete not only because some survived but also because desire, through remembrance and dialectical imagination, can achieve a kind of anamnestic solidarity (Lenhardt, 1975; Bloch, 1970; Benjamin, 1969) with past and present victims and thereby preserve the utopian *telos* of a desire unfettered by domination. By understanding the Holocaust and later monopoly capitalism in terms of this dialectical notion of desire, one can understand their institutional mobilization in powerfully depth-psychological terms — concentration camps as the absolute integration of subject and object, where subjectivity is exterminated — and, as well, protect a utopian imagery where desire lives to fight another day, notably through anamnestic solidarity: 'We shall never forget.'

### Behemoth: Explaining Jewish Otherness

Original critical theory had two interrelated aims. As I explained earlier in this book, the first was to explain the evolution within capitalism from entrepreneurial to corporate stages, focusing on growing state intervention in political economy and culture. Western Marxism sought to explain the collapse of the Second International and the demise of European proletariats as probable transformative agents (see Jacoby, 1981). The second aim, which I explore more fully here, was to address the alternation of myth and enlightenment as the basis of a philosophy of history that could, in larger terms, explain as well as resist fascism and its corporate integration. Such a philosophy of history, joined with postmodernism and feminist theory, can then plumb post-World War II capitalism for possible pockets of critical resistance, in the absence of Marx's fallen nineteenth-century proletariat.

It was the unprecedented evolution of capitalism, beyond Marx's original parameters, that led Horkheimer and Adorno to seek a dialectical philosophy of history that was less naïve than Enlightenment optimism, which equated intellectual and social progress with greater scientific certitude. The outbreak of World War I, which doomed the Second International and inspired the Bolshevik bowdlerization of Marx's emancipatory philosophy, clearly indicated that the 'expropriation of the expropriators' could be indefinitely postponed. Worse, it showed that Marxism itself had to be more clearly disentangled from the naïve progressivism of the Enlightenment lest it rush headlong into battle ill-equipped to understand the epochal ambiguity of the ideal of 'reason'.

To meet this challenge of providing Marxism with more circumspection and thus humility, Horkheimer and Adorno, as noted earlier, developed a concept of the 'dialectic of enlightenment', suggesting that the past has been marked by continual alternation between mythic belief and advances in enlightened understanding (Lenhardt, 1976). They developed the dialectic-of-enlightenment concept by drawing on the same Nietzsche appreciated by Derrida. They argue that the seemingly straightforward rationalism of western civilization is replete with mythic nuances that imperil an unproblematic reliance on science as a contemporary panacea. The Frankfurt critique of positivism suggests that it is dogmatic to enthrone scientific method as the only legitimate source of knowledge. They further debunk positivism as a will-to-power that in its own self-certainty, which eliminates all non-rational claims to knowledge, turns into an iron-clad mythology immune to all apostasy or opposition. Science as a total belief-system is intolerant of all otherness — that which cannot be seen, measured, manipulated, the veritable logic of positivism (fascism's epistemology and discursive strategy). Deviation is literally non-sense.

They apply this idea of a dialectic of enlightenment to show the historical specificity of the fascists' madness. Jews represent the 'Other' that the Nazis had to eliminate in order to mobilize Germans around the Aryan myth of racial superiority and national destiny. Unlike earlier forms of barbarism, however, fascism rested on a mix of the irrational and rational. Fascism was animated by a combination of mythic belief in national 'blood' and an operational efficiency, combining bureaucratic chain-of-command with cost-effective 'production' and disposal techniques in the camps.

Nazis used the Jews as an Other in order to demonstrate both their mythic superiority ('master race') and technological superiority and thus to mobilize the national state. Hitler in his manic, maniac madness struck a balance between mythic and rational elements of German self-understanding, harnessing medieval fears of Jews, gypsies and Slavs to the military mobilization of an entire society. He used Jewish otherness as an object for mass displacement of rage and anxiety in a Germany humiliated at Versailles and still undergoing the difficult transition from feudal to industrial stages of economic development. The Jewish Other did double duty as a mythic figure of anti-Christ and as the symbolic incarnation of the greedy businessperson, both objects of resentment among an increasingly insecure *petite bourgeoisie* and middle class.

The Frankfurt analysis of fascism, although far from homogeneous (Jay, 1973; Kitchen, 1976), suggests that the Germans used the Jewish Other to mobilize a threatened economic stratum and to divert what might otherwise emerge as political and economic revolt against a military-corporate élite. This mobilization of both power and passion could, however, only be achieved in the visible struggle between myth and scientific terrorism. It was insufficient for Germans simply to hate for it was unclear whether the mythic Other would survive its merely 'scientific' denunciation based on Aryan racialism. *Petit bourgeois* rage had to be externalized in both symbolic and organizational forms — yellow Stars of David and extermination camps — lest myth remain just that: an impotent belief-system, having no operational impact. Rage had to become a *text* for it to have meaning. Someone — what turned out to be many millions — had to be seen to suffer.

Critical theory suggests that this mobilization of German society was a crucial episode in the evolution of capitalism, in transition from mythic to rational modes. Their sociology of mobilization stressed that there must be an Other onto whom powerless economic strata could displace their own frustrations and resentment. In this sense critical theory's dialectic of desire, as I call it here, adds a crucial mediating element to Hegel's sketch of the Master-Slave relationship in *The Phenomenology of Mind* (the basis for Marx's subsequent dialectic of capital and labor; Hegel, 1910: p. 174; Marcuse, 1960: pp. 114–20). This mediating element is introduced historically in the development of capitalism in order to allow an already exploited group to vent its anger on an even weaker stratum. Marx paid insufficient attention to the role of an Other in solidifying a Slave-group's false consciousness. For that matter, Marx was as guilty of Enlightenment logocentrism as positivists. The Other is so repugnant to the Slave, and thus allows the Slave to take the Master's side in both thought and action, because the Other embodies the repressed desires of the Slave. The Slave is kept obedient because he or she both envies and resents the relative status of the Other. And Masters tame the Slave's buried desire for liberation by mobilizing him or her in an assault on the despised — and secretly envied — Other. Jews threatened embittered *petit bourgeois* Germans by their cultural and economic otherness, so easily caricatured by Nazi propagandists. Slaves are enlisted in campaigns of extermination and thus participate vicariously in the Master's power (Adorno's authoritarian personality) and, at the same time, avoid the desperate risk of liberation. Slaves regain feudal *Gemeinschaft* by persecuting those on the outside.

As well, Masters need an Other not only to distract their Slaves. The very existence of Others — embodying the non-identical, as Adorno termed it — implies an existence beyond enslavement. The Jews were not only portrayed by the Nazis as anti-Christ, appealing to Lutheran Germans' fear of damnation, but also as Bolsheviks (where, for example, the Protocols of Zion depict Lenin as a Hebrew speaker [Cohn, 1961]). The conjuncture of European Judaism and left-wing politics was of course no accident: outsiders gravitated to an ideology of liberation that promised to turn the world rightside up and give them a legitimate place in it. Judaism in addition possessed a universalistic element that could, if appropriately interpreted and shorn of dogmatic orthodoxy, allow all sorts of Slaves to fall under the umbrella of 'chosen people'.

Thus the Nazis had to obliterate the Jewish Other both to dissipate mass frustrations and to smash the dangerous idol of a utopian otherness, whether explicitly Zionist, Bolshevik or merely social democratic. In Adorno's terms, 'genocide is the absolute integration' (Adorno, 1973: p. 362). Backward German capitalism required unprecedented integration in order to catch up with the United States and England, which explains in part why capitalism in Victorian England (then the 'workshop of the world') could do without an external Other against which rage could be redirected and therefore expended. The Nazis fused myth and enlightenment in their monstrous way precisely because the feudal myths of blood and soil were then of more immediate relevance to their relatively backward historical situation.

From the standpoint of critical theory, then, the Other's function is primarily one of mobilization. Horkheimer and Adorno viewed fascism in a very real sense as the end of history beyond which there could be no positive reversals. This was precisely because 'absolute integration' was not a philosophical notion but forbiddingly human — expressed in the stick-like figures of camp survivors and in the wreck of Europe. Society became a 'universal context of guilt', both for survivors and perpetrators alike. In this regard the Frankfurt thinkers argued that the historical 'accident' of German fascism itself conveniently served as a hated, dreaded Other for the Allies, the conquest of which catapulted western capitalism into its mature stage of Keynesian state management. The peculiar admixture of German backwardness, breeding-ground for Aryan myth, and the quest for industrial mobilization, efficient extermination, enabled western capitalism to attain its immanent form in the totally administered society. It is precisely at this juncture that the millennial utility of the Jewish Other as a victim of Slaves' resentment appeared to become outmoded and ironically — absurdly, to the Frankfurt School's linear, liberal critics — strengthened the hand of total administration.

But even in 1940 Horkheimer recognized that the conquest of fascism by liberal capitalism would not unproblematically elevate enlightened rationality to a privileged position (see Horkheimer, 1973). Indeed fascism was seen to be the last attempt to justify domination on mythic — and hence criticizable — grounds. In advanced capitalism domination would be hinged around the post-mythological acceptance of assigned socio-economic duty, based on alleged laws of economics and social organization which, as I argued in chapter 2, are nothing but scripts of obedience. So according to the Frankfurt School, the conquest of fascism in an ironic sense removed any viable opposition to the total mobilization of society. While Aryanism was a myth that only hideously buttressed the 'rationality' of machine-age extermination, it is in the nature of myth by its very otherness — its non-operational character — to resist the arrogance of imperial science.

As dialectical thinkers the Frankfurt theorists did not choose belief or faith over enlightenment but rather wanted to debunk instrumental reason as an imposter for genuine Reason — insight into truth, freedom, justice. Fascism was the terminus of myth and at once a progenitor of a thoroughly mobilized society in which terror did not for the most part have to be employed to exact obedience (or if it was, it would not be seen as such — banalization of evil [Arendt, 1964]). Jews functioned as Others for the Nazis precisely because Germans had not been sufficiently 'freed' from mythic belief in blood, race, nation, God. The otherness of the Jews could be exploited in the context of post-Versailles Germany as a lever to unite Germans in the self-evident destiny of the Third Reich.

## Continuum: From the Holocaust to Friendly Fascism

According to the Frankfurt theorists the conquest of fascism only strengthened liberal-capitalism, replacing an overt authoritarianism with covert total administration and the mobilization of experience as depicted, for example, in Marcuse's (1964) *One-Dimensional Man*. With the emergence of western capitalism after World War II, otherness was internalized or 'introjected' in the increasing social and self-regulation of libidinal desire. This was regarded as an instance of *Aufhebung* by the Frankfurt School for they contended that mythic bases of domination were not at all eliminated in a reign of general freedom but were given a new, 'disenchanted' foundation in the technical values of pragmatism and scientism. Horkheimer's *Eclipse of Reason*, Adorno's *Negative Dialectics* and Marcuse's *One-Dimensional Man* chart this replacement of 'irrational' authority with a more 'enlightened' kind based on the superiority of scientific methods, now extended beyond the physical universe to the social, which in fast capitalism becomes a text that needs to be written by sociologizing ideologists (see chapter 2). In the nascent corporate stage of capitalism, the state's Keynesian role in stabilizing the economy had to be legitimated by economics, political science and sociology that urged the citizen to retreat from the public sphere of decision-making in return for modest doses of income and commodities consumed in 'leisure' time. In this regard, the function of the Other — in Germany, Jews and other non-Aryans — could ostensibly be dispensed with in a de-mythified stage of civilization in which positivism was not only a metatheory of science but a concrete text of consciousness and social regimentation: accommodation to 'the facts' as the epitome of 'reason'.

(Parenthetically, anti-Semitism in state-socialist societies like the USSR is still rampant, performing much the same function as in earlier fascism. In the USSR, the Other includes Jews, gypsies, non-Russians and especially the pathologically feared Chinese. It could be argued that state-socialist societies are in this sense somewhat less mobilized than their advanced capitalist counterparts, with external projection of rage onto a hated Other still in place. The Soviet equivalent of the Nazi's mix of mythic Aryanism and enlightened concentration-camp productivism is in their conjoined myth of the Party and the 'science' of psychiatric rehabilitation. But the Soviets at a time of *perestroika* are increasingly unable to control their satellite states or even internal dissent in the non-Russian republics.)

What, then, happened to the mobilizing, anxiety-dissipating Other in ascendant post-war capitalism? The dialectic of enlightenment is not halted, extermination actually achieving eternal integration in Adorno's terms, but gains a new world-historical form (Horkheimer and Adorno, 1972: pp. 200–8). The mythic Other of Judaism is now internalized as the external fascism of blood is 'introjected' (without of course ceasing to be externalized against scapegoats). The one-dimensional society, as Marcuse described it in 1964, is held together self-contradictorily by Slaves' (now bureaucratic workers') internal repression of the otherness of libidinal drives as well as by continued persecution of scapegoated minorities, especially unruly women. As Marcuse describes at length in his 1955 *Eros and Civilization*, social control is internalized precisely because the unprecedented economic growth made possible largely by the western defeat of the fascists now threatens to obviate the historical myth of eternal scarcity and induce modern Slaves to rebel against the false 'necessities' of alienated labor (Marcuse, 1955: pp. 71–95).

Thus the Frankfurt thinkers, particularly Marcuse in *Eros and Civilization*, attempted to explain the continuum of domination that allowed corporate capitalism to become a 'friendly' version of German fascism. Indeed the Frankfurt position suggests that capitalism is even more fully integrated in its post-war metamorphosis such that people are thoroughly inured to external terror and rather regard it as routine. The overt persecution of threatening Others — whether Jews, intellectuals, sexual deviants or members of the lumpenproletariat — is now joined by a deepening of covert self-regulation. As Marcuse suggests in his 1955 book on Freud, this surplus repression is self-repression beyond the technological requirements of obedience to assigned productive and reproductive roles, necessary in order to deflect workers from an increasingly obvious industrial surplus (that could liberate them from the realm of scarcity altogether). But he carefully notes that surplus repression does not eliminate the external estrangement of subject and object originally understood by Marx as the exploitation of labor power and the expropriation of surplus value. Nor does he suggest that the absolute integration of fascism has disappeared. Rather, the tyranny of desire has been totalized, where external fascism is reinforced by the internal fascism of surplus repression precisely in the sense that it is banalized and thus can proceed unhindered by moral qualms. As Adorno revised Hegel: 'The whole is the untrue'.

This 'friendly' postmodern fascism takes two forms, the first of which is characterized by the rigors of the so-called Protestant ethic, involving harsh self-denial of erotic energies — Marcuse's 'surplus repression'. Indeed it was this character-type that participated actively in the defeat of the Nazis, ushering in a subsequent post-war era in capitalism in which puritan self-denial could be eased. This is to suggest that there is a parallel of sorts between the external fascism of German anti-Semitism and the internal tyranny of surplus-repressive western puritanism. This is not to forget that racism was prevalent in pre-World War II American capitalism (and of course still is) but rather to suggest that racism in the US was less a phenomenon of total administration than a directly economic tyranny functional to the development of early mercantile capitalism in the United States, where slaves were a source of cheap labor.

The second form of tyrannized desire involves what Marcuse called 'repressive desublimation', release of frustrated erotic energy in narrowly sexual gratifications that by their very nature divert libido from attaining genuine fulfillment in 'erotized' activity. Truly liberated Eros for Marcuse would contain a 'rationality of gratification' — his version of early Marx's praxis — unrestricted to specialized bodily zones or to purely bed-time expression. In this sense, non-alienated labor, always the Marxist desideratum, would be both erotically gratificatory and socially productive, fulfilling what Marcuse in 1955 posited as our 'play-impulse' (Marcuse, 1955: pp. *vii–xi*). Repressive desublimation superficially loosens the shackles of bureaucratic regimentation in order to prevent puritanical abstinence from becoming too confining in an advanced stage of capitalism, in which the technological surplus is only too apparent. If Eros were unleashed to some extent (in a narrowly genital way, for example), bourgeois duty would seem increasingly irrational in an era of potential abundance. So desublimation must be allowed to take place in such a way that people are diverted from their genuine liberation, beyond capitalist scarcity, and at the same time heterosexualized in directly system-serving ways, where sex is bought and sold as a commodity.

This inauthentic desublimation is ambiguous because puritanism — aversion to the 'dirty' body — is never entirely vanquished; rather a repressively desublimated sexuality is to be both 'clean' and 'fun' in an era of moral 'maturity'. American advertisers sell toilet paper both as sexy-soft and as sterile-clean. Puritanism is *aufgehoben* in the interest of deeper administration of the organic body; we are kept busy in pursuit of sexual thrills and thus deflected from a more radical erotization of both our productive and domestic lives. Sexuality loses its taboo as an Other and becomes a 'healthy' expression of self, thus defusing its potential to erupt, properly politicized, in radical challenges to the present order.

This is why the 1960s counterculture, with its polygamous undercurrents, could be so easily coopted in the 1970s and beyond. This is precisely the issue I raise in chapter 10, where I discuss the cultural politics of postmodernism. 'Serial monogamy' is an example of repressive desublimation where we are allowed to loosen the strict bonds of life-long fidelity in the interest of sexual varietism — seen to be necessary for personal 'growth' — without undercutting the straight monogamous dyad resting essentially on patriarchal authority (although that too has undergone evolution towards 'liberated' equality-between-the-sexes, especially in the realization that women have both sexual and occupational 'rights', too; Shorter, 1975). In chapter 5, I discussed ways in which the discourse of feminism has been disciplined by mainstream sociology.

In this way, a polymorphous sexuality is kept at bay, harmlessly narrowed and discharged in leisure and consumer pursuits. Puritanism and its frustrated fascist irruptions were too archaic even in the beginning to survive for long as a useful technique of system-serving socialization. The notion of lifetime fidelity, coupled with 'irrational' notions about the dirty body, are offensive to the enlightened late twentieth-century rationalist. But contemporary desublimation, while ostensibly less repressive, is itself inauthentic precisely because it cannot be a legitimate substitute for our daily stint of alienated labor. Now as before, capitalism bears within it internal contradictions that threaten to erupt at any time. Today economic crises, in Marx's original sense of rampant unemployment and corporate stagnation, have been supplemented with what Habermas calls crises of motivation, where people are increasingly reluctant to accept soft-but-sterile toilet paper or sexual cheap thrills as adequate compensation for ceding their autonomy to élites, notably in the realm of work.

These desublimated needs are false because they do not adequately serve as balm for deeper wounds of self-abnegation and self-regimentation in an era when we could be freed from a regime of bureaucratized toil. Desire is tyrannized in late capitalism not only in the old sense of imprisonment, torture or harsh moral codes but now also in the sense that our public and private lives hold few lasting satisfactions, divested of all spontaneity and autonomy. Desublimation is engineered in order to keep us (especially women) from discovering the dirty sexuality that, once unleashed, would become what Horkheimer called a 'revolt of nature' against its enslavement (Horkheimer, 1974b: pp. 92–127).

So I am suggesting that the evolution from rigid sexual strictures of the nineteenth century and its more mythic Nazi-era perversions to the free-and-easy sexuality of pre-AIDS late capitalism was made possible by overall economic advancement which, in turn, required the body to be 'commodified'. Repressive desublimation releases some of the frustrations of people kept too long in the 'iron cage' of an early ascetic capitalism and intensifies our libidinal attachment to desired body-objects and commodities (O'Neill, 1972c: pp. 68–80). In this sense, the tyranny of desire — because it is fundamentally dialectical — sometimes involves the seeming desublimation of desire, producing Marcuse's robotized 'happy consciousness' of one-dimensional society. But the manipulation of deep subjectivity, even sometimes its apparent release in the heterosexualization of everyday life in late capitalism, is no less fascist, and even more effective, than the mythic fascism of the Nazi camps.

But the administered society is always dialectically balanced between capital and labor — or in my terms here between destructive and erotic energy. Yet as Horkheimer (1972b) suggested in his classic 1937 essay on 'Traditional and Critical Theory', the link between base and superstructure — in my case here, the economic-organizational interest in social control and the internalized tyranny of desire — is stronger in late capitalism and not weaker, despite some superficial appearances to the contrary. The Frankfurt argument has always been that the realm of the personal has become a crucial factor in economic and cultural reproduction ('objectivity of subjectivity'), and that it is precisely the appearance of the relative autonomy of subjectivity that allows its administration to be so successfully disguised and thus carried out.

The superficial liberal sexualization of everyday life in late capitalism does not therefore liberate basic desire but only adapts desire to system-serving functions. In this sense, repressive desublimation is itself a phase in capitalism's evolution, following fascism and surplus-repressive puritanism sequentially. In fact repressive desublimation may itself outlive its utility in the depressed capitalism of the 1990s. I suggest that the internalization of fascist social control is becoming externalized once again under pressure from new economic and socio-political crises of the sort discussed in the preceding chapter. As such — as the Frankfurt thinkers argued with prescience in the 1930s — domination would remain a continuum.

In fact, economic contraction increases class, race and gender exploitation as evidenced in the renewal of dominant-group rage against racial, ethnic and sexual minorities now including AIDS victims. Anti-Semitism is again on the rise, especially apparent in efforts, touched on below, to minimize the absolute horror of the Holocaust. It is not clear that the seamless introjection of domination in one-dimensional society will be increasingly projected onto the same Others used to mobilize Nazi Germany in the 1930s and 1940s. In this way, as rage against an irrational economic system increases, the routinization of terror will issue in the increasing dehumanization of everyday life as the system effectively reroutes that rage onto living symbols of deviant otherness. It is highly possible that advanced capitalist societies will return to the military mobilization of the Nazi period both to keep deviants in line and to divert aggressive energy into system-serving destructive and self-destructive acts. The growing efforts of Americans to arm themselves is only one of a myriad of illustrative examples of this.

## Anamnestic Solidarity: Remembrance as a Radical Response

This analysis of the merging of external and internal components of the tyranny of desire depicts a mobilized social order in which all experience is subordinated to the requirements of the preponderant objectivity of capitalist profit and social control. Extermination and terror do not disappear but rather are routinized: we become inured to televised horror stories of domestic and international bloodshed. One can speculate that the first discovery of the camps by the Allies provoked a kind of primordial shock (Brecht's estrangement-effect; see Marcuse, 1978: pp. 41–3) for which we were totally unprepared. Today, as tyrannized desire has been increasingly introjected by one-dimensional consciousness, we can even forget that we live under the shadow of the nuclear bomb, not to mention the daily atrocities of world capitalism and state-socialism. Even our vocabulary attests to the routinization of the horrible: extermination is sociologized into the more abstract and less revolting technical term 'genocide'.

The Frankfurt analysis of fascism, thus, refuses neither to relativize the Holocaust (as it is fashionable to do today in certain left circles, where it is offered as merely another instance of genocide), nor to absolutize it as the epicenter of decadent civilization. This deft balancing act resembles postmodernism at its best, as in the case of Foucault; history is viewed differentially, skeptically, optimistically all at once. For Adorno and Horkheimer, the Holocaust made incarnate the logic of enlightened civilization in the starkest possible terms, preparing us, as they tried to do in the 1930s and 1940s, for what was to come. It is not a question of whether we have made 'progress' or not but rather how the crude logic of the Nazis has been streamlined into a world-historical logic of absolute control in advanced capitalism that, according to Horkheimer and Adorno, began with the Enlightenment.

Marcuse's (1955) subsequent analysis of surplus repression added detail to Horkheimer and Adorno's earlier concept of the dialectic of enlightenment, which he reformulated in explicitly psychoanalytic terms. In this sense, he remained more dialectical than they, holding out hope, based on Freud, that the constructive energy within desire was ineradicable and could negate the destructiveness of Thanatos. Adorno and Horkheimer read Freud as a prescient prophet ('In psychoanalysis, only the exaggerations are true') where Freud despaired of the fate of civilization in his late works. The question of whether the erotic qualities in desire can be protected from desire's destructive-aggressive tendencies is resolved quite differently by Adorno and Marcuse, which explains why in the same historical period Adorno could write the resignatory *Negative Dialectics* — where he pronounces hope dead, gone up in the smoke of Nazi crematoria (Adorno, 1973a: pp. 361–5) — and Marcuse (1969) could fasten onto the New Left and its new subjectivity as a positive upsurge of ineradicable desire in his *An Essay on Liberation*. I suggest that this difference between resignation and hope hinges on different readings of psychoanalysis: Adorno took Freud more literally where Freud posited an eternal opposition between Eros and Thanatos — life and death instincts — while Marcuse suggested that the death instinct could be dialectically reformulated as the impulse to avoid not life but the pain of domination (Marcuse, 1955: pp. 214–15). Marcuse views the indestructibility of desire as the basis for eternal hope (see Agger, 1982). As long as our carnal subjectivity exists, even if only just this side of extermination, the social forces of total administration never quite succeed in robotizing us. There is, I suggest, a libidinal rebel in all of us that preserves both the dream and memory of liberation: an instinct to imagine, struggle and remember.

What, then, can be learned from this interpretation of the Holocaust as a moment in the evolutionary march of tyrannized desire? If one accepts that there is a dialectic of desire then one can — short of revolutionary hallucination — suggest a minimalist emancipatory program based on what I earlier called anamnestic solidarity. By vulgar-Marxist criteria, of course, there could be nothing more absurd than a notion of solidarity with the dead except perhaps in the form of socialist-realist monuments to heroes of the revolution. But I am suggesting that the Holocaust (along with other historical instances of the ultimate extermination of human beings) gives us material with which to bind ourselves to the dead through memory and thereby to restore our own emancipatory desire in a postmodern age where there is very little in the way of 'positive' revolutionary movements or examples. Solidarity in memory is a radical moment for it suggests to us, at least in the Nazi instance, that extermination failed to achieve absolute integration and that people survived who could recall the horror of it. Anamnesis of this sort energizes our rebellion in an age when we are habituated not only to forget the 'distant' past but to ignore even the flickering television images of daily brutality, even to cathect them as sado-masochistically thrilling. The analysis of one-dimensionality suggests, quite correctly I submit, that loss of memory is the most immediate threat to our rebellious interiority (*Innerlichkeit* — an early Frankfurt concept), without which we cannot even begin to think meaningfully about more direct political strategies (O'Neill, 1976).

The restoration of memory as a vital component of a dialectical imagination depends in the last analysis on a concept of libidinal desire that makes room for the possibility of the erotization of destructive energy, producing a rebellious instinct that holds out against the absolute integration of subject and object or, in terms of one-dimensional society, of consciousness and the totalized appearances and discourse of reality. This is to suggest that the death instinct, which accounts for the horrible betrayals of humanity that now seem to be 'second nature' — avoidable in mind because they have been banalized into an ever-the-same universal of everyday life — contains not only a rebellious impulse but an impulse to remember those who died in anonymity, uselessly. This is to read Marcuse against Adorno, who viewed the Holocaust as a complete metaphor for the subsequent totally administered order of post-war capitalism. The Holocaust is a profound metaphor for it shows us domination at its most totalizing, to be succeeded by later holocausts as well as by a radicalizing anamnesis on the part of those of us who still live, haunted by dreadful memories but, by the same token, not fully dehumanized.

That memory still exists indicates that the Holocaust is an ultimately incomplete metaphor for later capitalism. Memory's centrality to the dialectical project imposes on us the requirement that we must never forget, thereby dialectically giving us the power to remember and thus to resist the total manipulation of our desire, which mobilizes social amnesia as a tool for further blurring the distinction between what is and what might be (Jacoby, 1975). This is only a meager gain, to be sure, but at least it offers a third way between those who relativize the Holocaust as mere genocide (or as less, engaging, as some do today, in the offensive debate over death counts as a way of minimizing the 'final solution') and those for whom history stopped with Auschwitz. A notion of radical anamnesis at least sharpens consciousness in an epoch when consciousness above all is at stake.

Freudo-Marxism: Remembrance, like liberation, is a biological need. I am convinced that the essentialist excesses of mainstream psychoanalysis can be avoided in this Freudian-postmodern-feminist version of critical theory that I have tried to elaborate in this book. The notion of solidarity with the dead is a thoroughly postmodern notion inasmuch as it refuses the linear progressivism of modernism, for which the dead are just dust in the wind, not a dialectical resource for the radical imagination.

> This ability to forget — itself the result of a long and terrible education by experience — is an indispensable requirement of mental and physical hygiene without which civilized life would be unbearable; but it is also the mental faculty which sustains submissiveness and renunciation. To forget is also to forgive what should not be forgiven if justice and freedom are to prevail...Without release of the repressed content of memory, without release of its liberating power, non-repressive sublimation is unimaginable (Marcuse, 1955: pp. 212–13).

In the next chapter, I turn more fully toward a positive postmodern agenda of the establishment of a democratic public life through dialogue. Where in this chapter I discussed ways in which desire indomitably resists its total administration, even where resistance takes only anamnestic form, in the following chapter I encode polity-building practice directly in an ethic of public dialogue. Building on and extending Habermas, I develop a critical theory of dialogue that directly underpins my critical theory of public life. This chapter can be read as a Freudian-Marxist underpinning of Habermas' otherwise disembodied agenda of discursive will- and consensus-formation, discussed in the following chapter. The dialectic of desire grounds liberation in an embodied subjectivity, including the critical functions of memory. Too often, discussions of dialogue and discourse disembody consensus, whether in Mill or Habermas.

# Chapter 8

# The Dialectic of Dialogue

In the last chapter, I discussed ways in which solidarity with the dead through memory helps restore public life. Here, I turn more positively toward a vision and version of public life as achieved through dialogue, which is the centerpiece of any postmodern critical theory that values discourse and democracy but rejects their naïve Enlightenment formulation. I argued in the last chapter that people can seek dialogue with the dead as well as with their own buried desires as a way of keeping alive both the betrayal and promise of liberation. Here, I pursue the promise of dialogue as the basis of a political theory of radical democracy that I believe is essential for a feminist postmodern critical theory. In significant respects, my perspective on dialogue moves critical theory beyond Habermas' reconstruction of historical materialism as communication theory while preserving his vital stress on discursive democracy as the essence of a humane public life. Although I take issue with Habermas through my discussion of the counterpoint between Ackerman's radical liberalism and Habermas' own version of critical theory, my discussion of the social problems of public life is hugely indebted to Habermas' efforts to move critical theory beyond its foundation in the 1930s and into a more technologically advanced form of capitalism.

Habermas raises most of the right questions for a critical theory of public life, even though some of his answers are insufficient, provoking my feminist postmodern critical theory as a sympathetic response and rearticulation. In particular, Habermas does not sufficiently explicate his notion of consensus underlying the ideal speech situation (as Fraser, 1989, argues). It is possible to read his notion of consensus, to be achieved through democratic conversation, as somewhat logocentric in Derrida's terms, privileging talk over writing, a move that Derrida argues is the centerpiece of positivism (or the 'metaphysic of presence'). In other respects, too, as I develop in this chapter, Habermas does not push the emancipatory agenda of critical theory far enough, failing to appreciate the textual and technological possibilities of liberation opened up by his own communicative turn in critical theory. I take Habermas very seriously because he has offered the most ambitious transformation and extension of 1930s first-generation critical theory. I attempt to extend Habermas by challenging his communication-theoretic version of critical theory with insights from poststructuralism, postmodernism and feminist theory, much as Fraser (1989) has tried to do.

In this chapter I draw upon recent developments in political and social theory in order to address phenomena associated with the collapse of the public sphere in technocratic capitalism and, as well, both outline and organize possible social change in the future. In particular, I search for a cogent understanding of public political speech in Bruce Ackerman's (1980) reconstruction of liberalism, Jürgen Habermas' (1970b, 1971, 1973, 1975, 1984, 1987b) communication theory of society and in the tradition of western Marxism. Appropriately bonded through feminism and postmodernism, these theoretical traditions suggest that dialogue should be regarded as a source of the critique of the existing order, a trigger for fundamental challenges to that order and, finally, a model of all of our possible nondominating relationships with nature, symbol-systems, social roles, and other people in all of our productive and reproductive activities. This is to view communicative competence not simply as the capacity for interpersonal speech but also as a capacity for all sorts of productive and organizational activities, including reading and writing. Ultimately, I shall suggest that political dialogue between two enlightened interlocutors can be a model of our involvements with others, texts and nature according to which our self-externalizing activity both fulfills our own expressive needs and respects the rights and needs of 'the Other', be it human or nonhuman. In this way, dialogue is conceptualized both as a means of discrediting and overcoming exploitative institutional arrangements and as an imaginative model of free human activity.

## Critical Theory's Changing Metaphors

Marx's original critique of ideology was directed at what he regarded as the illegitimate self-reflection of a market economic system, presented by Smith and Ricardo in terms of allegedly harmonious laws of supply and demand that benefit worker and capitalist alike. He felt that this was mystifying because the capitalist social system does not in fact reward buyer and seller equally but tends to enslave those who sell their labor power in return for a wage. In Marx's era, thus, capitalist ideology was political-economic in a direct sense, suggesting to workers that they could seek modest rewards for obedience to these laws of supply and demand in the bartering of their individual labor-power. Early capitalist ideology, functioning effectively to keep workers harnessed to their prescribed roles in the creation of private profit, was grounded in this notion that there is a 'fair exchange' between workers and capitalists.

In later technocratic capitalism, however, with the further evolution and expansion of the state's role in economics and culture, a growing rigidity in the division of labor and increasing technological planning generally, the discourse of ideology has changed, as numerous neo-Marxist theorists of the capitalist state have discussed (Schroyer, 1973; Miliband, 1969; Mandel, 1975). Market laws regulating exchange have been largely replaced by sociological laws of a complex division of labor, to be efficiently coordinated by technical experts in business and government. The individual is no longer promised rewards for obedience and industriousness through the main chance of entrepreneurial success, conjured up in the imagery of the frontier (e.g., 'get rich quick', 'the self-made man'). Instead the person is to legitimate the social order by relinquishing an active participatory role in the marketplace and politics in exchange for greater material comfort and occupational security.

Where early market ideology involved discursive claims about the alleged rationality and moral inviolability of contracts ('fair exchange'), ideology in the technocratic stage of capitalism is propped by the sociologically ratified notion of the inevitability of *socially structured silence* about political and economic decision-making in a 'complex' society. This version of social fate is scripted by the textwriters of discipline, including positivist social scientists, as I discussed in chapters 2 and 5. This later version of ideology promotes an absence of dialogue between experts and citizens about what are portrayed as arcane matters of esoteric science and high technology. The scientization of ideology thus goes hand in hand with this structured silence among citizens; as I shall discuss below, certain contemporary neo-Marxists like Habermas characterize the social outcome of this silence as the collapse of the public sphere, describing the institutional consequences of people's retreat from participation in the economy and polity, formerly oriented to the personal accumulation of wealth and power in an earlier stage of capitalism. According to them, this does not alter the deep structure of capitalism in the sense that it erases class conflict but on the contrary allows a state-managed capitalism to survive in a technologically sophisticated corporate era. Indeed, the very evolution of capitalism necessitates this shift from the imagery of busy entrepreneurialism to structured silence about what are regarded as issues beyond the ken and competence of citizens.

A critical theory of dialogue extrapolates from and thus in a sense revises Marx's critique of political economy without losing sight of his basic structural understanding of capitalism, which remains central in this book. Critical theory focuses on ways in which discourses of politics, economics and social organization become vehicles of domination in an advanced stage of capitalism, promoted by and promoting what Marx originally called 'false consciousness'. In the technocratic stage of capitalism economic and political élites require social distance between themselves and the masses in order to function unencumbered as steerers of a complex social system. Ideology in contemporary capitalism must induce silence about these matters lest citizens begin to question the whole ethos of technocratic management. Their passivity is induced by suggesting the existence of symbol systems and technical understandings 'inherently' too complicated for democratization. Thus the monopoly of capital goes hand in hand with the monopoly of both information and dialogue chances. From early childhood we are taught in numerous explicit and subtle ways to accept the fact that we inhabit a complex society requiring a hierarchical division of labor and narrow occupational specialization. Accordingly, we are taught to refrain from dialogic, and thus political and economic, intervention in realms that are defined as beyond the boundaries of our competence to play assigned or inherited social roles.

The guardians of science and technology become ideologists in this stage of capitalism on the basis of their monopoly of symbolic and discursive power. We legitimate élites precisely because we believe that their status is based on technical understandings inaccessible to us and on their ability to write specialist prose. Accordingly, we refrain from dialogue and discourse because we believe that we would otherwise jeopardize our opportunities for a limited degree of mobility promised by ideology in technocratic capitalism. In effect, we silence ourselves by neutering our political imagination and retreating from the public sphere because we believe (falsely, according to Marxists like Habermas and me) that self-directing action is impossible in a complex world of institutional giants. And in many obvious ways we find it easier to accept narrowly circumscribed role playing along with the public silence this implies than it would be to challenge the conventional technocratic wisdom by refusing to cede all decision-making power to 'higher' authorities. Most people, after all, are willing to trade work-a-day alienation for modest levels of creature comforts in postmodern leisure time so long as we can depend on the system-steering competence of élites who make these comforts possible by keeping capitalism off the shoals of economic crises. This is precisely the image of 'postmodernity' that I interrogate in my concluding chapter.

A critical theory of dialogue, thus, addresses the ideology of technocratic guidance that sanctions nondialogic relations between élites and masses on the basis of the alleged inherent complexity of technical languages and system-steering roles, much as Marx addressed the ideology of a market system through his original critique of bourgeois political economy which made particular economic arrangements into a fact of nature and self-evident morality. Critical theory attempts this task of demystification by positing our innate capacities for world-making activity, including writing and reading social texts, thus freeing us (and we ourselves) from bondage to what is scripted ideologically as our social fate. I want to trace the roots of this theory in the liberalism of Ackerman, the communication theory of Habermas and the work of other neo-Marxists, critical theorists, postmodernists and feminists. Ackerman starts us on our way by sketching a delegitimating role for political speech; Habermas takes us further by offering, through his innovations in communication theory, a basis for an ideology-critique of technocratic capitalism. But neither thinker allows us sufficiently to broaden this delegitimation and ideology-critique into actual transformative activity that, I shall argue, rests on a deepening of the very concept of 'dialogue' to include not only interpersonal communication and writing but also our productive involvements with nature. In this sense, my critical theory of dialogue has three interrelated components: a conversational and textual basis for delegitimating a given social order, through which the powerless engage the powerful in initial justificatory dialogues; a critique of the dominant ideology of technocratically induced silence that uses the public experience of delegitimation as a spur to further, more ideologically sophisticated, political speech; and a sketch of concrete social and political action suggested by insights into our inalienable capacity for competent involvement in person–nature, person–symbol and person–person dialogues. Such a theory, based on a deepened concept of communicative competence involving instrumental, cognitive, textual and organizational dimensions, may help us better understand the historical metamorphosis of capitalism as well as achieve fuller awareness about the character of domination in its recent technocratic form.

## Ackerman's Immanent Critique of Liberalism

In spite of its avowed liberalism, Bruce Ackerman's 1980 book, *Social Justice in the Liberal State*, may in certain respects belong as much to the emergent tradition of neo-Marxism as to liberal political philosophy, a notion he hints at in an early footnote reference to parallels between his own work and that of Habermas (Ackerman, 1980: p. 10). Indeed I read Ackerman's theory of justice as a more fruitful contribution to a Marxian-inclined critical theory of dialogue than to a liberal tradition that (it may be unfair to say) is quite dead. Ackerman would reject this assessment of liberalism, although his sustained critique of earlier utilitarianism and social contractarian thinking only serves to vitiate his own contention in this regard. The peculiar thing about Ackerman's argument for liberalism is that it continually runs up against the thoroughly illiberal principles and practices of every known mode of capitalist social organization, including our own technocratic variety. This does not come as a complete surprise to Ackerman, especially where in Part Three of his book he moves 'from ideal to reality', an aspect of his self-understanding as a liberal that I shall take up shortly.

Ackerman wants to ground an authentic liberal political philosophy in new terms. He regards Bentham's utilitarianism as well as Hobbesian and Lockean social contract theory as specious because, in somewhat different ways, they all presuppose an external, mythic standard for entering into a social compact, the utilitarian a standard for deciding the 'greatest good for the greatest number' and the contractarian a pre-historic ground unadulterated by worldly interest from which mythic men and women are said to have entered into a social contract. Most of the book, in fact, is taken up with delightful mock dialogues between various speakers that are designed to reveal the inherent problems of both of these philosophical approaches. Ackerman is instead in search of a real-world ground for a liberalism that dispenses with fictions such as 'greatest good for the greatest number', 'state of nature' or Rawls' 'veil of ignorance', the most recent statement of social contract theory. Ackerman seeks a principle of liberal justice that can allow committed liberals to assail illegitimate power structures. He terms this the principle of 'Neutral dialogue', his core idea, offered in the beginning and then unraveled through the course of his book.

A power structure is illegitimate if it can be justified only through a conversation in which some person (or group) must assert that he or she is (or they are) the privileged moral authority: Neutrality. No reason is a good reason if it requires the power holder to assert (a) that his or her conception of the good is better than that asserted by any of his or her fellow citizens, or (b) that, regardless of his or her conception of the good, he or she is intrinsically superior to fellow citizens. Ackerman uses this principle of 'Neutral dialogue' as a ground of a liberal political theory that provides citizens with the means of delegitimating corrupt power structures. 'Unconstrained power talk' is the type of dialogic relationship he proposes between individuals, and presumably between individuals and institutions, who seek to establish the legitimacy of a political relationship. Through fascinating mock dialogues Ackerman probes the strength and range of this dialogic principle of justice. Predictably, he finds it a very powerful tool for ensuring and maintaining the legitimacy of truly liberal states. But here he is forced to confront the distinction between regimes that are liberal only in name (such as our own) and regimes that are genuinely based on the principle of Neutral dialogue. Thus he introduces a tripartite distinction among three types of theory, relevant to three types of actual and possible regimes. 'Ideal' theory hypothetically presupposes a 'new world' to be colonized by ideal citizens who possess what Ackerman calls a 'perfect technology of justice' (Ackerman, 1980: p. 21) capable of readily implementing the substantive conclusions of Neutral dialogue.

He quickly notes that the assumption of a perfect technology of justice in ideal theory does not deny the existence of material scarcity. Indeed the central problem for liberal theory, as Ackerman conceives of it (and, in fact, of all political theory including that of Marx), is to justify certain distributions of scarce resources in a way that does not violate his guiding principle of Neutral dialogue. It is only as a means of unraveling the consequences of the assumptions behind conversational neutrality (namely that conceptions of the good are equally valid and that people are intrinsically equal to each other in a moral sense) that he postulates a perfect technology of justice unconstrained by the ambiguities inherent in the concept of economic trade-off. As Ackerman is well aware, his exercise in creating an ideal theory of liberal dialogue quickly runs up against the harsh reality of the absence of perfect technologies of justice which could ensure what he calls 'undominated equality' for all. 'Second-best' theory, thus, is charged by him with determining ways of ensuring maximum social justice in possible future societies in which there are all sorts of trade-offs between the abstract goal of undominated equality and the practical necessity of fostering a technology that is to improve the quality of life for all. It is because we do not live in an ideal world in Ackerman's sense that we, as presumably committed liberals, must figure out *how* to ensure the aims of Neutral dialogue (Ackerman, 1980: p. 23).

But in Part Three of his book, 'From Ideal to Reality', and, revealingly, in chapter 8, entitled 'Exploitation', Ackerman moves closer to a critical perspective on the possibilities and constraints of dialogue that in many ways is similar to the Derridean critique of logocentrism. He recognizes that not all 'liberal statesmen' (in name only) will relinquish illegitimate power to dialogic partners — the humble petitioners and angry rebels of the exploited. Thus 'third-best' theory must deal with the question of real-world exploitation, monopolies of power and wealth that do not admit of dialogic justification on grounds of conversational Neutrality (Ackerman, 1980: pp. 232–3).

What is to be done if power holders refuse to join justificatory dialogues and by their actions (and inaction) imply that they are morally superior to others beneath them, and have a superior conception of the good? This is a central problem of all political theory written under the cloud of structured social inequality. Ackerman has done an important job, I believe, in taking traditional liberalism out of the ethereal realm of utilitarianism and social contract theory and placing it instead on the terra firma of real-world social interaction. This supports a critical theory of dialogue precisely where it offers a standard with which to assess the legitimacy of power structures, namely adherence to principles of Neutral dialogue in pursuit of undominated equality among people. This is an innovation in democratic theory because it suggests a delegitimating criterion — failure to engage in dialogue with interlocutors or, once engaged, to offer an adequate justification of one's advantages — that is vital for a critical theory of society today, as I outlined it in the preceding section and shall elaborate below.

In this sense, I read Ackerman as much less a liberal than he thinks he is or, perhaps better said, a truer liberal than most and for that reason an authentic democratic Marxist (in his ethics, if not his strategic theory of liberation, of which he has none). His concept of Neutral dialogue as an archetype of all substantively free social relationships is remarkably similar to Habermas' own notion of the 'ideal speech situation', discussed in the next section, which I regard as among the most important contemporary extrapolations of the original Marxist critique of domination even if it lacks a certain poststructural circumspection about the opacity and undecidability of language. If Habermas is a Marxist (and in the important sense of the term connoting allegiance to the dialectical analysis of the evolving contradictions of capitalism I certainly think he is), then Ackerman, too, shares many of his Marxist insights, notably about the stultifying character of structured public silence in illegitimate social orders. Most of Ackerman's swipes at the 'Marxist' tradition, as he construes it, are clearly aimed at Lenin's 'democratic centralism', a euphemism for iron-fisted Communist Party authority, and not at the dialectical-democratic core of Marx's thought that I am drawing upon here (Ackerman, 1980: p. 263).

My contention is that Ackerman's liberalism, based on a concept of legitimate and illegitimate political dialogue, is virtually identical to the possible ethical core of a democratic Marxism. His characterization of the relationship between individual and community is so reminiscent of 1844 Marx (Marx, 1961), of subsequent existential-Marxists like Maurice Merleau-Ponty (1964a, 1964b), and of those Eastern European Marxists who dwell on the component of 'praxis' and democratic community in early Marx like Adam Schaff (1970), Gajo Petrovic (1967), Mihailo Marković (1974) and Svetozar Stojanović (1973) that one is surprised that Ackerman does not note the parallel. I think he is unaware of it, just as most Marxists are unaware of the power of liberalism in providing a sane conception of some sort of contractual or consensual basis for a future humane socialism — a Marxist 'new social contract', or, indeed, new dialogic contract:

> No longer does liberal thought revolve around the dichotomy
> that opposes individual to community; instead, the substance
> of individual rights is constructed through a social dialogue;
> the triumph of individualism, a social triumph (Ackerman,
> 1980: p. 347).

I regard Ackerman, in spite of his avowed liberalism, as belonging very much to the vanguard of this ethical tradition, which one might characterize as Humean-Marxist, mixing skepticism about overarching rationality with the idealistic passion that wants to bring reason into the world. Unlike most liberal theorists of justice, he imbeds ethical principles in the very structure of grounded behavior — Neutral dialogue, as he calls it — and does not relegate it to a set of principled abstractions. In terms of a critical theory of dialogue, this has the powerful consequence of providing an interpersonal litmus test with which we can evaluate all present and future action on dialogic grounds and thus ensure that our verve for a new social rationality does not get the better of our fragile bond to the community and thus lead us up the garden path (timeworn, to say the least) of intellectual and political arrogance. Ackerman derives living principles of what I regard as socialist justice from the very structure of speech itself (much as Habermas does in his development, described below, of a 'universal pragmatics' of communicative action [Habermas, 1979]). Ackerman offers us a tool with which to guarantee that public speech in an ideal socialist state does not itself degenerate into silence under pressure from those who have appointed themselves the guardians of public truth. In spite of the seeming logocentric biases of this position, which appears to privilege speech over writing (hence inviting political tyranny, according to Derrida), I would argue that the ideal-speech situation could as well be formulated as an ideal-text situation. In other words, many of the dialogic implications of my perspective on public speech apply equally to writing and reading, which I view essentially as public performances. Unfortunately, Habermas has not developed the possible rapprochement of his critical communication theory and poststructuralism/postmodernism because he rejects what he takes to be the neo-conservative implications of postmodernism (see Habermas, 1987a).

> These, then, are four of the main highways to the liberal state: realism about the corrosiveness of power; recognition of doubt as a necessary step to moral knowledge: respect for the autonomy of persons; and skepticism concerning the reality of transcendent meaning (Ackerman, 1980: p. 369).

These four notions all derive from the central principle of Neutral dialogue, that none of us conceives of himself or herself as morally superior to any other or believes that he or she, unlike they, enjoys privileged access to knowledge of the good. The very act of speaking and listening presupposes some commitment to these notions. It allows us to derive a practical ethics and code of justice, not from abstract desiderata that necessarily clash with a harshly constraining reality in which loving one's neighbor and obedience to the Golden Rule are prerogatives only of the well-off and secure, but from what we actually do: we speak and write to each other in hope of sharing our common humanity, however buried or distorted, and of buffering our mortal aloneness. The concept of dialogue is such a powerful idea for socialists and feminists because, appropriately reinterpreted in critical terms, it suggests an ethics based on the mutual respect of all 'speakers' who enjoy roughly equal dialogue-chances. It offers us the hope, if not further assurances, that a humane socialist-feminism is practicable as long as we commit ourselves, first, to talk to each other about our differences and to keep talking no matter how much we may differ and, second, to ensure an egalitarian distribution of dialogue-chances. It is abundantly clear that a dialogic ethics without a properly materialist foundation in a society of real equality will prove as irrelevant as a 'socialism' that submerges ethics in the abstractions of economic theory.

However, in spite of his convergence with democratic Marxism in this ethical sense, Ackerman's liberalism fails as ideology-critique because he has no structural understanding of the historical roots of exploitation in a particular economic system that uses a political superstructure, including liberal political philosophy, simply as a prop. He cannot go beyond delegitimation, once accomplished (and read in the surrounding silence of failed dialogue-attempts) toward social change. He cannot answer the implicit question 'what happens (and what ought to happen) when dialogue breaks off?' In spite of his innovative and important immanent critique of the *laissez-faire* individualism of earlier contractarian liberalism and his attempt to reground liberal ideals in a dialogic, communitarian philosophical anthropology almost identical to that of 1844 Marx, Ackerman ends up in the traditional impasse of liberalism: political democracy is contradicted by economic and ideological domination.

This is the concern of third-best theory, to which a critical theory of dialogue definitely belongs. With Marx and subsequent neo-Marxist theorists of domination, discussed in the next two sections of this chapter, I contend that in a capitalist society dialogues between powerful and powerless either do not take place (for example, the depoliticization of politics [Arendt, 1958; O'Neill, 1972b], end of ideology [Bell, 1960], rise of mass society, collapse of the public sphere) or else are illusory, only contributing to the strengthening of a fraudulent liberal ideology. Ackerman fails to develop a theory of ideology that would allow him to understand the politically mobilizing functions of (failed) dialogue-attempts. He has no sociology of social movements that would allow him to broaden the one-to-one structure of his modal dialogues. He lacks a theory of real (third-best) social structure and a theory of social change suited to it. Marxists believe that structured exploitation will lead either to silence among contesting interlocutors or the reinforcement of cosmetic ideological props of a 'civic culture' (Almond and Verba, 1966). Ackerman's constrained power talk will almost immediately be halted in silence, and his important philosophical effort obscured, unless he is to develop a counterpart critique of ideology that makes the recognition of dialogic possibilities the spark of social change and not merely a justificatory litmus test in a society that, as Ackerman himself recognizes, justifies itself not through dialogue but only through ideologically fostered images of the inexorable domination of masses by élites. If we twist Ackerman's liberal theory of dialogue into a Marxist mode it will be possible to make the concept of dialogue much more powerful both as a prod to counterideological consciousness and as the actual organizing principle of a new social order. Enter Habermas.

## Communicative Competence, the Critique of Ideology and Social Change: Habermas and the Neo-Marxist Tradition

I have argued so far that Ackerman's theory of dialogue cannot suffice as a critical theory because it does not mobilize the consciousness of the exploited to challenge the present system and to work toward a new one. Ackerman does not consider failed dialogues, which predominate in technocratic capitalism. While he does suggest that certain dialogues either broken off in silence or ended with illiberal assertions of superior moral privilege can delegitimate certain states, he does not inquire about what the failure of such dialogues would mean either ideologically or in terms of possible social change. It is clear that Ackerman views technocratic capitalism as more or less intractable and thus his important philosophical exercise has very little direct political relevance save to demonstrate that most societies are illegitimate on dialogic grounds. A critical theory, however, must move beyond the recognition of illegitimacy toward the renewal of dialogues that spark radical social change. I believe that Ackerman, unlike other liberal thinkers, brings us to the edge of this social change by focusing on the delegitimating potential of dialogue. He cannot move further, given his background assumption about the inexorability of technocratic capitalism and, even more fatally, his inability to break completely with liberal individualism which assumes that people today can actually make themselves heard in dialogic encounters with dominant institutions. He does not invest dialogue with sufficient political and critical content, and thus he can neither take concrete steps beyond the principled recognition of corrupt systems nor move beyond the logocentrism of his position toward a more Derridean appreciation of textual politics or a more feminist appreciation of the permeable boundary between public/productive and private/reproductive spheres (see Fraser, 1989).

Beyond Ackerman, however, I believe there are all sorts of dialectical possibilities for new dialogues not rooted in distorted and dominating communication. In the work of Jürgen Habermas, the original Frankfurt School theorists (Marcuse, 1955, 1964, 1969; Horkheimer and Adorno, 1972; Adorno, 1973, 1974a; Horkheimer, 1972a) and other neo-Marxists, notably Antonio Gramsci (1971), Jean-Paul Sartre (1963, 1965a, 1965b, 1976), Maurice Merleau-Ponty (1964a, 1964b, 1972, 1973) and Marxian-humanist thinkers from Eastern Europe (Kolakowski, 1968, 1969, 1978; Kosik, 1976), I think we have the missing resources for a more complete critical theory of dialogue which would deepen some of Ackerman's concerns and turn them full face in the direction of democratic Marxism. I want to take up where I believe Ackerman leaves off with the delegitimation of corrupt states, ending in conversational silence. I suggest two other political functions of dialogue that together satisfy my earlier characterization of a critical theory as one that uncovers the ideological self-representation of a given society and at the same time projects the image of a different future which can mobilize the disadvantaged to take political action.

I do not think Ackerman makes sufficient use of the ideology-critical potential of dialogue because he is still too entrapped in logocentric models of discourse that rest on the assumption of unproblematically lucid two-way communications between fully rational speakers. Thus he takes for granted that the disadvantaged can actually muster the dialogic resources with which to challenge the federal government and ATT (American Telephone and Telegraph) and, as well, that the government and ATT are rational speakers committed to the ground rules of Neutral dialogue. Aided by the communication theory of Habermas, I want to move beyond Ackerman, who has at least raised the question, to explore two political functions of dialogue in a third-best social order. Taking up where Ackerman leaves off, I shall begin with an analysis of the consequences of failed dialogues for the disadvantaged. By tracing these consequences, I think we can arrive at a full-fledged critical theory of dialogue that significantly broadens the notion of political speech and hence of community-building public discourse.

Beyond the initial recognition that our social order is illegitimate, forged in the crucible of failed dialogue between powerless and powerful, there are two additional political functions of possible dialogue in a third-best social order. The first is what I shall call learning to speak politically, in response to initial dialogic failures and the mounting evidence that a social order is illegitimate; the second is, on that basis, learning to play, and to organize democratically, heretofore restricted social roles, thus broadening the very concept of dialogue beyond purely interpersonal speech to include person-nature and person-symbol relations. In his notion of Neutral dialogue Ackerman assumes sufficient linguistic competence in both interlocutors to assure that question and answer are unproblematically understood and thus a consensus achieved. He therefore does not consider the possibility that serious communicative distortions resulting from a highly skewed societal distribution of wealth and power may prevent speakers from successfully entering into such dialogues in the first place, or at least pursuing them beyond their initial opening moves. This is especially crucial where we consider the difficulties writers face in getting published, distributed, tenured, read. He does not adequately consider the difficulty many of the disadvantaged will have in entering dialogue in the first place, equipped with insufficient conceptual sophistication, publication outlets or faith that the future could be different to raise their political frustration above the level of raw resentment.

While in a third-best world dialogue ends in silence because the wealthy and powerful do not accede to demands for power by the dispossessed, *something* politically significant may be going on. This is precisely what Ackerman misses since he is interested mainly in the formal properties of possible dialogues, in the Kantian sense, and not in actual dialogues. Although he criticizes Rawls for his background assumptions of the 'veil of ignorance', behind which contractors know virtually nothing about themselves or the world, his own interlocutors are equally without flesh and blood. Real (powerless) people, once they try to engage the powerful in justificatory talk, are rarely satisfied with the recognition that the regime is illegitimate; instead they are passionate in their mounting newfound resistance to insufficient dialogic justification of what they regard as unjust. Ackerman's speakers exhibit no passion in their speech (a peculiar and notable characteristic of most of his dialogues) because their passion, in legitimate ideal and second-best states, is presumably to be expressed in other domains. Politics for them is only an abstraction, a pro forma contract-forming obligation that otherwise distracts them from more important concerns. And that is perhaps the way it should be. I believe that Marx, unlike most Platonist-inspired liberals, shares this view that politics is a temporarily necessary but intrinsically unrewarding activity that in an ideal state would be dispensed with in favor of the deeper self-expressive joys of living. In a third-best state, however, political speech about perceived injustice is not an arid obligation like trooping to the polls or taking a pledge of allegiance but a vital concern because, after all, lives are at stake.

What actually happens is that the disadvantaged, after sustained reflection on unbearable misery and growing willingness to take risks (of censure, unemployment, prison, silence), learn to speak politically: they begin, however haltingly and inarticulately (not having received higher education in the protocol of pseudo-liberal democracies), to engage the powerful in talk. Welfare mothers might stage a rally protesting cutbacks in their allowance; ethnic minorities might take to the streets in violent rage against institutionalized prejudice; workers might try to unionize. This is the language of critique, engaged in when people no longer accept the image that society is governed by incontrovertible laws that, in our own third-best state, compel the many to concede all system-steering rights to the few. To speak politically is a product and a cause of the critique of an ideology that legitimates silence and civic obedience in return for certain modest material rewards and a limited degree of occupational and status mobility. When the poor become too poor, however, dialogue may be joined. Even if it ends in silence, as always it must in an exploitative society, consciousness has been raised and the ground prepared for further speaking, writing and acting, albeit of a sort that transcends the established ground rules of political discourse in technocratic capitalism.

Habermas' work underpins this notion that entry into dialogue is a deeply political act. First in *Knowledge and Human Interests* and then in *Legitimation Crisis, Communication and the Evolution of Society* and *The Theory of Communicative Action*, Habermas develops a systematic understanding of this technocratic ideology that replaces the earlier entrepreneurial version. I read Habermas essentially as trying to concretize the earlier Frankfurt School theory of domination hinged around Horkheimer and Adorno's (1972) concept of a totally administered society that defies all political escape routes and Marcuse's (1964) notion of one-dimensionality. In effect, domination is a state of being in which people are not only economically exploited but also stripped of psychic, linguistic and textual vehicles of resistance. The one-dimensional society is simply that of all-enveloping silence, where the technocratic managers of capital do their work unhindered by the need to provide discursive justifications of their authority in the public sphere, nor to disclose who actually wrote the social texts of fast capitalism that script the quotidian for 'readers' — citizens.

Habermas has assimilated this analysis of technocratic domination, conceived by the original Frankfurt theorists in response to fascism and the corporate capitalism that overcame fascism, and tried to put it on solid foundations both epistemologically and empirically. As such, most of his work attempts to show that this imperial scientific-technical worldview — beyond values, morality, political choice — can be delegitimated by understanding the deep structure of human rationality, which he divides into three parts: instrumental scientific-technical action (the person acting productively on nature), self-reflective action (the person thinking about himself/herself and his or her world), and communicative action (people talking and — a Derridean would add — writing together). He suggests that speech categorically differs from instrumental action and thus cannot be reduced to it by appealing to allegedly self-evident grounds of truth in making claims both about the world and about values. He supports this argument on the basis of insights into the nature of the social world, constituting what one commentator has called his 'transcendental anthropology' (Lenhardt, 1972). In earlier work Habermas concentrated on defining the boundary between instrumental action and self-reflection, whereas in more recent work he has developed his thoughts on the uniqueness of communicative action and sought a teleology of social freedom in the very structure of our dialogic encounters.

I read him as the first theorist sympathetic to Marxism to take seriously this matter of the political content of dialogic challenges to a scientific-technocratic ideology that enforces structured silence as a means of domination. His work is so important because he addresses concretely the nature of a critique of ideology appropriate to the technocratic stage of capitalism. For Marx, in early capitalism the critique of ideology was directly political-economic because the central mobilizing issues then were life-and-death matters of material deprivation. While economic exploitation has obviously not disappeared (since ours is a capitalist system skewed in favor of a single class), the character of ideology has changed in such a way that people are now induced to support the system not because they accept the notion of 'fair exchange' in the marketplace and thus retain the optimism (and accept the desperate risks) of the entrepreneurial profit-seeker but because they are presented with technocratic 'laws' of socio-economic complexity that sanction élite governance and correspondingly inhibit public participation in the polity and economy. As I argued in chapter 2, sociology itself purveys these laws, its ideology becoming socio(onto)logical, hence seamless. Drawing on the work of scholars in other areas of linguistic investigation like Noam Chomsky and Karl-Otto Apel, Habermas has addressed this issue in terms of what he calls 'communicative competence' (see Chomsky, 1966, 1972; Apel, 1971, 1980).

He argues that on the basis of what he regards as a false perception of necessity, people acquiesce in technocratic guidance and fail to overcome their own communicative incompetence socially engendered in the technocratic stage of capitalism. He places discourse (if not, explicitly, writing) squarely in the center of his version of critical theory because he regards the loss of people's 'dialogue chances' as the most fundamental mode of ideological dominance in advanced capitalism. The binding force of the ideology of fair exchange rooted in the labor contract has been superseded in importance by the monologic stance of technical experts and scientists who retain power on the basis of claims about the purely instrumental character of politics as well as of their monopoly of the means and mode of literary production. As capitalism has evolved into a complex social and economic system in which relations between the classes are mediated by the welfare state, issues of communicative competence have become more central because the character of legitimation is no longer defined simply as obedience to free market contracts (although, of course, concepts of the inviolability of contracts and private productive property are still fundamental in contemporary capitalism) but rather as obedience to technocratic élites and the roles they assign the rest of us in the division of labor. Legitimation today, Habermas suggests, rests on public willingness to renounce communicative competence and thus political activity.

His challenge to the authority of scientific-technical ideology takes the form of an argument not that instrumental rationality (governing person-nature productive relationships) is invalid *per se* but that it is illegitimate when extended into the arena of intersubjective behavior. Habermas distinguishes between the types of rationality that govern person-nature and person-person relationships because he wants to circumscribe the role of an imperial scientism and not rule it out of court altogether. He does not oppose instrumental reason in the service of a productive technology that frees us from odious and time-consuming labor but the invasion of this mute rationality of control into an arena that ought to be properly governed by a 'universal pragmatics' of communicative praxis. He suggests that this communicative rationality is animated by the desire to achieve conversational consensus, based on what he calls 'the power of the strongest argument'. 'Distorted' communication, in turn, is speech governed by the instrumental motive of control (for example, propaganda, browbeating, 'of course' statements).

Habermas distinguishes between everyday language and what he calls discourse, which closely resembles what Ackerman calls Neutral dialogue. Discourse is speech that suspends all conversational motives other than that of reaching an understanding, to be achieved by withholding judgments about the superiority of certain values and the existence of certain states of affairs. Interlocutors thus enter an 'ideal speech situation' in which they seek consensus on the basis of the power of the strongest argument, uninhibited by communicative distortions. And an ideal speech situation can be entered only when people enjoy more or less equal chances to participate effectively in dialogues. Habermas thus secures a normative basis for critical theory in the very structure of discourse itself, arguing that the ideal speech situation can be the model of an ideal society in which all sorts of activities are democratized and opened to general public participation, one of the guiding values of my feminist postmodern critical theory.

While Habermas' ideal speech situation is remarkably similar to Ackerman's Neutral dialogue, it goes a step beyond it in attempting to generalize justificatory discourses to other sorts of activities heretofore closed off from broad public participation. Ackerman does not recognize, as I remarked above, the critical power of his own concept of dialogue because he assumes that such political speaking will only involve the matter of legitimation and delegitimation. He does not recognize, as Habermas does, the enormous ideology-critical potential of a theory of dialogue applied to technocratic capitalism for he does not understand the occluding, distorting effects of ideology. In developing his theory of dialogue, Habermas draws inspiration from the model of the psychoanalytic encounter precisely where psychoanalysis attempts to liberate the patient from self-imposed inhibitions that lead him or her to engage in the repetition of unhappy behavior. Habermas in effect is saying that the proletariat as a collective subject can liberate itself from technocratic ideology by recognizing its basic opportunity for engaging in uninhibited dialogues about political and economic matters. Communicative competence is gained when the powerless respond to failed justificatory dialogues not with self-imposed political inhibitions (public apathy, false consciousness), resting on the post-ulate of a language of science and technology that only a few can master, but with renewed political speaking and acting.

## Completing a Critical Theory: From Dialogue to Praxis

Yet Habermas, as Marcuse (1978–79) has convincingly argued (see Agger, 1976b, 1979b), restricts dialogue to the realm of interpersonal behavior on the basis of his transcendental reconstruction of rational-ity in *Knowledge and Human Interests* and thus cannot go beyond his teleology of conversational consensus. At best, for Habermas, a critic-al theory of dialogue can lead to awareness of the importance of democratizing dialogue chances — learning to argue politically with usurpers of scientific-technical expertise — but not, as for early Marx and the original Frankfurt School theorists including Marcuse, of radically reconstructing dialogue itself, including not only inter-personal communication but all of our productive entanglements with texts, culture, economics, the external world and with one another. Habermas only takes Marxism one step, albeit a crucial one, beyond Ackerman's immanent critique of liberalism. Where Ackerman recog-nizes the delegitimating potential of dialogue, and Habermas the democratizing and mobilizing potential of failed dialogues, I believe there is a further stage in a critical phenomenology of political dia-logue which I will call the impulse to reconstruct all 'dialogues' between people and between humanity and nature, involving both textuality and technology. Insight into this further stage in the trans-formative potential of political dialogue is provoked by postmodern-ism and feminist theory, both of which emphasize the politics of textuality in a way that is useful for an emerging intertextual critical theory. Where Habermas foresees the restoration of communicative competence among the disadvantaged as an outcome of failed dia-logues, affording them a newfound transcendental self-understanding as rational speakers, I suggest that there is a final stage in this phe-nomenology of political speech at which people learn to play and to coordinate heretofore restricted social roles, thus achieving real work-ers' control in Marx's original sense. This final stage emerges from the mobilizing insight, won at stage two, that people need not accept structured silence but can legitimately enter public dialogues and pub-lic writing otherwise reserved for élites. Beyond this mobilizing in-sight, they realize not only that they can enter such dialogues but that they can engage in a whole series of socially, textually and technologi-cally transformative activities from which structured silence in the service of a tight capitalist and sexist division of labor has heretofore excluded them.

Entering into political dialogue, then, can finally lead to entry into the self-management of all political, economic, cultural, sexual and social activities, a vision expressed throughout socialist utopian imagery from 1844 Marx to Marcuse and beyond. Habermas cannot go beyond the initial restoration of communicative competence, expressed as the urge to enter into heretofore restricted political dialogue with a scientific-technical élite, because he too strictly separates instrumental from communicative action; he cannot glimpse the possible reconstruction of person-nature relationships in the realm of productive work, but only (and, of course, significantly) of communicative relations among people trying to decide on qualitatively distinctive uses of instrumentally rational science, technology, and labor. Habermas is therefore prevented from understanding that the democratization of dialogue chances can ultimately lead to the democratization and qualitative reconstruction of work, techne and textuality as well as public dialogue, in Marxian terms serving to transform both the relations and mode of production and, feminism adds, reproduction.

I want to suggest that we can view dialogue not simply in the rationalistic terms of discursive speech among interlocutors but also as textual and productive work on nature and with others. Ackerman's modal first question — Why should you have what I do not? — is the basis for Habermas' subsequent critique of technocratic ideology that can ultimately ignite a full-fledged movement for radical social change incorporating public desire not just to 'speak' democratically but also to produce and reproduce democratically, across and among roles heretofore considered off limits to mute consumers of élite prescription. This deepens the notion of dialogue by using Marx's original imagery of the unity of productive and creative activity to suggest that egalitarian dialogic relationships, the essence of an authentic socialism, can exist between humanity and nature through work and writing, as well as among people trying democratically to dispose of a surplus product provided by an advanced technology.

To learn to speak politically is insufficient if it is not joined to participatory role playing across the wide range of the social, textual and sexual division of labor. While the liberation of communicative competence goes a long way toward both delegitimating the technocratic state and sparking critical public consciousness about social purposes, it stops short, in Habermas' version, of sparking a movement toward social change advocating full participation in the many segmented roles in the socio-sexual-textual division of labor. A critical theory of dialogue is completed, I am suggesting, by binding together Ackerman's notion of delegitimating dialogue, Habermas' stress on the possible democratization of dialogue chances, and a vision of the despecialization and cooperative coordination of all productive and reproductive roles conceived of as 'dialogues' between humanity and nature, humanity and symbols, and people and each other. In particular, feminism, poststructuralism and postmodernism help broaden Habermas' notion of dialogue in these ways. While Habermas allows us to turn Ackerman's edifying liberalism into critical Marxism, Habermas' own thought, I am suggesting here, is itself incomplete without further support from theorists in the 'western Marxist' tradition as well as from feminists, poststructuralists and postmodernists who in some respects retain more of early Marx's totalizing vision than Habermas has.

These theorists, writing in opposition to the 'scientific socialism' of the Second International and the centralist tradition of Leninism as well as to Marxism's own sexism, add to critical theory the idea that the 'process' and 'product' of social change, as well as production and reproduction, ought to blur to the point of indistinguishability. To separate process and product in the name of revolutionary expediency will only invite a protracted period of authoritarian rule that, as we recognize in hindsight when evaluating the Soviet Union, tends to be self-perpetuating. Thus these theorists have argued that democratic and communitarian values must inform the socialist struggle from the beginning and should not be postponed to a distant future, the apocryphal judgment day when perfect 'synthesis' arises from capitalist 'thesis' and socialist 'antithesis'. In addition, the collapsing of product and process in the class struggle has given rise to the idea, perhaps most coherently expressed in Gramsci, that intellectuals and the public are to be perpetually in dialogue: theorists will use people's experience of capitalist alienation as a resource for their more structural analysis of systemic crisis points, which they can then return to the proletariat and other social groups in the form of ideology-critique and even strategic insight and thereby facilitate their informed action. Gramsci, in much the spirit of my critical approach to dialogue, spoke of 'counterhegemonic' activity as that de-mystifying, consciousness-raising dialogue between intellectuals and citizens, and among citizens, that instructs them in their own dialogic and hence political competence (Gramsci, 1971: pp. 332–5).

This renegade, antiauthoritarian tradition in Marxism, feminism, poststructuralism and postmodernism stresses the possibility of closer harmony between productive and reproductive activity. Not only can the relations of production and reproduction more rationally and democratically distribute wealth and organize intimacy but also the very 'mode of production' (labor, science, technology, textuality) can be qualitatively altered, especially in an advanced era where a sophisticated technological infrastructure frees us from the most odious forms of what Marx called 'necessary labor'. Marcuse's (1969: pp. 17–30) 'new sensibility' discovers that productive labor can retain its instrumental character oriented to the reproduction of the species while also being experienced as a form of self-creative freedom. This would have the effect of blurring Habermas' distinction between techne and praxis and overturning all of the fateful dualisms of subject and object, pleasure and pain, play and work that needlessly keep us in harness to a tight social and sexual division of labor. Given our immense productive capacity today, Marcuse argues, we can be freed from most types of instinctually ungratifying work and instead engage in mature self-expressive activity more nearly on the blurry boundary between the rationality of instruments and the rationality of fantasy, imagination and the erotic body.

My version of dialogue retains this western-Marxist and feminist aim of the full emancipation of labor based on a blurring of productive, reproductive and creative work. My concept of dialogue stresses the transformative possibilities inherent in the blossoming of full self-expressive competence, no longer restricted to speech but now including all aspects of our productive, reproductive, textual, technological and organizational involvements. I am saying not only that people can learn to speak politically as a response to failed dialogue in the technocratic stage of capitalism, as Habermas powerfully argues, but that they can also engage in work, intimacy and writing that joins humanity and nature in nonantagonistic relations and thus allows them to enjoy work that is at once creative and productive, overcoming the dualism (which Habermas retains) of freedom and necessity. This suggests dialogic relations between human and nonhuman nature in which we accord nature a certain aesthetic standing, perhaps even 'natural rights' (Leiss, 1972). Thus (and this is very much in the spirit of Ackerman's urging that as a condition of Neutral dialogue we bequeath to our children a world which is not plundered and despoiled) we shall recognize that our own social freedom depends in large measure on how well we master, and not exploit, the natural environment. Indeed, the boundary between our own instinctual nature and nature 'out there' cannot be as sharply drawn as philosophers in the Cartesian tradition, including Habermas, have tried to do.

But my theory of dialogue offers an additional, even more powerful, component of a full-fledged Marxian perspective on the emancipation of labor that can further underpin Ackerman's delegitimation strategy and Habermas' critique of technocratic ideology. Not only can the concept of dialogue be extended to govern nonantagonistic relationships between human and nonhuman nature, revealing the prospect of work as genuinely creative praxis, but it can also serve to open up heretofore restricted and bureaucratically administered roles in the division of labor. Indeed, western Marxists (notably the French existential-Marxist Cornelius Castoriadis, 1973–74, 1984, 1987; also see Singer, 1979, 1980) have offered a trenchant critique of heavy bureaucratic specialization and organization, achieved through what Weber (1947) called 'imperative coordination.' If work were reconstructed dialogically, not only would we enjoy 'dialogue' with the nonhuman environment and thus build its 'needs' into the calculus of our own needs, but we would also learn to master and carry out a variety of roles heretofore restricted to élites and on that basis develop *dialogic organizations and a dialogic public sphere* not dependent on bureaucratic coordination but on cooperation among all communicatively competent workers. 'Dialogue' thus contains the triple promise of qualitatively different orientations to nature, to symbol-systems and social roles heretofore reserved for élites and accredited professionals, and to other people who share the labor, reproduction and writing with us. Even more important than the implications of treating nature as a dialogue partner, albeit a silent partner, in the human enterprise are the political implications of new dialogic relations both to complex symbol systems and occupational roles and to our fellow human beings, auguring not only new relationships to nature but a whole new set of productive and reproductive relationships.

The most pernicious consequence of structured public silence in technocratic capitalism is the institutionalization of a trained incapacity to participate fully in productive and reproductive relationships (including textuality) and their organization. The neutering of human imagination and self-expression is an absolutely vital requisite of domination in advanced capitalism. As Basil Bernstein (1971) and Paulo Freire (1970) have both argued, the more that symbolic codes and cultural production outlets are restricted, the more powerless we become in face of preponderant scientific-technical expertise. Both Ackerman and Habermas miss the crucial political salience of restricted symbolic codes, Ackerman because (as a liberal) he is concerned only with explicitly justificatory dialogues, and Habermas because (as a Cartesian and Kantian) he draws such a heavy line between symbolic codes in the world of science and technology, on the one hand, and communicative praxis, on the other. I think they both fail to appreciate how the assumption of dialogic competence presupposes a deeper competence to understand and use symbolic codes and thus how a critical theory of dialogue must contain a notion of our competence not only to speak politically but also to master all productive, reproductive, textual, technological and social relationships (although it is clear to me that Habermas comes much closer to this understanding than does Ackerman; see O'Neill, 1976).

Such a theory must address not only person-nature and person-symbol relations but the person-person relations involved in actually organizing a new mode of production and reproduction. Weber articulately defended a technocratic ideology based on the exploitation of nature, the élite monopoly of restricted symbolic codes, and the universality of bureaucratic organizations in industrial society. His vindication of bureaucracy as a handmaiden of economic efficiency rests squarely on what amounts to his defense of the notion of differentially distributed communicative competences. For Weber, 'rational' criteria of (capitalist) efficiency dictate a tight bureaucratic organization of labor. But it is not clear that either society as a whole must contain a rigid division of labor (defended, on the level of sociological theory, by Emile Durkheim) or, particularly, that the workplace, in the interest of efficiency, requires a minute 'technical' division of labor epitomized by the assembly line, enshrined as the engine of capitalist productivity by Frederick Taylor, the founder of industrial sociology and the 'scientific management' of labor (Taylor, 1919, 1947). The western Marxist and feminist traditions suggest not only that people can gain competence in heretofore restricted symbolic codes but that they can also more or less spontaneously engage in the cooperative, nonbureaucratic administration of the workplace and home, where they move easily across roles and take an active hand in coordinating the ensemble of such roles.

In conclusion, communicative competence as I have elaborated it can be seen to involve three interrelated types of competence, beyond the capacity simply to articulate political grievances (Ackerman) and, once freed from the allure of a technocratic ideology that urges us to cede all decision-making functions to élites, to discuss alternative uses of labor, science and technology (Habermas): an instrumental competence to work on nature in a way that both humanizes the worker by blurring the boundaries among his or her productive, reproductive and creative efforts and respects the standing of the external world conceived as a dialogue-partner; a cognitive and textual competence to master and use complex technical codes and the socio-economic roles they underpin, allowing us to move more easily across the social and sexual division of labor; and an organizational competence that allows people to cooperate in the coordination of their various productive relationships without succumbing to bureaucratic administration by managerial élites.

I have argued that dialogue can do more than convince us that technocratic capitalism is illegitimate and that people can regain their decision-making voices by seeing through the occluding ideology of an imperial scientism. Dialogue, when fully emancipated from the technocratic worldview that reduces speech to an instrument of control, can also join us in new ways to the world and to each other, enabling us not just to talk together in making political decisions formerly reserved for élites but also to write and work together harmoniously both to reproduce the species and to fulfill our deep existential urges to mold nature creatively. Communicative competence in this sense is nothing less than a competence to manage all the facets of our lives in transcending an ideology that robs us both of our political voices and our substantive social and economic freedoms of self-creation.

A critical theory of public life relies on a theory and practice of dialogue both to pierce ideological illusions through enlightening discussion and to prefigure the very polity that dispenses with socially structured silence and hierarchized state-managed knowledge. In the next chapter, I take up this theme again when I consider why public discourse has declined and what role critical theory must play in reversing that decline. Habermas is a central figure in my discursive critical theory. Yet Habermas is also an ironic example of a critical discourse theorist who diminishes discourse and hence democracy by virtue of his own teutonic example of esoteric writing. I will argue that critical theory must bear some responsibility not only for theorizing the decline of public discourse but also for reversing that decline in the example of its own language game, which must be optimally democratized.

Anyone can preach dialogue, discourse and democracy. But such recommendations must be encoded in language that appeals to the broadest possible polity. Restricted linguistic codes inherently hierarchize knowledge and power. This is not to call for slang or argot as politically sufficient in themselves. Deconstruction shows how simple translation from one code to another involves all sorts of interpolative constructions requiring imagination and guesswork. Only to 'simplify' critical theory banalizes it, especially where its dialectical insights must work themselves out in the dialectic of lucidity and opacity. Difficulty educates and clarity obfuscates at a time when advertising slogans substitute for thought. Baudrillardian simulations make anything out of anything — freedom out of shopping malls and credit cards, justice out of military technologies, truth out of mathematical symbolism.

Although this chapter ends on a high note, empowering dialogue to change the world by democratizing knowledge and discourse, I need to return to the simultaneously hermeneutic and political problem of educating the educator that has bedeviled radical movements from the beginning. In what language is political education to be conducted? From what power position? To what end? With what syllabus? These are burning questions for the left, especially when postmodern skepticism about 'grand narratives' of global change abounds. In the following two chapters I conclude this book by engaging with these questions; I consider concretely what it means to live a radical life at a time when everything is susceptible to commodification and integration — critical theory, feminism and postmodernism no less than other trends.

*Chapter 9*

# Theorizing the Decline of Discourse or the Decline of Theoretical Discourse?

Where in the last chapter I developed a version of critical theory as a theory of dialogue and discourse, in this chapter I ask a host of questions about how radical intellectuals by attempting to create a new public sphere in which people participate dialogically and democratically can avoid a new vanguardism, reinforced by the hierarchy of élite discourse over more plebeian dialects. There is a telling irony about critical theories that preach democracy undemocratically. Unless radical intellectuals address this irony without succumbing to a disingenuous populism that celebrates the false consciousness of the quotidian, we will only repeat epochal problems of educating-the-educator. Elitism reproduces itself on the left as well as the right. This fact must be faced squarely by those who profess to love humanity and hate oppression; those of us who are not part of the solution remain part of the problem. This chapter does not argue for sheer dedifferentiation, as if the despecialization of theoretical language will solve all of our problems. It simply acknowledges the irony of élite radical discourses and tries to work around it creatively. In particular, I consider what it means to be a postmodern intellectual, turning postmodernism further in the direction of critical theory. Thus, this chapter and the following chapter return to some of the themes raised in chapter 1, where I first posed the possible synthesis of critical theory and postmodernism.

### Theory as Public Speech

My interest in this chapter is the public sphere, the polity. I am concerned to trace the decline of the public sphere to certain structural and cultural elements of literary political economy in late capitalism — the institutional ways in which writing and reading are organized. Drawing on the analysis presented in chapter 4, my argument here is that writers no longer write sharp, imaginative, accessible prose for general readers because they are compelled by the profit and discipline requirements of mass culture and academia respectively to narrow their focus and domesticate their arguments. In this sense, I analyze the decline of discourse both in terms of economic and ideological factors, thus continuing the long tradition of western Marxism (e.g., Agger, 1979a) that refuses to separate these two dimensions of social reality (Horkheimer, 1972b).

I characterize the rampant loss of public voice as the decline of discourse (see Agger, 1990). The decline of discourse matters because accessible speech and writing connect us to an authentic realm of political discussion and practice otherwise controlled by élites (O'Neill, 1972b; Habermas, 1975; Sennett, 1978; Agger, 1985). Unwittingly, people who theorize about politics, especially leftists, often contribute to the specialization and professionalization of public language by composing themselves in ways accessible to a few hundred, not a few hundred million (Jacoby, 1987). The left critique of declining discourse ironically only compounds the problem.

Part of this is inevitable. Analyses of what is going wrong with our literary political economy cannot proceed without some reliance on abstract and technical concepts, whether words like 'commodification' or 'hegemony'. Of course, these terms can be defined and hence democratized; they must be, if we are to create the populist polity in which what Habermas calls dialogue chances and what Derrideans call textuality (McCarthy, 1978: pp. 306–10) are democratically distributed. But in this chapter I argue that social analysis and diagnosis can proceed without involuted technical categories only deepening the problem they originally intended to address. The Frankfurt School (e.g., Marcuse, 1969) has called this prefiguration — the inescapable fact that what we do and say in the present helps create a certain future in its image. For example, oppressing our colleagues and comrades out of alleged revolutionary exigency only entrenches authoritarianism, albeit flying different flags. By the same token, writing as if people could understand it and join one's discourse dialogically helps create that very polity, albeit in halting, accumulating steps.

It is unlikely that any literary product will have the same sweeping impact as Marx's *oeuvre*. Writings are too readily coopted by the culture industry for all that, either defused as the ravings of lunatics or sold profitably as evidence of the system's alleged openness (e.g., what happens when academic presses publish left-leaning work). Yet *writings matter* if only because they are matter; they exist as what Wittgenstein (1953) called 'forms of life', 'language games' with their own interpretive and dialogical rules. Textual politics is not all politics, yet it is undeniably political, especially in light of a theory of ideology that attunes itself to the way popular discourse helps maintain the *status quo*. Thus, people who theorize discourse must attend to their own complicity in worsening the very problem they bemoan — here, the erosion of a genuinely public language with which to create a new polity and hence a whole new world.

British analytic philosophers continually lament the inability or refusal of European social theorists to write clearly (see Gellner, 1959). They read obscurantism as incorrigible élitism and infantilism. It is not as simple as that if only because the complex world requires a good deal of conceptual and empirical complexity in order to be understood. International capitalism demands training in sophisticated economic theory, just as cultural criticism forces one to study labyrinthine interpretive theories. But that does not mean that critical theorists ought to ignore the prefigurative implications of their own writing for the very polity they so desperately desire. C. Wright Mills, a self-styled 'plain Marxist' (1962), argued eloquently against academic obscurantism (1959), showing in the example of his own work an admirable ability to write clearly about broad-gauged issues of social criticism.

Russell Jacoby (1987) is correct to lament the absence of the accessible public book typified by those of Mills. Of course, as he well knows, this is largely conditioned by literary political economy itself. Commercial publishers want blockbusters and hence they avoid controversy. Academic publishers demand intellectual conformity plus the rarefied, stultified methodological apparatus of 'scholarship'. And Mills' own house, Oxford University Press, has become largely a trade publisher concerned to make money. But Jacoby correctly holds writers, especially left-wing ones, responsible for blithely complying with these external imperatives, even endorsing them. Most left academics are no less obscurantist than centrist and right-wing ones; their commitment to élitist academese outweighs their political commitment to a democratic world. The example of Habermas is prominent here. He writes about the importance of 'universal speech situations' and democratized 'dialogue chances' in a code that is difficult to crack without years of training in European philosophy and social theory. He justifies this literary strategy as an attempt to legitimate critical theory in the bourgeois university. But that is a meager benefit when balanced against the loss of his public voice. Where C. Wright Mills influenced and energized the New Left, particularly the Port Huron Statement of the original Students for a Democratic Society (SDS), Habermas' comments about the 'colonization of the lifeworld' by oppressive 'systems' provoke little but ennui. His architectonic Parsonian Marxism produces footnotes but not political passion. One has to dig deep beneath the surface of his text, as I have done in this book, to find the secret heartbeat at the core of every literary act.

Neoconservatives valorize plain language simply to restrict public access to élite codes of power (see Freire, 1970; Bernstein, 1971; O'Neill, 1976). In no way should the left take all the blame for the gaping distance between élites and publics today. But the left cannot ignore its own victimization by academic discourse that reproduces hierarchy and conformity. Left critics must write straight ahead through the thickets of confusion and complexity confronting any responsible social analyst; this confusion and complexity *can be simplified*, even if one must acknowledge that simplification always threatens to recede deconstructively into the murky soup out of which clarification initially arises in a bold stroke. That nothing is simple today is all the more reason for theorists to write simply and forcefully.

We must avoid the methodologization of this notion of public discourse, however, whereby we try to translate difficulty into simplicity directly. There are no one-for-one principles of translation or semiotization according to which we can replace a complex concept with a simpler, terser one. The responsibility for writing public discourse is more a matter of temperament and style than a methodological injunction to craft brief sentences. As Adorno shows in his most powerful and penetrating prose, dialectical allusion is often clearer than the linearity pretending to grasp complexity in monosyllables. As I argued in my introduction, the principle of public speech and writing involves a commitment to *political education*, the systematic enhancement and transformation of consciousness that allows the disempowered to learn and use complex languages and thus to challenge power.

Today, especially in North America, political education smacks of agitprop. It might better be called consciousness raising, a concept developed by the women's movement in response to the male supremacy of the New Left. Or simply call it public discourse. It matters little what pedigree we give our commitment to creating a new polity in which dialogue chances are more or less equal. This commitment has been called many things: socialism, feminism, democracy etc. Whatever words we use to talk about the restoration of the public sphere, we must recognize that our analytic and diagnostic language itself bears responsibility for the world we would create. Intellectuals are political actors; hence we must address the politics of intellectuality.

## The Politics of Textuality/Intellectuality

As I said earlier, textual politics are politics, although not all politics. Literary political economy helps us understand what happens to writing and writers when they become merely white-collar employees (Mills, 1951), losing both autonomy and vision. They work, write and live for others, whether in popular culture (advertising, journalism, trade fiction, television, movies) or in academia. Their literary craft is dictated by their status as wage laborers in the culture industry, no matter that they are white-collar workers with ample emoluments, even corporate benefit packages. The commodification of culture inevitably degrades it where it blocks critical imagination by diverting thought into the narrow profit and disciplinary requirements of popular culture and academia.

Literary political economy, which I derive from a postmodern version of cultural studies emphasizing its liberatory possibilities, has both economic and ideological features. After all, the decline of discourse has both objective and subjective dimensions — what editors decide the market will bear and what writers write. On the one hand, the commodification of literary activity turns writing into yet another exchange value and writers into wage and salary slaves. On the other hand, literary political economy involves hegemony, a dominant culture of ideas and values reproduced by these literary underworkers. It is still true (viz. *German Ideology* [Marx and Engels, 1947]) that the ruling ideas are the ideas of the ruling class, propagated through what Horkheimer and Adorno (1972: pp. 120–67) called the culture industry. Original Marxism was long on economic analysis of commodification but short on ideological and cultural critique showing the interconnection between profit and political/ideational/cultural hegemony. Marx's model of ideology was simplistic; he characterized ideology as a 'camera obscura' through which people are coaxed to view the world upside down.

Gramsci's (1971) notion of hegemony renders the discussion of ideology more sophisticated. One cannot trace hegemony to an original conspiracy of editors, publishers and producers any more than one can reduce each and every cultural expression to the profit motive *per se*. There is dissonance around the edges of the late-capitalist totality, notably including postmodernism itself which, in significant respects, veers away from traditional bourgeois concepts of modernity, the subject, reason, values etc. Although Lyotard's (1984) affirmative version of postmodernism is affiliated to the project of capitalist modernization (e.g., for all practical purposes Bell [1960] = Lyotard [1984]), postmodernism addresses and legitimates a much more complex late capitalism (Jameson, 1984b, following Mandel, 1975) in which 'difference' (Derrida, 1976) is supposedly the best post-modern, post-capitalist, post-rationalist principle of integration. Of course, this is fraudulent; difference, once deconstructed, can be traced to all the usual centers and samenesses of capital, gender, race. As I argue in the next chapter, postmodernity is no more pluralist than modernity; in fact, to the extent to which postmodernism functions as an occluding ideology duping people about the prevalence of real difference, postmodernity regresses *behind* earlier stages and versions of modernity that ambivalently contained both the project of general enlightenment and liberation (viz. Habermas' [1981a, 1987a, 1987b] valorization of enlightenment), on the one hand, and cooptation/coercion/discipline, on the other.

The culture industry is not a mystery. It involves considerations of cultural corporate concentration, market, ratings, cosmopolitanism and literary imagination. All of these things can be viewed materially without reducing cultural products simply to market reflexes or to conspiracies of publishers and editors. What Gramsci called hegemony as a way of updating Marx's earlier notion of ideology can be traced to the political economy of literary production, involving both institutional and motivational features. Surely the culture industry would grind to a halt without willing writers. Just as surely, words are a big business, highly constraining the authorial choices available to writers today.

In this sense, then, modernity and modernism are somehow more dialectical than postmodernity and postmodernism, which flatten bourgeois civilization into a Nietzschean tableau of eternal presentness. Marcuse (1955) already carefully explained late capitalism's need for 'repressive desublimation', loosening discipline's hold on people lest they chafe too much against early-Protestant superego restraints. Postmodernism in Lyotard's (1984) neoconservative variant theorizes and legitimizes this repressive desublimation, outfitting the world in Gucci clothes, feeding them American fast-food as well as Americanized 'foreign' food, entertaining them with the 'pastiches' and 'collages' (Jameson, 1984b) of cultural expression drawn from diverse historical and global sources, and housing them in a postmodern cityscape apparently adding soul and depth to the usual modernist skyscrapers, offices and factories. Indeed, I have serious doubts that Jameson's own (1984b: p. 92; 1988) strategy of 'cognitive mapping' can help overcome the very 'multinational capitalism' he decries. But I do not pretend to have a better strategy if by that one means a definitive program of agitational political tactics.

As such, as I suggested in chapter 1, postmodernism is both an economic and cultural phenomenon, what Jameson (1984b) appropriately called the 'cultural logic of late capitalism'. I want to suggest a version of postmodernism much more closely affiliated to the culture-critical project of western Marxism, especially the Frankfurt School (Kellner, 1988). I (e.g., Agger, 1989a, 1990) derive an empirical and dialectical sociology of culture from postmodernism, notably a theory of literary political economy allowing me to address the decline of discourse in concrete terms. What writers write and how they live are largely dictated by the forces of literary commodification. As such, literary liberation must address the culture industry squarely and neither lament the passing of a golden age that never existed (e.g., freelancing) nor burden heroic, solitary writers with the weight of the world. Writers can only do so much to change things, although it is undeniable that they must involve themselves in overall social change — the politics of textuality/intellectuality. This will help transform the culture industry and thus dominant ideology in general.

To work through an alternative postmodernism not beholden to Lyotard's (1984) aversion to the grand 'metanarratives' of history — Marxism, feminism, etc. — we must split postmodernism into affirmative and dialectical moments. With Jameson (1984a, 1984b,

1988), Kellner (1988, 1989a, 1989b, 1989c), Aronowitz (1981, 1988, 1990), Huyssen (1984, 1986) and others, I believe that we can salvage the emancipatory and critical insights of postmodernism in a way that dialectically preserves the continuity between modernity and post-modernity. This is especially relevant where we use postmodernism against itself to combat the quiescent 'postmodernism' (e.g., Lyotard, 1984; Kroker and Cook, 1986) celebrating the putative end of modernity as our collective liberation from the 'metanarratives' of universal liberation. Theoretical pedigree is relatively unimportant here. One could as easily suggest that postmodernism is a radical modernism, emphasizing Marx's own modernist penchant for a universalistic philosophy of history preserved in the work of western Marxists, particularly the thinkers of the Frankfurt School (e.g., Adorno, 1973; Habermas, 1984, 1987b).

In effect, then, my dialectical version of postmodernism issues in a radical cultural studies (Denzin, 1991). This approach to cultural analysis and criticism that explains and opposes the decline of public discourse in terms of concrete structural arrangements of writing and reading is political work in its own terms. It is critique of ideology, deriving from but going beyond Marx's (Marx and Engels, 1947) classical model of ideological unmasking, which is now rendered textual via poststructuralism and postmodernism. I conduct the critique of bourgeois postmodernism from within the rhetorical frame of reference of postmodernism itself precisely in order to implode it, a strategy of what the Frankfurt theorists called immanent critique. I believe that we have not yet arrived at the end-of-the-modern, post-modernity, but only new iterations and variations of the same world-historical capitalism first addressed by Marx and later by feminists and opponents of racism and the domination of nature. In this sense, the postmodern agenda is the end-of-history as depicted by Marx — the transcendence of global alienation. And one of the most significant routes toward this end is a version of radical cultural studies that squarely addresses what Horkheimer and Adorno (1972) called the culture industry. Postmodernism functions empirically, critically and politically as a theory of cultural production and reception explaining the ways in which ideology is scripted by people for people, hence hinting at its transformation.

Unfortunately, textual politics have a decidedly ambiguous status in American higher education and American letters generally, especially on the left. This relates to larger questions about the role of critical intellectuals, which I want to address further in this chapter. First, here, I discuss the false duality of materialist and idealist perspectives on the politics of intellectuality and then I conclude with a discussion of postmodern intellectual life (although I should properly call that post-postmodern if we are talking about postmodernism as affirmative ideology and not as critical theory).

The ambiguous status of textual and cultural politics on the left has very much to do with the classical problem of economism in Marxism. Although Horkheimer (1972b) definitively laid to rest the notion that Marx was economistic or reductionist in his method, thus suggesting a critical theory that closely linked economic with cultural and ideological processes, the Frankfurt School's perspective on cultural politics is far from universally accepted on the left. More orthodox Marxists reject what they take to be the untoward focus on culture on the part of western Marxists and others heavily involved in literary theory and cultural criticism. Although I believe that they are wrong not to recognize the embeddedness of literary political economy in political economy generally, culture critics tend to fetishize textuality to the exclusion of almost everything else (see Agger, 1989a).

This fetishism ignores the political economy of textuality and intellectuality. Poststructuralists and postmodernists fond of Derrida's notion that the text has no outside only continue a line of argument embraced earlier by the New Criticism (Ransom, 1941; for a critique, see Fekete, 1978). This is ironic in that poststructuralist and postmodernist literary criticism formulated itself in opposition to the textual objectivism of New Criticism, where each text is treated on its own terms. As I read it, this is only a family difference. Derrida, and later those Americans like de Man who have methodologized poststructuralism into deconstruction (e.g., the Yale School), also close off textuality from a kind of social reading, although deconstruction valuably expands the notion of the text from literature *per se* — the actual pages on which it is inscribed — to all manner of social and cultural expressions. Poststructuralist sociologists even write books called *Society as Text* (Brown, 1987), reflecting this tendency to extrapolate the notion of textuality from the authorial product *per se* into a veritable ensemble of interpersonal and cultural expressions. The poststructural and postmodern fetishes of textuality (Agger, 1989a: ch. 6) miss the dynamic, non-identical relationship between (material) text and (material) world, ignoring literary political economy altogether.

But textuality *is* a political battleground and must be addressed materially, albeit in a way that recognizes that the 'texts' of ideology are often concealed in what Baudrillard (1983) calls simulations, littering the quotidian landscape of postmodern lifeworlds. Ignoring postmodern textual politics is tantamount to ignoring ideology which, as Marx, Lukács and the Frankfurt theorists knew, is a crucial political factor in its own right. Indeed, as I noted earlier in this book, Horkheimer's (1972b) original 1937 article on 'Traditional and Critical Theory' argues that political economy includes both economic and ideological elements *that are virtually impossible to separate*. Regrettably, though, once one enters into the thicket of conceptual, interpretive and empirical problems surrounding the radical sociology of culture, notably the close examination of the culture industry, one is almost inevitably trapped on the sticky fly-paper of literary and cultural theory oblivious to the material nature of textuality. Deconstruction, fetishized in American departments of English and Comparative Literature, is one result; it is typically apolitical, precious and pretentious. In claiming the world for textuality (Derrida: the text has no outside), this textualism loses the world. Stanley Fish's influential book *Is There a Text in This Class?* (1980) needs to be reformulated materially. Indeed, John O'Neill has done so (1991). He asks: Is there a class in this text? Not frequently enough, in the work of the deconstructors.

Stanley Aronowitz remarked that some postmodernists invest themselves so deeply in literature and the literary that their *soi-disant* Marxism loses its political coordinates. Aronowitz lamented the degeneration of critical literary theory into aestheticism. He said that he can write of Dickens and still ground his argument in empirical political theory — what for the left are the bread-and-butter issues of the theory/practice merger. Here, Adorno's later considerations of aesthetic theory (e.g., 1984) suggest the impasse of Frankfurt critical theory, later occasioning the Kantian and Parsonian Marxism of Habermas (1984, 1987b). Adorno's *Negative Dialectics* (1973a) suggests an ideology-critical agenda for critical theory that by *Aesthetic Theory* (1984) he had largely foresworn in favor of a critical theory ensconced in aesthetic interpretation and opposition. Although there is much that is attractive about the various Frankfurt perspectives on aesthetic politics (Agger, 1976a), Marcuse and Adorno (*The Aesthetic Dimension*, 1978) retreat to aesthetic expression as adequate (or the only available) modes of political resistance, the fateful trajectory of Marcuse's Great Refusal (1964: p. 257). Interestingly, the trajectory of Jameson's own work from *Marxism and Form* (1971) to *The Political Unconscious* (1981) has been similar, threatening to lose touch with the political moment of aesthetic theory in favor of a highly self-referential theory of interpretation.

Empirically, Adorno, Marcuse and Jameson are correct; late capitalism swallows virtually every resistance and opposition, requiring dissent to find unconventional, even nondiscursive, forms. This is the essential message of the theory of the culture industry, and one that is central to my argument here. I accept Frankfurt aesthetic theory as far as it goes. But aesthetic theory almost inevitably becomes aestheticism, an approach to cultural studies that sacrifices political critique to the disciplinary project of interpretation. To be sure, we can and must redefine the region of the political. Culture is not a world apart from political economy and thus our criticism must address culture in thoroughly material terms, asking phenomenologically how, where, why, when and what real flesh-and-blood writers can write in order to avoid the implosive tendencies of aesthetic commodification.

The Frankfurt School's aesthetic theory, especially pre-*Aesthetic Theory*, kept this firmly in mind. Some of Adorno's discussions of television (1954), radio (1945) and journalism (1974b) are unparalleled examples of materialist cultural criticism that avoids its own empty methodologization. Tellingly, Adorno's World War II exodus in the US, when he collaborated first with Paul Lazarsfeld, one of the doyens of sophisticated social-science research methodology, and then with the California social psychologists on *The Authoritarian Personality* (Adorno *et al.*, 1950), was among his most productive periods in terms of this nuanced cultural criticism and media studies (Adorno, 1969). After he and Horkheimer returned to West Germany, Adorno reverted to earlier, more apocalyptic and philosophically abstract modes of theorizing (Jay, 1984a). The politically promising sociology of culture that Adorno and some of his other Frankfurt colleagues like Marcuse had begun during the 1940s gave way to the world-historical musings of *Minima Moralia* and *Aesthetic Theory*.

It is important to note that the issue here is not simply political pessimism or the lack of it (Slater, 1977; Agger, 1983). Orthodox Marxists who ground optimism in a socialist dialectic of nature mislead themselves as much as do postmodernists who disdain political discourse as shabby and out-of-date. Pessimism and optimism are temperamental categories, nothing more. Political predictions are empirical, nothing less. Adorno's lack of hopefulness during the post-World War II reconstruction period, when capitalism rebuilt itself on a global scale, thus integrating aspects of fascism (Foucault's disciplinary society), was largely justified on the evidence. Yet Adorno's ventures in aesthetic theory closed off some very real political possibilities. Of course, were he alive today, he might well recant some of his strictures on the impossibility of political resistance. Adorno was much less a metaphysician than met the untutored eye. As Jay (1984a) and Ryan (1982) have pointed out, there are some important continuities between Adorno's critical theory and both poststructuralism and postmodernism. The postmodern problematic only emerged in somewhat clearer light since Adorno's death, making it difficult to predict whether he would have approved of a left version of postmodernism. Perhaps an engagement with the problematic of modernity and postmodernity (e.g., Habermas, 1981a) would have softened Adorno's commitment to purely aesthetic resistance or led him to reformulate that resistance in a more political-economic direction, like my work here. My version of critical theory is scarcely imaginable without Adorno's concept of negative dialectics (1973a), indeed without the example of his whole *oeuvre*.

But the tone of my discussion here is precisely the problem with theory today. People's search for pedigree becomes all-consuming; we forget the empirical and political issues of the day in favor of scholarship, the career capital of academics. Then again, intellectuals almost inevitably become academics in late capitalism. The intellectual as a social category is nearly archaic. To talk about the politics of intellectuality is really to talk about the relationship among academics, university, state and culture. My analysis here is a contribution to that discussion, although I need to extend that discussion into a fuller consideration of intellectuality and intellectual life today. Who/what is the postmodern intellectual?

## The Postmodern Intellectual

Above all, the postmodern intellectual is a writer; that is my theme. Whether writers today are intellectuals is another question. My answer is largely negative. Writers do everything but think, indentured to producers, publishers, studios, editors, department heads, promotion-and-tenure committees. I obviously include myself in this. Obscurantism is a virtually unavoidable outcome of academic discourse in the late-capitalist university. People like Jacoby (1987) who rail against academization are voices in the wilderness. But I decided to compose this chapter in a more pedestrian discourse than some of my earlier work and certainly than my intellectual heroes like Adorno. We must write *as if* there were an intelligent public capable not only of understanding what we are saying but of joining us in community-building dialogue.

This is to say that we must take Habermas' (1979) *ideal speech situation* seriously as a radical goal. In doing so, we must not exempt ourselves as intellectuals and writers from the requirement of public discourse; indeed, we prefigure the world of the future in what we do and write today, including how we treat our intimates and how we articulate our larger political aims. Habermas is right that it is impossible to understand our own political and cultural formation without having tackled Plato, Kant, Hegel, Marx, Freud, and Habermas himself. But Habermas wants dialogue chances and thus power to be democratized. Therefore his own discourse bears examination as a prefigurative medium. He only invites scorn by those who hold him out as an example of yet another phony radical unwilling to talk to the people in a language they can understand.

Above all, the postmodern intellectual will accept responsibility for creating the ideal speech situation and hence the democratic polity. Interestingly, American feminists have been more sensitive to the constitutive nature of their own discourse, indeed to the whole politics of language, than have most male leftists. This might reflect only the fact that Marxism derives canonically from the hallowed *oeuvre* of Marx and his epigones; feminism is only as old as yesterday and thus it poses fewer interpretive and devotional problematics (quickly being remedied by the involution of the French poststructuralist feminists!). But I suspect it reflects something deeper: American feminists may be more democratic than American and European male leftists, an issue addressed by those who trace the origins of feminism in the male-dominated New Left (e.g., Evans, 1980).

The parallel between western Marxism, and particularly critical theory, and feminism has been noted before (Marshall, 1988; Agger 1991b). But critical theorists, with few notable exceptions, have been unable or unwilling to jettison their own élite symbolic codes for more accessible ones; they have never overrated the agitational possibilities of critical theory. And American feminists, although more discursively democratic, have been short on totalizing social theory, frequently failing to articulate their own critique of male supremacy in terms of a larger theory of class, gender and race interrelations. This has slowly begun to change, especially where critical theorists and feminist theorists are starting to recognize not only their own possible political mutuality but the extraordinary fact that their critiques of sexist capitalism are very similar at root (e.g., Marshall, 1988; Fraser, 1989).

*The postmodern intellectual is post-specialist and post-élitist*, even if his or her theoretical discourse is sometimes fine-grained and complex. Where the world's difficulty provokes analytical difficulty, the postmodern intellectual must work as hard as possible to prevent difficult language from sedimenting itself into a code so impossibly restricted that public comprehension and hence consensus formation — political mobilization — are thwarted. That is the nub of the issue; intellectuals today fail to engage (and enrage) the public because they have either neglected or forgotten the political role of intellectual activity. Habermas, other critical theorists, left feminists, poststructuralists and postmodernists want to restore a decent, democratic public sphere. That is all the more reason why they must prevent the decline of their own discourse lest they merely reproduce hierarchies in their own lives and practice, notably the hierarchy of writers over readers. In the next section, I will discuss more concretely the nature of public voice. Here I want to consider just where intellectuals have failed to attend to the politically constitutive nature of their own discourse as a way of suggesting some remedies, below.

The modernist intellectual is typified by Marx, Beckett, Adorno, Benjamin, Beauvoir, Sartre, Habermas. The modernist intellectual feverishly wants things to change, to improve, and thus devotes his or her intellectual energy to dissecting and diagnosing the dismal present. Marx's engagement remains exemplary for this intellectual archetype. Where Marx in the *Manifesto* called working people to arms, suggesting to them their own world-historical opportunity for ending class society, in *Capital* he analyzed the functioning of capitalism in rigorously detailed terms, authoring Marxism as a dialectical science of society. Unfortunately, at least among Marxists and Marxologists, the second book has received much more interpretive attention than the first. After all, it is longer, denser, more susceptible to close hermeneutic work signalling devotion. And it purports to lay the foundation for Marxism as a systematic social theory or science. Similarly, Adorno's essays (e.g., 1967) blaze the way for his dense philosophical (1973) and aesthetic-theoretic (1984) works. They are thus read as preparatory, even if Adorno intended them as self-sufficient in their own right.

Modernist left scholarship almost inevitably intends itself as a dialogue with other intellectual specialists. Most fail to examine or counteract the irony that these very leftists argue for the democratization of dialogue chances. Modernist intellectuals fail to descend from the rarefied heights of scholarship, interpretation and historiography to the terra firma of public discourse. Indeed, many of us on the critical left have become adept at defending our aloofness in terms of our own empirical theories of late capitalism that explain the cooptation of intellectual work in convincing terms (e.g., Marcuse's 1964 *One-Dimensional Man*). Although this defense is credible, it fails to move beyond itself toward a theoretical practice — public discourse — that empowers non-specialists to join the debates.

At one level, then, the postmodern intellectual must deal with the hierarchy of intellectuals over citizens in much the way Marx and Gramsci (1971) first formulated the problem. Marx prophesied an all-round individual capable of shifting from one role to another without taking on their life-long imprints (Marx and Engels, 1947); Gramsci suggested an organic intellectual devoted to a 'philosophy of praxis' that explicates the necessity of democratizing intellectuality. These modernists took seriously their own responsibility for transcending the very world making them writers and others readers. That is why both Marx and Gramsci took pains to elaborate the political role of radical intellectuals.

Although the Frankfurt theorists were also committed to a democratic public sphere (e.g., Habermas, 1975; Keane, 1984), they were less convinced than Marx and Gramsci that modernity could be rearranged in significant ways. If Marx was an early modernist, Adorno was a high or late modernist, if not sufficiently postmodern in the way he theorized the relation between intellectuals and public life. And if Adorno was a late modernist, Habermas is a late-late modernist, given the circumlocutions of his highly byzantine critical theory. Irony abounds here for Habermas (1981a) was among the first to take Lyotard to task for betraying the project of the Enlightenment and hence of modernity. Perhaps he realizes that his commitment to ideal speech and his inability to engage in it are clearly contradictory! I fully agree with his condemnation of Lyotard's postmodernism as neoconservative in its thoroughgoing anti-Marxism.

A genuinely postmodern intellectual would not have to recant the radical theories and perspectives of earlier modernists, notably Marx and Marxists. In fact, I believe that one cannot inhabit the contemporary world and hope to improve it without being powerfully energized by the modernist impulse, dating all the way back to the Enlightenment. Nietzsche's critique of the Enlightenment only goes so far. At a certain point, his negation must be negated and we must salvage what we can from the *philosophes'* vision of a new world, albeit refusing Comte's imagery of a benevolent reign of technocrats. Modernism, however, fails precisely where it is élitist; modernists in one way or another endorse vanguardism — the notion that societies will only change where small groups of leaders enforce discipline on the masses, leading them out of the wilderness. In this sense, modernism inhibits democracy.

The issue is not whether the masses need leadership, education, enlightenment. That is certainly not arguable in the era of the culture industry and authoritarian state (Horkheimer, 1973). But modernist intellectuals embrace their own vanguard roles too cavalierly, unself-consciously lapsing into esoteric language that only perpetuates itself 'after' the revolution, in spite of Marx's, Gramsci's and Freire's warnings to the contrary. Indeed, for Marxist intellectuals to warn themselves and others against vanguardism is thoroughly ironic for it was Marxism itself that gave birth to the notion of ideology-critique, if also to the notion of educating the educator, ever the left-modernist dilemma. We can read Marx in a host of different ways. I choose to read Marx as humble before the task of political education. I think he understood how precarious it was for intellectuals and tacticians to exploit the communicative and intellectual incompetence of the masses, especially on the part of those who proclaimed that the élitist state would wither away after capitalism.

But, after Marx, we have Marxists, feminists, critical theorists, poststructuralists and postmodernists who do not heed his warning. We assume that educating-the-educator is no longer problematic since we all sport doctoral degrees from the finest institutions of higher education, have healthy curricula vitae full of erudite publications, and possess the gift of professional gab which we refine at professional meetings and in the classroom. *Theory talk is inevitably rarefied these days, only compounding the problem of political education.* This is the legacy of modernism to which a genuinely radical postmodernism must be a response. Modernist theorizing is so Apollonian, so elevated, that virtually no one can climb these mighty peaks without years of acclimation, not just trusty road-maps. Unavoidably, this entombs theoretical conversation in the university, ensuring that theory itself will not help revivify the public sphere — ever our most important political agenda.

Even to utter these thoughts will earn the disrespect of my left colleagues who have worked so hard to learn Kant, Hegel, Marx, Freud, Frankfurt, deconstruction, feminism. I am not pulling rank, although I have spent my share of time sweating through this arduous apprenticeship. But there is something profoundly unreflexive about theory that forgets its own connection to the body politic (O'Neill, 1972c), even hastening the dissolution of this connection. Modernity is permeated by expert cultures disempowering those on the outside.

The most constitutive expert culture is called capitalism, as Marx recognized, but there are others, too. One of the aims of an interdisciplinary critical theory is precisely to weave together a narrative about how these expert cultures fit together and, together, sustain themselves. We use a variety of terms like capitalism, sexism and racism to do this job. But we must also attend to critical theory itself as an expert culture that inhibits its own democratization, hence democracy in general.

This is less a doctrinal question than one of temperament. My left comrades are committed to democracy as a radical endpoint. But too few of them are genuinely democratic in spirit; hence they ignore the contribution their own argot makes to hierarchy, empowering only those who speak and write European high theory. Theory has become an academic specialty, not a mode of address to the political world. How many theorists address the flesh-and-blood individuals who could not care less about Kristeva and Habermas but care desperately that the world be a less hellish place? Theory is a modernist project in that it does not doubt the legitimacy of its own epistemological privilege. Left theorists ironically would end capitalist modernity by professionalizing and specializing their discourse even further. But this only further marginalizes critical theory as well as entrenching expertise.

Postmodern intellectuals must question the contribution of intellectual and political modernism to the very world we all profess to oppose. At the same time, we must not recant the liberating modernism of the Enlightenment, Marxism, feminism etc. The alternative to capitalist modernity, with its self-perpetuating expert cultures, is not counter-modernity — a left Luddism. The only suitable alternative is a rethinking of the modern in a way that makes writers responsible for their own agitational and rhetorical stance toward the masses. Whether this means we should simply democratize our language is a question I take up shortly, in this chapter's final section. I suspect it is not as simple as that for theory must overcome the tendency of all intellectuality since the Greeks to seal itself off hermetically from the ebb and flow of everyday life. Even Marxists have not learned enough from Marx about how to engage theory with the non-expert cultures occupied by most of the world's billions in order to change the very valence of intellectuality, making it 'committed' in Sartre's (1965b) terms.

The postmodern intellectual must address his or her public role politically; this inevitably requires some degree of de-academization, of distancing from the lifeworld of professional journals, books, conferences, classrooms. I am not suggesting that intellectuals deny their intellectuality, embracing whatever excrescence of so-called popular culture is most current or profitable. American survey research knows nearly everything there is to know about public opinion. Instead, postmodern intellectuals must find a way to offer their discourse as a rule of societal reconstruction, neither shrinking from analytical difficulty and abstraction nor ignoring the tendency of theory itself to become a hierarchical language game — just another expert culture to which access is granted through credentialing processes. Postmodern intellectuality must invent itself, and thus a whole new world, without renouncing the liberating tendency of genuine modernism.

## An Agenda of Radical Cultural Studies

This suggests a postmodern research agenda to be formulated in a democratizing rhetoric that I call *the public voice.* Let me describe this agenda and then conclude with a few comments about the public voice. Of course, these two things are inseparable; I am not distancing the topics of radical writing from writing itself. Methodology will not win the day, especially where methodology has itself become a suffocating expert culture. Programmatism must already write in the voice it recommends. That is one of the key postmodern insights. Writing is already a social practice; it creates a new public world through its own prefigurative example as a form of life. Although writing is not all of politics, textual politics is definitely an arena and vehicle of the political, especially in a fast capitalism in which images, concepts, advertising dominate our public discourse. Ignoring cultural politics is self-defeating for those who would both decode and transform the public sphere.

In this sense, we theorists must cease our exhaustive and exhausting exegetical work (haven't we learned enough already about the classics of high theory?) and instead turn our attention to critiques of the culture industry — political education, critique of ideology or consciousness raising. Theoretical lineage matters less than the deconstructive practice of opening seemingly deauthored cultural texts to the reality of their own artifice, thus inviting new texts; I have done this with regard to positivist social science (Agger, 1989b). One of the central claims of a radical postmodernism is that cultural discourses do not just fall from the sky but can be traced backward to authorial gestures that could have been made differently. In this sense, postmodernism explodes the distinction between high and low culture, or at least renders that distinction inherently dialectical at a time when it is difficult to draw a clear line between them. The culture industry mobilizes all sorts of texts against the threat of utopian imagination — popular culture more than high culture, in fact. For this reason, a radical cultural studies must address these entwining texts as political practices, refusing to ignore them simply because they are pedestrian. Their pedestrian character is precisely their efficacy when it comes to shutting down political imagination.

Deconstruction can become a vital critical methodology once liberated from its fetishism in English departments as yet another interpretive perspective on the literary canon. Derrida meant for deconstruction to undo the hidden contradictions and ironies of texts that are otherwise smoothly integrated into the world as the truths they purport to contain. Deconstruction lets authorial artifice shine through, revealing, for example, network television to be a corrigible, deliberate product of busy scribes and not the intractable piece of nature it often appears to be, as close to hand as the remote-control channel changer. As such, by 'reading' television (e.g., Miller, 1988) through the deconstructive lens of radical cultural studies we can not only undo its hold on us but even *rewrite* it, or at least formulate a possible television appropriate to a socialist-feminist-postmodernist society.

I have formulated my version of cultural studies as literary political economy, thus stressing the connection between the study of literary commodification on the one hand and literary hegemony on the other. These things are fundamentally inseparable. Television's thirst for profit is reflected in, and reproduces, the way in which television is a screen of power (T. Luke, 1989) basically vitiating critical intelligence and utopian imagination. My discussion of textual politics here demonstrates the possible relevance of literary political economy to a larger discussion of the future of the public sphere especially as I focus on the nature and status of the postmodern intellectual.

## The Public Voice

Let me return to the role of postmodern intellectuals, having suggested that our primary political work will fall under the rubric of radical cultural studies (once armed with literary political economy). As I indicated, to programmatize a postmodern research agenda is absolutely inseparable from a discussion of (and in) the postmodern critical voice — the language game of postmodernity, one might say. I have already lamented the tendency for modernist intellectuals to deny their own embeddedness in a self-reproducing expert culture, suggesting by implication a postmodern intellectuality opposed to the cult of its own expertise. At some level, we must admit that intellectuals are still occupants of a rare and privileged social stratum and thus have a peculiar political opportunity unavailable to almost everyone else. Political education assumes that some need education more than others; my point here is that political educators — postmodern intellectuals — must never forget that their discourse itself, notably its attitude toward its own monologic tendencies, has extraordinarily powerful implications for the 'content' of the education to be imparted. It is one thing to preach democracy; it is quite another to preach democracy democratically, as if one is really willing to generalize one's communicative competence over a whole society such that readers become writers, hence efficacious and critical citizens.

Can we meaningfully talk of intellectuals as a distinct social stratum when everyone is capable of engaging in creative intellectual discourse or simply public speech? I think not, although we are very far from that day. How many radical intellectuals are willing to relinquish their own privilege? How many really embrace lifeworld-grounded ideal speech — democracy — in Habermas' terms? Fewer than one would expect if one focuses on radicals' unwillingness to open up their self-perpetuating rhetoric. This is to understand left obscurantism as a purposeful strategy and not just an occupational hazard. Political vanguardism plays out on rhetorical and epistemological levels.

Postmodern intellectual discourse is just discourse itself — public speech spoken in an accessibly public voice. In this sense, discourse is an antidote to left fascism. Let me define public voice, recognizing that any definition of that voice must already speak in it. *By public voice I am referring to the way postmodern discourse is non-technical but nonetheless can understand, and even use, technical language where necessary: public voice expertly subverts its own expert culture,* broadening communicative competence as well as utopian imagination far beyond its own academic ranks.

It is a mistake to confuse public voice with ordinary language; ordinary language is riddled with unconsciousness, acquiescence, lapses and contradictions where public voice comprehends the deformation of discourse in thoroughly political terms. British analytic philosophers who mute the esoteric tones of high theory do so not in order to create the ideal speech situation but simply to undercut radical insight delivered complexly. Public voice does not shrink from difficulty or abstraction but labors hard to make these maximally accessible, in the process educating itself about its own unreflected reliance on categories and catechism. Too many theorists use their technical conceptual apparatus without really thinking about the utility of their neologisms. Theory deconstructs itself where it tries to break its own dependence on a theoretical apparatus that essentially robs thought of vitality. We must try to remember what sharp concepts meant before they became dulled by their ceaseless repetition. Words like domination, oppression, freedom, liberation can be restored to meaningfulness if we work hard to counteract their tendency to become clichés, used whenever we cannot solve intellectual and political problems in their own terms.

Public voice abhors the decline of discourse into clichés, although it does not for that reason dispense with all technical language, as intellectual Luddites might. As Freire (1970) amply demonstrated, the process of 'conscientization' requires a political pedagogy empowering the disempowered to understand and use languages heretofore reserved for élites. Expert culture in defending its own privilege gives expertise a bad name, as much on the left as in the mainstream. There is simply no excuse for theorists to invest so much in their own rhetoric that they forget how to think beyond the received wisdom of their particular language games. I could repeat terms like 'decline of discourse' or 'literary political economy' a million times without getting them genuinely to solve intellectual problems. In my recent work, including this book, I have tried to write in a way that invites the citizen-reader to develop a facility with the occasional theoretical digressions required to raise my writing from mere description to analysis and diagnosis. After all, against Lyotard's postmodernism, the world's totality cannot be grasped without the aid of totalizing categories like exploitation, domination, hegemony and patriarchy.

This is a delicate balance: on the one hand, we must use abstract concepts to understand the mammoth structuring forces invading and constituting our lives. On the other hand, we must avoid the ritualization of these categories lest they cease to do useful analytical work. Most important, we must *democratize expert cultures of all sorts*, including the culture of theory. This democratization does not just flatten theory talk into prosaic terms of everyday usage; that would only rob critical categories of their diagnostic ability. Rather, my conception of self-deconstructing/democratizing theory trades on theoretical insights without turning theory itself into a new force of mystification. Democratizing expert language reinvents language, overcoming the distinction between quotidian discourse and a more rarefied code heretofore monopolized by jealous professionals, including the left.

This reinvention of language is easier said than done. I fully intend this work to contribute to that reinvention, moving back and forth between theory and a lower-level discourse unashamed of its popular nature. The decline of discourse will be reversed only if we transform popular culture so that it incorporates heretofore recondite elements of expert discourse, *transvaluing the very distinction between lay and expert rationalities*, the project of postmodern intellectuals. It is a profoundly political project today given the enormous power of the culture industry and its textual politics. It takes little rigorous research to show that television, journalism, science have constitutive roles in shaping the body politic and thus in perpetuating an unequal distribution of wealth and power. Writers write discourse commodified and displaced into the 'texts' of popular and academic culture. As such, they could reinvent these texts as well as the whole world to which they are addresses.

I am not simply saying that postmodern writers will comprise a new vanguard for that whole military metaphor of tactics and conquest is inappropriate to radical democracy. Yet writers matter because writing matters; we who compose are firmly ensconced in literary political economy, which is part of a larger political economy generally. Our words are converted into economic, cultural and career capital. They have enormous political impact if what we write is sucked into the vortex of the culture industry both as a mode of production and reproduction. A playful deconstructor might say that our words constitute a cultural *vortext*. In any case, writers, including academics, constitute an important class and cultural fraction. Ideology is written through us and thus it could be written differently. Of course, solitary literary heroism will have little impact on the machine of cultural production. It is precisely for that reason that I call for critical writers to develop a public voice with which to enter into dialogue with those convinced that the present social order is inherently intractable or, as some say, postmodern.

Ultimately, the problem with postmodernism as a discourse is that it pretends too clean a rupture between the fluid period of industrializing modernity and the present period of hardened postmodernity. One cannot date or periodize the shift between the two anymore than one can specify the transition between feudalism and modernity. Certainly postmodernity did not dawn on the morning after the publication of Lyotard's *The Postmodern Condition: A Report on Knowledge*. Existentialism reminds us that history is open; there are no certainties, either about the eternity of social perfection or the inevitability of decline. Instead, history is indeterminate, as such susceptible to transformations. Dialecticians — better, call us ironists — recognize that in transforming the world we are ourselves transformed. Or, more aptly, we cannot change things without working to change ourselves in the process. Otherwise, change is chimerical; things stay the same, albeit under different flags, different regimes.

I would prefer to see modernity and postmodernity as a continuum, a perpetual set of possibilities. We will not escape modernity unless we fry and chill ourselves into nuclear winter, the only conceivable end-of-history. Short of that, we will face a future somehow continuous with the past and present and yet also open to being radically rerouted. Writing as public speech is a way of inserting ourselves into history, a way of making a difference. In any case, capitalism requires writing in order to script the products, lifestyles and imagination appropriate to it. Commodities must be textualized just as texts become commodities themselves. Otherwise, they will fail to traffic in the marketplace, appearing to be the false needs (Marcuse, 1964; Heller, 1976; Leiss, 1976) they really are. And without a restless, frenetic consumerism, capitalism grinds to a halt, just as Marx perspicaciously foresaw. At root, literary political economy exists to prime the general economy (in which texts, too, acquire exchange value or sign value).

It is tempting to end this chapter by methodologizing my notion of public voice, offering inflexible criteria by which we can judge talk as public or not. But that is foreign to the dialogical, dialectical project of genuine discourse, which responds to the world and to other interlocutors in a comprehensible, comprehending sense making. We must work hard to be understood, just as we want to raise the level of understanding. A nation that watches *Miami Vice* and *White Christmas*, reads *People* and tabloids, and votes for Ronald Reagan and then the Bush-Quayle ticket must be addressed in its own pedestrian terms, although without forgetting that the point of public discourse is to remake the polity by democratizing expert culture (hence blurring the boundary between lay and expert rationalities).

This is political education in the best sense of the word. But that is not to endorse didacticism any more than it is to eschew polemic and passion. One of the left's historic problems has been its inflexibility with regard to what is now tellingly called political correctness. Apart from some general commitments to life, liberty and social justice, public life necessarily defies the institutional ritualism that all too quickly leads to a combination of tyranny and mass apathy. There are no singular or simple answers to what ails us apart from some general observations about the colonizing imperatives of capital, patriarchy, racism and the domination of nature (e.g., Habermas 1984, 1987b). The most pressing political work ahead is the critique of ideology, revealing the aporias of literary claims about the rationality of reality. We literary workers must deconstruct cultural claims made on behalf of the present order of things as a way of reauthoring the world.

We must recognize that we are being used as conduits of ideology and ontology. As I discussed in chapter 5, it seems that books (scripts, advertisements, journal articles etc.) write authors, not the other way around. Literary political economy fosters this illusion; in fact, writers write the texts of ideology further diminishing our public competence to think, speak, write and act in ways that answer to our fundamental human needs. No matter how impenetrable the dense web of capitalist textual politics, no matter how disempowered the solitary author, *ideology does not fall from the sky; it is composed by people working in the service of ideology, the busy wage slaves of the culture industry*. Even to recognize this is a step in the right direction, toward a public literary culture. Of course, recognizing it is not enough. We must reauthor the whole public world, not just theorize about what is going wrong.

In this sense, writers who attain public voice must narrate the world anew, suggesting heretofore suppressed social possibilities in believable, convincing terms. Marxists and to a lesser extent feminists make little headway in North America because their scant imageries of a different world are too remote from North American experience. The working-class white people and minorities who voted for Reagan and Bush are not addressed by political education relying heavily on European left theory; no matter how comprehensible, *The Communist Manifesto* does not play in Peoria. It likely never will. American leftism (Agger, 1979a; Kann, 1982) must speak American. That is, we on the left must pay attention to the thematic issues of our time, as well as to the current nadir of political consciousness, and not hope to transmit the truths of high European social theory by injection or hypnotism. Although we have learned from Marx, Lukács, Frankfurt,

Gramsci, feminism, we must cease an exegetical mode of political education. Even if ordinary working-class and middle-class Americans would sit still for courses in the Basic Texts of Modern Marxism, the point is not to impart book knowledge of these canonical writers and texts but to help average Americans apply notions like domination, hegemony and alienation to their own daily lives and then to reinvent their sense of what is possible.

Ultimately, our political education will be a dismal failure if we do not empower these dulled readers to become writers themselves. Everyone can learn the public voice, at least to the extent to which people begin to resist élite culture on the local level. If this sounds like a Tocqueville version of American Marxism and feminism, so be it. The New England town meeting is our own equivalent of the Paris Commune and we must respect this difference lest we doom ourselves to irrelevance. This does not mean that we theorists and writers should recant the analytical and diagnostic apparatus of Marxism-feminism but only that we must generalize the liberatory insights of this tradition to a generic public practice; here, I call it public voice, although, obviously, we could name it differently.

The notion that everyone can and must become writers — public speakers — is genuinely radicalizing at a time when virtually everyone capitulates to the imperatives imposed on them by experts. Critical theorists (e.g., Mueller, 1973; Wellmer, 1976; Habermas, 1979, 1984, 1987b) have made communication thematic precisely because the monopoly of wealth and power is reinforced, and reinforces, the monopoly of information, expertise and dialogue chances. The culture industry both creates false needs and diverts us from true needs. To the extent to which culture could be scripted differently, the notion that everyone can produce culture is potentially powerful. A radical version of cultural studies represents what I think is most enduring about the long legacy of critical theory since Marx. But it is imperative that cultural studies resist its own academization; works about culture written by and for other specialists only compound the problem. For this reason, critical theorists must carefully examine their own unreflected reliance on élite discourse. Critical theory can and must be written in a new voice; I have called this the public voice, suggesting the political relevance of critical theory at a time when both criticism and theory are only academic projects. Reversing the decline of discourse begins at home.

In this chapter I have made use of postmodernism as a version of critical theory, returning to my earlier attempt in this book to establish the grounds for a feminist postmodern critical theory. Unfortunately, postmodernism has tended to lose its sharp critical edge, becoming an establishmentarian ideology used to disqualify radical social change. As Habermas (1981a) noted, postmodernity is celebrated as the end of ideology, auguring an eternal present in which possessive individualists turn away from the grand narratives (Lyotard, 1984) of social change and instead turn inward. The cosmopolitan, cynical self shuns politics as irremediably venal. This postmodernism is especially characteristic of public life in an age of decline. In the next chapter, I address this phenomenon, viewing an affirmative, mainstream postmodernism itself as a social problem that blocks transformative projects.

# Chapter 10

# Postmodernity as a Social Problem

In this concluding chapter I caution against an embrace of post-modernism, even though I have self-consciously affiliated myself to a critical theory that makes ample use of certain postmodern as well as feminist insights. Postmodernism in its establishment versions ignores social problems of the public sphere altogether, resolving postmodern anxiety with doses of commodities and commodified popular culture. The postmodernism hawked on every yuppie street-corner must be rejected by those seriously concerned with transforming large-scale social structures. In fast capitalism, cultural and intellectual trends are ephemeral, the postmodernism craze included. Unfortunately, the establishment postmodernism so prevalent today blocks attempts to reformulate a radical vocabulary of social change, among both femin-ists and Marxists. In this final chapter, I examine the modalities of the culture industry's own postmodernism which, as I conclude, is far removed from the radical Nietzschean transvaluation of all values that converges with what Marxists later called the critique of ideology. Instead of being critique of ideology, which it could be in its best sense, an affirmative postmodernism lamely celebrates the end of ideology, hence hastening it.

## Is Postmodernism the Solution or the Problem?

Postmodernism is just about the hottest cultural and intellectual trend around. People across the humanities and social sciences publish articles and books and organize conferences and panels on postmodernism. 'Pomo' has become a minor cottage industry, giving bored post-leftist academics something new to do and read. Although, as I have demon-strated in this book, there is a great deal to be said about the more theoretical versions of postmodernism that seriously engage with world-historical issues of social theory and social change, I am more concerned in this chapter with postmodernism as ideology — or, more precisely, with postmodernism as the end of ideology, which it intends to be. Here I am not talking mainly about the literate post-modernisms of Baudrillard (1983), Lyotard (1984) and Foucault (1976, 1977, 1980), although in this chapter I allude to these people in passing, but about the postmodernism of the American cultural establishment and culture industry — what I am calling a *New York Times* postmodernism (see Gitlin, 1988). This concluding chapter is designed as a political introduction to the fads and fashions of *New York Times* postmodernism. I am mostly dismissive of this version of postmodernism, although I have suggested repeatedly in this book that one can merge certain postmodern insights with the political and theoretical agenda of the Frankfurt School, neo-Marxism and feminism. I am increasingly convinced that the mainstream discourse of postmodernism, like those of *perestroika* and post-Marxism, is merely the latest, trendiest attack on the left. I want to conclude this book by suggesting some ways in which postmodernism not only ignores social problems but becomes a problem in its own right.

My critique will possibly be heard as yet another attack on heterodox European theory that breaks the mold of Marxism-Leninism. But we must not be bound by the simplistic dichotomies that force us to choose between Marxism and postmodernism. One can (and must!) fashion a Marxist version of postmodernism as well as a postmodern Marxism that genuinely contributes critical insights to new social movements. Aronowitz (1990), Huyssen (1986), Kellner (1989b), (Best and Kellner, 1990), Jameson (1981), T. Luke (1989), Fraser (1989) and I (1990) have offered examples of this convergence. Here, I criticize an establishment version of postmodernism in order to demonstrate the affinity between a peculiarly uncritical post-modernism, on the one hand, and perennial bourgeois social thought, on the other. Intellectual fads must be resisted and debunked, the hoopla surrounding postmodernism especially. This does not preclude a serious engagement with the discourse of the postmodern, which remains one of the most exciting theoretical challenges. It simply acknowledges that such engagements do not typify the celebration of postmodernism currently taking place across the university as well as in mainstream culture at large. Like all celebrations, this one must be viewed skeptically, especially from the vantage point of critical social theory.

Here I consider the tendencies of a glitzy, Manhattanized post-modernism to monopolize the terrain of cultural production and reception, as well as of the capitalist built environment. One finds postmodernism as an identifying slogan in nearly every avant-garde bookstore, magazine, television show and movie as well as in the buildings and malls housing cultural producers and consumers. A stroll through Soho and Tribeca in New York or along Queen Street West in Toronto indicates the cultural hegemony of postmodernism, where hipsters dressed in black stroll and shop and dine under the *Zeitgeist* of the postmodern, whatever that is supposed to mean.

Postmodernism does mean something in these formulations and manifestations; it represents a thoroughgoing aversion to political discussion and contestation, embodying the narcissism addressed by Lasch (1979) as early as the late 1970s.

It is not strictly accurate to conflate Lyotard's (1984) nuanced, if relentless, critique of Marxist grand narratives with the mannered postmodernism of the New York galleries, clubs and critics. At least, Lyotard, like Daniel Bell (1976) before him, was aware of Marxism, recognizing it is a genuine subversion of capitalist pluralism. Thus, one could argue with Lyotard in his own terms, as Habermas (1981a) has done. The people who sell and live postmodernism in the US do not inflate their participation in the *Zeitgeist* with a serious ideological critique of the left. In fact, they do not view themselves in terms of a philosophy of history at all. For them, postmodernism is largely a consumer movement.

Where in the preceding chapter I distinguished between Lyotard's version of Bell's end-of-ideology and postindustrial-society theses, on the one hand, and a radicalized postmodernism with a political intent, on the other, here I want to discuss a third variant of postmodernism that in some respects is really a subcategory of Lyotard's neoconservative version, although without the philosophical patina of an engagement with Nietzsche and Heidegger. This *New York Times* version of postmodernism is simply not theoretical enough to warrant extended discussion as a full-fledged version of cultural and social theory, although it is prevalent as a cultural attitude today. It is the sort of postmodernism found in *Rolling Stone*, mentioned in the *Times*, developed in *New Yorker*, and cited in urbane Sunday supplement pieces on the cultural beat as well as in various critical and trade publications on the arts. This *NYT* postmodernism epitomizes a range of cultural attitudes and gestures encoding deeper political content. Of course, the essence of postmodernism is to conceal politics underneath the veneer of the rejection of politics, now as before a posture of value freedom. Unlike the more self-consciously ideological approaches of Lyotard and Bell, this *NYT* postmodernism is not defined by its opposition to left-wing radicalism. Rather, it is signified by Lasch's (1979) narcissism, Macpherson's (1962) possessive individualism and Marcuse's (1955) repressive desublimation. Not that these are texts read by *NYT* postmodernists! But they help explain some of the valences of this postmodernism especially as it issues in the distinctive cultural creation and criticism typical of this perspective. In the rest of this chapter, I will itemize some of the features of this untheorized postmodernism in order to uncover its secret political affiliations.

## Modalities of Affirmative Postmodernism

*NYT* postmodernism rejects political discourse as out of date, shabby, irrelevant. Politics is not a venue of meaning because all political movements and personalities are viewed as venal to the point of Nixonian absurdity. One might periodize *NYT* postmodernism as post-Watergate, although there were stirrings of this postmodernism in the counterculture, further demonstrating a certain distance between *NYT* postmodernism and Bell's end-of-ideology perspective, especially as rendered in his (1976) book *The Cultural Contradictions of Capitalism*. As Gitlin (1987) indicates, one must divide the 1960s into a genuinely political rump (e.g., the Port Huron statement of the early SDS) and a depoliticized counterculture devoted to many of the same cultural significations as *NYT* postmodernism.

The aversion to politics is more temperamental than doctrinal. Since Marxism is not a specter haunting the US, American postmodernism, unlike the French variety, does not take its bearings from a considered rejection of Marxism. Again, one is tempted to periodize this postmodern denial of the political as a particular feature of the post-baby boom generation. But that is strictly incorrect. Yuppies, born in the post-war baby-boom, are quintessentially postmodern in their consumerist individualism and political cynicism, and they derive whatever semblance of theoreticity they possess from periodicals like *The Times* and *Esquire* as well as from television shows like *Thirtysomething*. The apolitical post-baby boom cohort is no more apolitical than its Yuppie predecessors. The only difference perhaps is that Yuppies can fall back on the rhetoric of the 1960s as disingenuous proof of their social commitments — disingenuous, because the lion's share of baby-boomers in the 1960s were dope-smoking conformists and not serious political rebels.

*NYT* postmodernism endorses consumer capitalism and hence, by implication, rejects the possibility of radical social change — e.g., socialism. If issues of social change are addressed at all, they are addressed piecemeal. A more structural radicalism is regarded as hubris. Radicals themselves are branded as failed personalities somehow still mired in the adolescent passions of the 1960s. Although in other respects *NYT* postmodernism places value on retro gestures that encompass the less political manifestations of the counterculture (like the Rolling Stones appearing in Budweiser ads and McCartney shilling for VISA cards), the angry radicalism of the 1960s is dismissed as both antediluvian and excessive. At best, mainstream postmodernism is liberal on social issues like a woman's right to have an abortion, the First Amendment and the environment but conservative on fiscal matters.

*NYT* postmodernism celebrates popular culture unashamedly, failing to make distinctions (which are rejected as modernist and mandarin). This robs postmodernism of the ability to expose and debunk the political codes of culture. Postmodern cultural criticism adds value to the popular, which is thoroughly commodified. This valorization of popular culture reinforces a common generational experience of the world, albeit mass-mediated, which substitutes for real community. Every baby-boomer understands that we are defined by common televisual events like the broadcast of the Kennedy assassinations or the first moonwalk. But what we want to remember about these collective experiences are not simply the events themselves but the text and texture of the cultural experience of identity formation watching Dan Rather break the first news from Dallas and living the event from Friday through the funeral cortège. These experiences are focused retrospectively not on what they were and what they meant but on the ways they formed us, affording us both identity and meaning. My own adolescence, which is typical in this respect, can be reproduced diachronically in terms of how the mass-mediated unfolding of these events and experiences paralleled and signified my own passage through successive stages of the life cycle, especially adolescence. A pedestrianized, depoliticized postmodernism helps us reexperience these mass-mediated public events for their contributions to our own ego formation, which is threatened by all of the colonizing forces threatening to turn us into what Lasch (1984), borrowing from the Frankfurt School, called minimal selves.

Although I decry this banalization of postmodern cultural criticism, especially where I (Agger, 1991a) contend that a radical cultural studies is the single best incarnation of the erstwhile critique of ideology, there is no denying the impact of this sort of retrospectively self-referential analysis of culture. Like most baby-boomers, I too reexperience myself in terms of my participation in these aspects of the popular, although for me most of these events take on a more political significance inasmuch as they help me chronicle my own formation as a social critic, not a contented Yuppie. One of the reasons why academic baby-boomers are attracted to cultural studies is because we experience our own selfhoods in terms of their constitution by the popular, refracted through the retrospective analysis of these public spectacles in which we can relocate central aspects of our ego formation.

There is nothing wrong with wanting to understand one's own constitution by the popular, especially where the popular encodes deep political meanings. For example, the television to which we were exposed in the 1950s and 1960s tried to turn us into men, women, parents, citizens and consumers. But *NYT* postmodernism prevents us from critically examining our differential experiences of the popular as well as the hierarchies of access and accumulation imbedded in it. It is far more important that the media presented a manufactured Vietnam war than that we came of age watching the coverage of the Tet offensive, which we then insert retrospectively into the reconstructed pastiche of our identity formation — just another relativized cultural experience that we examine self-referentially but not also in terms of the million Vietnamese who died during the war.

The reexperience of the formation of self through pop-culture analysis is less important than the critical evaluation of ways in which the popular is itself a differential field that not only constitutes us but also deceives us in fundamental respects. After all, the mass-mediation of social reality proceeds apace; the lessons we learn about the spectacularization of the 1960s (see Debord, 1972) can be applied today in helping us resist the most insidious aspects of cultural and personality formation, as well as the deflection of political mobilization, at the hands of popular culture. As I develop in my (1991a) book *Cultural Studies as Critical Theory*, a radical cultural studies can help us read and resist mass culture as what Adorno (1973: p. 406) called 'an objective context of delusion.'

*NYT* postmodernism purposely replaces substance with style, installing ironic detachment as the central social value. But neither cynicism nor irony is an appropriate political posture, especially where so much is going wrong. Both accelerate the venality of politics and the commodification of public discourse. Post-baby boomers are especially impervious to social problems, which they perceive to have little relationship to their own lives devoted to the consumption and celebration of commodified popular culture. Teachers of social science confront a growing psychologism on the part of students, which inures them to larger structural understandings of what is going wrong. We cannot simply lay this episodically at the door of the Reagan and Thatcher regimes, as some critics do. Certainly the 1980s were not an aberration in the sense that they are now over and will not reoccur. The privatization of social issues is part and parcel of capitalism. We noticed this self-aggrandizing privatization during the 1980s because it was especially pronounced in the images of the homeless huddled outside Trump Tower. Some leftist critics of this socio-political ennui blamed it on the putatively new ideology of postmodernism, failing to recognize that narcissism and possessive individualism are ways in which capitalism defends itself against the threat of collective insurrection.

As I noted earlier, *NYT* postmodernism has a soft spot for the environment. It is easy for Yuppie and post-Yuppie possessive individualists to relate to the degradation of the built and natural environments because they relate so obsessively to commodities. Ironically, postmodern environmentalism commodifies environmentalism while indicting the commodification of the environment. Witness the numerous corporate tie-ins to the environmental movement; companies sell environmental awareness as proof of their own social concern. This is not to deny the possibility of a radicalized environmentalism (see Leiss, 1972) but only to note the self-contradictory postmodernization of environmentalism in the context of capitalist consumerism.

## Postmodernism, Post-Marxism, Postindustrialism

These four features of an affirmative postmodernism contribute to the blockage of a genuine radical cultural critique that can intervene in the cultural field as a counterhegemonic force of its own, which is the central purpose of my version of critical theory presented in this book. The postmodernization of everyday life is a thin veneer for its further depoliticization, which has been gathering momentum since the collapse of the First International and the dream of an international socialist revolution. The postmodernism of shopping malls and *Miami Vice* ends ideology yet again, defusing political disputation in the name of the so-called end of history — a warmed-over version of Bell's (1973) postindustrialism. Of course, neither ideology nor capitalism has ended, in spite of the ridiculous spectacularization of the 'end of communism', which, in fact, only signals the failure of Stalinist command economies that western Marxists have denounced for the past seventy years. Postmodernism does not best Marxism any more than *perestroika* does; it simply transmogrifies anti-Marxism into another cultural commodity, readily gobbled up by the cultural and political establishment.

Indeed, the end-of-ideology thesis, captured figurally and gesturally in the lived experience of postmodernity (see Harvey, 1989), props up capitalism by diverting attention from substantive social, economic and cultural alternatives. As Horkheimer and Adorno (1972) noted in the 1940s, the culture industry exists in large measure to represent capitalism as a rational social order, hence perpetuating the very commodification of all experience that gives the lie to the postulate of substantive rationality.

Horkheimer and Adorno were first exposed to Hollywood culture and American mass media in the 1940s, when they developed the theory of the culture industry. Where half a century ago ideology could be more readily debunked as egregious falsification, today ideology has gone underground, encoded in the Baudrillardian simulations (see Baudrillard, 1983) of what I (Agger, 1989a) have called fast capitalism, in which the boundary between the textual and material has virtually disappeared, disabling social criticism as a result. As I discussed in chapter 3, texts today commanding experience are not found between covers but dispersed in the imagery, infrastructure and discourse of a postmodernized everyday life — what Baudrillard (1983) calls hyperreality — in which people believe that we live at the edge of the end of history, in the eternal present posited by Nietzsche as the fateful destination of the Enlightenment gone wrong.

Nietzsche despised the linear liberalism and rationalism that enthroned itself mythologically as a new religion of positive thinking. But *NYT* postmodernists do not read Nietzsche. Thus, they cannot appreciate the ways Nietzsche grounds both the Frankfurt School's

Marxism, on the one hand, and the postmodernism of Lyotard and Foucault, on the other. The closest they get to Nietzsche is Ayn Rand, a central possessive-individualist culture hero. The *NYT* postmodernism that dominates our urban environment and its urbane cultural discourse celebrates what Nietzsche viewed as the antithesis of reason. Meaninglessness is frozen into a monument to capitalism, which is now neologistically called postmodernity. But capitalism is thoroughly modernist in its essential logic; postmodern architecture and culture only embellish a modernist public space with trivial borrowings from premodern epochs (see Gottdiener, 1991), producing the trivially different buildings that dominate the skylines of Manhattan, London, Houston and Atlanta. We have not yet entered a genuine postmodernity, which would have to be post-capitalist. We can make a halting step toward that genuine postmodernity by reversing the momentum of the postmodernizing culture industry that eschews ideology while perpetuating it at every turn.

The establishment postmodernism that I decry threatens to engulf postmodern tendencies in social science and the humanities. Although I and others have tried to borrow the more critical insights of postmodernism and poststructuralism in our own theorizing (e.g., see Fraser, 1989; Best and Kellner, 1990), I hesitate to endorse the postmodernization of sociology when postmodernism typically is yet another version of post-Marxism. This is not to say that Marxism is a monolith; the critical feminist-Marxism that I advocate gave up on state socialism long before it was fashionable on the American left to do so. The attempt to pit Marxism against postmodernism obscures their possible interpenetration and dialogue. Nevertheless, we who care about the structural roots of social problems should be on guard against an affirmative version of postmodernism at a time when the celebration of the so-called end of Marxism becomes what Hegel (1966: p. 70) called a 'bacchanalian whirl in which no member is not drunken'.

In this book, I have tried to blend postmodernism with other themes in critical theory and feminism in order to produce a useful critical theory of public life. As this chapter demonstrates, certain versions of postmodernism function ideologically where they oppose the very radicalism giving rise to my proposed theoretical synthesis. This demonstrates again that subversive ideas can be deployed against themselves when they are reduced to clichés. Notwithstanding that, I am hopeful that postmodernism, like feminism, poses a fundamental challenge to Marxism that can only be met by rethinking some basic Marxist positions on the relationship between discourse and social change. Like feminism, postmodernism helps Marxism strengthen itself at a time when the nineteenth-century prophesy of class struggle seems extremely remote from the passions and problematics of the day. I have attempted to preserve Marx's vision of a better society by formulating it in discourse-theoretic terms, with the aid of postmodernism and feminist theory. Against the commodified postmodernism discussed in this chapter, I believe that we can revivify the public sphere and transform our political agenda, but only if we rethink aspects of Marxism that have lost their vitality and relevance today. A feminist postmodern critical theory contributes to this rethinking, affording us a powerful perspective with which to address social problems of modernity and postmodernity — including theory's own obfuscation of these social problems. It remains to be seen whether feminist postmodern critical theorists can address the public in comprehensible, compelling terms, deacademizing their own discourse. I hope that my book has at least raised the possibility of this deacademization.

# References

ACKERMAN, B. (1980) *Social Justice in the Liberal State*, New Haven, Yale University Press.

ADORNO, T. (1945) 'A Social Critique of Radio Music', *Kenyon Review*, **8**, 2, pp. 208–17.

ADORNO, T. (1954) 'How to Look at Television', *Quarterly of Film, Radio and Television*, **3**, pp. 213–35.

ADORNO, T. (1967) *Prisms*, London, Neville Spearman.

ADORNO, T. (1969) 'Scientific Experiences of a European Scholar in America', in FLEMING, D. and BAILYN, B. (Eds) *The Intellectual Migration*, Cambridge, MA, Harvard University Press.

ADORNO, T. (1973) *Negative Dialectics*, New York, Seabury.

ADORNO, T. (1974a) *Minima Moralia*, London, New Left Books.

ADORNO, T. (1974b) 'The Stars Down to Earth: The Los Angeles Times Astrology Column: A Study in Secondary Superstition', *Telos*, **19**, pp. 13–90.

ADORNO, T. (1984) *Aesthetic Theory*, London, RKP.

ADORNO, T.W., ALBERT, H., DAHRENDORF, R., HABERMAS, J., PILOT, H. and POPPER, K. (1976) *The Positivist Dispute in German Sociology*, London, Heinemann.

ADORNO, T.W., FRENKEL-BRUNSWIK, E., LEVINSON, D. and SANFORD, R.N. (1950) *The Authoritarian Personality*, New York, Harper and Row.

AGGER, B. (1976a) 'On Happiness and the Damaged Life', in O'NEILL, J. (Ed.) *On Critical Theory*, New York, Seabury.

AGGER, B. (1976b) 'Marcuse and Habermas on New Science', *Polity*, **9**, 2, pp. 151–81.

AGGER, B. (1977a) 'Dialectical Sensibility I: Critical Theory, Scientism and Empiricism', *Canadian Journal of Political and Social Theory*, **1**, 1, pp. 3–34.

AGGER, B. (1977b) 'Dialectical Sensibility II: Towards a New Intellectuality', *Canadian Journal of Political and Social Theory*, **1**, 2, pp. 47–57.

AGGER, B. (1979a) *Western Marxism: An Introduction*, Santa Monica, CA, Goodyear.

# References

AGGER, B. (1979b) 'Work and Authority in Marcuse and Habermas', *Human Studies*, **2**, pp. 191–208.

AGGER, B. (1982) 'Marcuse's Freudian Marxism', *Dialectical Anthropology*, **6**, 4, pp. 319–36.

AGGER, B. (1983) 'Marxism "or" the Frankfurt School?', *Philosophy of the Social Sciences*, **13**, 3, pp. 347–65.

AGGER, B. (1985) 'The Dialectic of Deindustrialization: An Essay on Advanced Capitalism', in FORESTER, J. (Ed.) *Critical Theory and Public Life*, Cambridge, MA, MIT Press, pp. 3–21.

AGGER, B. (1989a) *Fast Capitalism: A Critical Theory of Significance*, Urbana, IL, University of Illinois Press.

AGGER, B. (1989b) *Reading Science: A Literary, Political and Sociological Analysis*, Dix Hills, NY, General Hall.

AGGER, B. (1989c) *Socio(onto)logy: A Disciplinary Reading*, Urbana, IL, University of Illinois Press.

AGGER, B. (1990) *The Decline of Discourse: Reading, Writing and Resistance in Postmodern Capitalism*, London, Falmer Press.

AGGER, B. (1991a) *Cultural Studies as Critical Theory*, London, Falmer Press.

AGGER, B. (1991b) 'Critical Theory, Poststructuralism and Postmodernism: Their Sociological Relevance', *Annual Review of Sociology*, **17**, pp. 105–31.

AGGER, B. (1991c) *Beyond the End of Ideology: Marxism, Critical Theory, Postmodernism*, Evanston, IL, Northwestern University Press.

AGGER, B. (1992) *Do Books Write Authors? Gender, Class and Critique in the Age of the Blockbuster*, Durham, NC, Duke University Press.

ALEXANDER, J.C. (1990) 'Commentary: Structure, Value, Action', *American Sociological Review*, **55**, pp. 339–45.

ALMOND, G. and VERBA, S. (1966) *The Civic Culture*, Palo Alto, Stanford University Press.

ALTHUSSER, L. (1969) *For Marx*, London, Allen Lane.

ANTONIO, R. (1983) 'The Origin, Development and Contemporary Status of Critical Theory', *Sociological Quarterly*, **24**, pp. 325–51.

ANTONIO, R. and KELLNER, D. (1991) *Theorizing Modernity*, London, Sage.

APEL, K-O. (1971) *Hermeneutik und Ideologiekritik*, Frankfurt, Suhrkamp.

APEL, K-O. (1980) *Towards a Transformation of Philosophy*, London, RKP.

ARAC, J. (Ed.) (1986) *Postmodernism and Politics*, Minneapolis, University of Minnesota Press.

ARATO, A. and GEBHARDT, E. (Eds) (1978) *The Essential Frankfurt School Reader*, New York, Urizen.

ARENDT, H. (1958) *The Human Condition*, Chicago, University of Chicago Press.

ARENDT, H. (1964) *Eichmann in Jerusalem*, New York, Viking.

ARONOWITZ, S. (1981) *The Crisis in Historical Materialism*, New York, Praeger.

ARONOWITZ, S. (1988) *Science as Power: Discourse and Ideology in Modern Society*, Minneapolis, University of Minnesota Press.

ARONOWITZ, S. (1990) *The Crisis in Historical Materialism*, 2nd ed., Minneapolis, University of Minnesota Press.

BARTHES, R. (1970) *Writing Degree Zero*, Boston, Beacon Press.

BARTHES, R. (1974) *S/Z*, New York, Hill and Wang.

BARTHES, R. (1975) *The Pleasure of the Text*, New York, Hill and Wang.

BAUDRILLARD, J. (1975) *The Mirror of Production*, St. Louis, Telos Press.

BAUDRILLARD, J. (1981) *For a Critique of the Political Economy of the Sign*, St. Louis, Telos Press.

BAUDRILLARD, J. (1983) *Simulations*, New York, Semiotext(e).

BEAUVOIR, S. DE (1953) *The Second Sex*, New York, Knopf.

BECK, E.M., HORAN, P.M. and TOLBERT, C.M. (1978) 'Stratification in a Dual Economy: A Sectoral Model of Earnings Determination', *American Sociological Review*, **43**, pp. 704–20.

BECKER, H. (1966) *Outsiders: Studies in the Sociology of Deviance*, New York, Free Press.

BECKER, H. (1986) *Writing for Social Scientists*, Chicago, University of Chicago Press.

BELL, D. (1960) *The End of Ideology*, Glencoe, IL, Free Press.

BELL, D. (1973) *The Coming of Post-Industrial Society*, New York, Basic Books.

BELL, D. (1976) *The Cultural Contradictions of Capitalism*, New York, Basic Books.

BENHABIB, S. (1984) 'Epistemologies of Postmodernism', *New German Critique*, **33**, pp. 103–26.

BENHABIB, S. (1987) *Critique, Norm and Utopia*, New York, Columbia University Press.

BENJAMIN, W. (1969) *Illuminations*, New York, Schocken.

BERMAN, A. (1988) *From the New Criticism to Deconstruction: The Reception of Structuralism and Post-structuralism*, Urbana, IL, University of Illinois Press.

BERMAN, M. (1982) *All That is Solid Melts into Air*, New York, Simon and Schuster.

BERNSTEIN, B. (1971) *Class, Codes and Control*, London, RKP.

BERNSTEIN, E. (1961) *Evolutionary Socialism*, New York, Schocken.

BEST, S. (1989) 'The Commodification of Reality and the Reality of Commodification: Jean Baudrillard and Post-Modernism', *Current Perspectives in Social Theory*, **9**, pp. 23–51.

BEST, S. and KELLNER, D. (1988a) '(Re)Watching Television: Notes Toward a Political Criticism', *Diacritics*, **17**, pp. 97–113.

BEST, S. and KELLNER, D. (1988b) 'Watching Television: The Limits of Postmodernism', *Science as Culture*, **4**, pp. 44–70.

BEST, S. and KELLNER, D. (1990) *Postmodern Theory*, London, Macmillan.

BLAU, P.M. and DUNCAN, O.D. (1978) *The American Occupational Structure*, New York, Free Press.

BLOCH, E. (1970) *Philosophy of Hope*, New York, Herder and Herder.

BLOOM, A. (1987) *The Closing of the American Mind*, New York, Simon and Schuster.

BLUESTONE, B. and HARRISON, B. (1982) *The Deindustrialization of America*, New York, Basic Books.

BOGGS, C. (1983) 'The Intellectuals and Social Movements: Some Reflections on Academic Marxism', *Humanities in Society*, **6**, pp. 223–39.

BOGGS, C. (1986) *Social Movements and Political Power: Emerging Forms of Radicalism in the West*, Philadelphia, Temple University Press.

BOSE, C. (1985) *Jobs and Gender: Sex and Occupation*, New York, Praeger.

BOURDIEU, P. (1984) *Distinction: A Social Critique of the Judgment of Taste*, Cambridge, MA, Harvard University Press.

BOURDIEU, P. (1988) *Homo Academicus*, Cambridge, England, Polity Press.

BRAVERMAN, H. (1974) *Labor and Monopoly Capital*, New York, Monthly Review Press.

BREINES, P. (1985) 'Redeeming Redemption', *Telos*, **65**, pp. 152–8.

BRODKEY, L. (1987) *Academic Writing as Social Practice*, Philadelphia, Temple University Press.

BROWN, R. (1987) *Society as Text*, Chicago, University of Chicago Press.

CALLINICOS, A. (1985) 'Postmodernism, Post-structuralism and Post-Marxism?', *Theory, Culture and Society*, **2**, pp. 85–101.

CASTORIADIS, C. (1973–74) *L'Expérience du Mouvement Ouvrier*, Paris, Union Générale d'Editions.

CASTORIADIS, C. (1984) *Crossroads in the Labyrinth*, Brighton, Sussex, Harvester Press.

CASTORIADIS, C. (1987) *The Imaginary Institution of Society*, Cambridge, England, Polity Press.

CHODOROW, N. (1978) *The Reproduction of Mothering*, Berkeley, University of California Press.

CHOMSKY, N. (1966) *Syntactic Structures*, The Hague, Mouton.

CHOMSKY, N. (1972) *Studies on Semantics in Generative Grammar*, The Hague, Mouton.

CICOUREL, A. (1973) *Cognitive Sociology*, New York, Free Press.

CIXOUS, H. (1986) *Inside*, New York, Schocken.

CLEAVER, H. (1979) *Reading Capital Politically*, Austin, University of Texas Press.

COHN, N. (1961) *The Pursuit of the Millennium*, New York, Harper and Row.

COLEMAN, J. (1990) 'Commentary: Social Institutions and Social Theory', *American Sociological Review*, **55**, pp. 462–3.

COLLINS, R. (1975) *Conflict Sociology*, New York, Academic Press.

COLLINS, R. (1990) 'Cumulation and Anti-Cumulation in Sociology', *American Sociological Review*, **55**, pp. 462–3.

THE CONFERENCE BOARD OF ASSOCIATED RESEARCH COUNCILS (1982) *An Assessment of Research-Doctorate Programs in the United States: Social and Behavioral Sciences*, Washington, DC, National Academy Press.

CONNERTON, P. (1980) *The Tragedy of Enlightenment*, Cambridge, England, Cambridge University Press.

COWARD, R. and ELLIS, J. (1977) *Language and Materialism: Developments in Semiology and the Theory of the Subject*, London, RKP.

CULLER, J. (1982) *On Deconstruction: Theory and Criticism after Structuralism*, Ithaca, NY, Cornell University Press.

DAVIS, K. and MOORE, W.E. (1945) 'Some Principles of Stratification', *American Sociological Review*, **10**, pp. 242–9.

DEBORD, G. (1972) *Society of the Spectacle*, Detroit, Black and Red Press.

DENZIN, N. (1986) 'Postmodern Social Theory', *Sociological Theory*, **4**, pp. 194–204.

DENZIN, N. (1989) *Film and the American Alcoholic*, New York, Aldine-DeGruyter.

DENZIN, N. (1990) 'Reading Cultural Texts', *American Journal of Sociology*, **95**, pp. 1577–80.

DENZIN, N. (1991) 'Empiricist Cultural Studies in America: A Deconstructive Reading', *Current Perspectives in Social Theory*, **11**, pp. 17–39.

DERRIDA, J. (1976) *Of Grammatology*, Baltimore, Johns Hopkins University Press.

DERRIDA, J. (1978) *Writing and Difference*, Chicago, University of Chicago Press.

DERRIDA, J. (1981) *Positions*, Chicago, University of Chicago Press.

DERRIDA, J. (1987) *Glas*, Lincoln, NE, University of Nebraska Press.

DEWS, P. (1984) 'Power and Subjectivity in Foucault', *New Left Review*, **144**, pp. 72–95.

DEWS, P. (1987) *Logics of Disintegration: Post-Structuralist Thought and the Claims of Critical Theory*, London, Verso.

DIESING, P. (1982) *Science and Ideology in the Policy Sciences*, New York, Aldine.

DIESING, P. (1991) *How Does Social Science Work?: Reflections on Practice*, Pittsburgh, University of Pittsburgh Press.

DONOVAN, J. (1985) *Feminist Theory*, New York, Ungar.

DOOB, C.B. (1985) *Sociology: An Introduction*, New York, Holt, Rinehart and Winston.

DOUGLAS, J. (1981) *Observations of Deviance*, Lanham, MD, University Press of America.

References

DOWLING, W. (1984) *Jameson, Althusser, Marx*, Ithaca, NY, Cornell University Press.
DURKHEIM, E. (1950) *The Rules of Sociological Method*, Glencoe, IL, Free Press.
DURKHEIM, E. (1966) *Suicide*, New York, Free Press.
EAGLETON, T. (1976) *Marxism and Literary Criticism*, London, Methuen.
EAGLETON, T. (1983) *Literary Theory: An Introduction*, Minneapolis, University of Minnesota Press.
EAGLETON, T. (1985) 'Marxism, Structuralism and Poststructuralism', *Diacritics*, **15**, pp. 2–56.
ECO, U. (1979) *The Role of the Reader: Explorations in the Semiotics of Texts*, Bloomington, Indiana University Press.
EISENSTEIN, Z. (Ed.) (1979) *Capitalist Patriarchy and the Case for Socialist Feminism*, New York, Monthly Review Press.
EITZEN, S. (1985) *In Conflict and Order: Understanding Society*, 3rd ed., Boston, Allyn and Bacon.
EITZEN, S. (1988) 'Textbook Writing: Asymmetries and Issues in the Publisher–Author Relationship', *Teaching Sociology*, **16**, pp. 390–3.
ELSHTAIN, J. (1981) *Public Man, Private Woman*, Princeton, Princeton University Press.
ENGELS, F. (1935) *Socialism: Utopian and Scientific*, Chicago, Charles H. Kerr.
EVANS, S. (1980) *Personal Politics: The Roots of Women's Liberation in the Civil Rights Movement and the New Left*, New York, Vintage.
EWEN, S. (1974) 'Advertising as Social Product', in REID, H. (Ed.) *Up the Mainstream*, New York, David McKay.
FEATHERSTONE, M. (Ed.) (1988) *Postmodernism*, Newbury Park, CA, Sage.
FEKETE, J. (1978) *The Critical Twilight: Explorations in the Ideology of Anglo-American Literary Theory from Eliot to McLuhan*, London, RKP.
FEYERABEND, P. (1975) *Against Method*, London, RKP.
FISCHER, M. (1985) *Does Deconstruction Make a Difference?*, Bloomington, Indiana University Press.
FISH, S. (1980) *Is There a Text in this Class?: The Authority of Interpretive Communities*, Cambridge, MA, Harvard University Press.
FOUCAULT, M. (1970) *The Order of Things*, New York, Pantheon.
FOUCAULT, M. (1976) *The Archaeology of Knowledge*, New York, Harper and Row.
FOUCAULT, M. (1977) *Discipline and Punish: The Birth of the Prison*, London, Allen Lane.
FOUCAULT, M. (1978) *The History of Sexuality*, Vol. 1, New York, Pantheon.
FOUCAULT, M. (1980) *Power/Knowledge*, New York, Pantheon.
FRASER, N. (1984) 'The French Derrideans: Politicizing Deconstruc-

tion or Deconstructing the Political?', *New German Critique*, **33**, pp. 127–54.

FRASER, N. (1989) *Unruly Practices: Power, Discourse and Gender in Contemporary Social Theory*, Minneapolis, University of Minnesota Press.

FREIRE, P. (1970) *Pedagogy of the Oppressed*, New York, Seabury.

FRIEDAN, B. (1981) *The Second Stage*, New York, Summit Books.

FRIEDRICHS, R. (1970) *A Sociology of Sociology*, New York, Free Press.

GADAMER, H-G. (1975) *Truth and Method*, New York, Seabury.

GALBRAITH, J.K. (1967) *The New Industrial State*, Boston, Houghton Mifflin.

GARFINKEL. H. (1967) *Studies in Ethnomethodology*, Englewood Cliffs, NJ, Prentice-Hall.

GELLNER, E. (1959) *Words and Things*, London, Gollancz.

GIDDENS, A. (1973) *The Class-Structure of the Advanced Societies*, London, Hutchinson.

GILBERT, G.N. and MULKAY, M. (1984) *Opening Pandora's Box: A Sociological Analysis of Scientists' Discourse*, Cambridge, England, Cambridge University Press.

GITLIN, T. (1987) *The Sixties: Years of Hope, Days of Rage*, New York, Bantam Books.

GITLIN, T. (1988) 'Hip-Deep in Postmodernism', *The New York Times Book Review*, **6**, November, pp. 1, 35–6.

GOFFMAN, E. (1961) *Asylums*, New York, Doubleday.

GOFFMAN, E. (1974) *The Presentation of Self in Everyday Life*, New York, Overlook.

GOODE, E. (1984) *Sociology*, Englewood Cliffs, NJ, Prentice-Hall.

GOTTDIENER, M. (1985) 'Hegemony and Mass Culture: A Semiotic Approach', *American Journal of Sociology*, **90**, pp. 979–1001.

GOTTDIENER, M. (1990) 'The Logocentrism of the Classics', *American Sociological Review*, **55**, pp. 460–2.

GOTTDIENER, M. (1991) 'Space, Social Theory and the Urban Metaphor', *Current Perspectives in Social Theory*, **11**, pp. 295–311.

GOTTDIENER, M. and LAGOPOULOS, A. (Eds) (1986) *The City and the Sign: An Introduction to Urban Semiotics*, New York, Columbia University Press.

GOULDNER, A. (1970) *The Coming Crisis of Western Sociology*, New York, Basic Books.

GRAMSCI, A. (1971) *Selections from the Prison Notebooks*, London, Lawrence and Wishart.

HABERMAS, J. (1970a) 'Technology and Science as "Ideology"', in HABERMAS, J. *Toward a Rational Society*, Boston, Beacon Press.

HABERMAS, J. (1970b) *Toward a Rational Society*, Boston, Beacon Press.

HABERMAS, J. (1971) *Knowledge and Human Interests*, Boston, Beacon Press.

# References

HABERMAS, J. (1973) *Theory and Practice*, Boston, Beacon Press.
HABERMAS, J. (1975) *Legitimation Crisis*, Boston, Beacon Press.
HABERMAS, J. (1979) *Communication and the Evolution of Society*, Boston, Beacon Press.
HABERMAS, J. (1981a) 'Modernity versus Postmodernity', *New German Critique*, **22**, pp. 3–14.
HABERMAS, J. (1981b) 'New Social Movements', *Telos*, **49**, pp. 33–7.
HABERMAS, J. (1984) *The Theory of Communicative Action*, Vol. 1, Boston, Beacon Press.
HABERMAS, J. (1987a) *The Philosophical Discourse of Modernity*, Cambridge, MA, MIT Press.
HABERMAS, J. (1987b) *The Theory of Communicative Action*, Vol. 2, Boston, Beacon Press.
HALLIN, D. (1985) 'The American News Media: A Critical Theory Perspective', in FORESTER, J. (Ed.) *Critical Theory and Public Life*, Cambridge, MA, MIT Press.
HARTMAN, G. (1981) *Saving the Text: Literature, Derrida, Philosophy*, Baltimore, Johns Hopkins University Press.
HARVEY, D. (1989) *The Condition of Postmodernity*, Oxford, Basil Blackwell.
HASSAN, I. (1987) *The Postmodern Turn: Essays in Postmodern Theory and Culture*, Columbus, OH, Ohio State University Press.
HAZELRIGG, L. (1989) *Social Science and the Challenge of Relativism*, Vols. 1–2, Gainesville, FL, University Presses of Florida.
HEGEL, G.W.F. (1910) *Phenomenology of Mind*, New York, Macmillan.
HEGEL, G.W.F. (1966) 'Preface to *Phenomenology of Mind*', in *Hegel: Texts and Commentary*, KAUFMAN, W. (Ed.) Garden City, NY, Anchor Books.
HELD, D. (1980) *An Introduction to Critical Theory*, Berkeley, University of California Press.
HELLER, A. (1976) *The Theory of Need in Marx*, New York, St. Martin's.
HERRICK, R. (1980) 'Nineteen Pictures of a Discipline: A Review of Recent Introductory Sociology Textbooks', *Contemporary Sociology*, **9**, pp. 617–26.
HESS, B. (1988) 'In Defense of the Introductory Textbook', *Teaching Sociology*, **16**, pp. 403–4.
HESS, B.B., MARKSON, E.W. and STEIN, P.J. (1985) *Sociology* 2nd ed., New York, Macmillan.
HIRSCH, E.D. (1987) *Cultural Literacy*, Boston, Houghton Mifflin.
HORKHEIMER, M. (1972a) *Critical Theory*, New York, Herder and Herder.
HORKHEIMER, M. (1972b) 'Traditional and Critical Theory', in HORKHEIMER, M. *Critical Theory*, New York, Herder and Herder, pp. 188–243.
HORKHEIMER, M. (1973) 'The Authoritarian State', *Telos*, **15**, pp. 3–20.

HORKHEIMER, M. (1974a) *Critique of Instrumental Reason*, New York, Seabury.

HORKHEIMER, M. (1974b) *Eclipse of Reason*, New York, Seabury.

HORKHEIMER, M. and ADORNO, T.W. (1972) *Dialectic of Enlightenment*, New York, Herder and Herder.

HUGHES, H.S. (1975) *The Sea Change: The Migration of Social Thought, 1930–1965*, New York, Harper and Row.

HUYSSEN, A. (1984) 'Mapping the Postmodern', *New German Critique*, **33**, pp. 5–52.

HUYSSEN, A. (1986) *After the Great Divide: Modernism, Mass Culture, Postmodernism*, Bloomington, Indiana University Press.

INSTITUTE FOR SOCIAL RESEARCH (1972) *Aspects of Sociology*, Boston, Beacon Press.

IRIGARAY, L. (1985) *This Sex Which is Not One*, Ithaca, NY, Cornell University Press.

JACOBY, R. (1975) *Social Amnesia*, Boston, Beacon Press.

JACOBY, R. (1981) *Dialectic of Defeat*, New York, Cambridge University Press.

JACOBY, R. (1987) *The Last Intellectuals: American Culture in the Age of Academe*, New York, Basic Books.

JAGGAR, A. (1983) *Feminist Politics and Human Nature*, Totowa, NJ, Roman and Allenheld.

JAMESON, F. (1971) *Marxism and Form*, Princeton, Princeton University Press.

JAMESON, F. (1972) *The Prison-House of Language*, Princeton, Princeton University Press.

JAMESON, F. (1976–77) 'Ideology of the Text', *Salmagundi*, **31**, pp. 204–46.

JAMESON, F. (1981) *The Political Unconscious: Narrative as a Socially Symbolic Act*, Ithaca, NY, Cornell University Press.

JAMESON, F. (1984a) 'The Politics of Theory: Ideological Positions in the Postmodernism Debate', *New German Critique*, **33**, pp. 53–65.

JAMESON, F. (1984b) 'Postmodernism, or the Cultural Logic of Late Capitalism', *New Left Review*, **146**, pp. 53–93.

JAMESON, F. (1988) 'Cognitive Mapping', in NELSON, C. and GROSSBERG, L. (Eds) *Marxism and the Interpretation of Culture*, Urbana, IL, pp. 347–57.

JAY, M. (1973) *The Dialectical Imagination*, Boston, Little, Brown.

JAY, M. (1984a) *Adorno*, Cambridge, MA, Harvard University Press.

JAY, M. (1984b) *Marxism and Totality*, Berkeley, University of California Press.

JENCKS, C. (1987) *Post-Modernism: The New Classicism in Art and Architecture*, New York, Rizzoli.

JOHNSON, R. (1986–87) 'What is Cultural Studies Anyway?' *Social Text*, **12**, pp. 38–79.

KAMMEYER, K.C.W. (1988) 'Are Sociology Textbooks Really So Bad?' *Teaching Sociology*, **16**, pp. 424–7.

KANN, M. (1982) *The American Left*, New York, Praeger.

KEANE, J. (1984) *Public Life and Late Capitalism*, Cambridge, England, Cambridge University Press.

KELLNER, D. (1981) 'Network Television and American Society: Introduction to a Critical Theory of Television', *Theory and Society*, **10**, pp. 31–62.

KELLNER, D. (1984–85) 'Critical Theory and the Culture Industries: A Reassessment', *Telos*, **62**, pp. 196–206.

KELLNER, D. (1988) 'Postmodernism as Social Theory: Some Challenges and Problems', *Theory, Culture and Society*, **5**, 2/3, pp. 239–69.

KELLNER, D. (1989a) 'Boundaries and Borderlines: Reflections on Jean Baudrillard and Critical Theory', *Current Perspectives in Social Theory*, **9**, pp. 5–22.

KELLNER, D. (1989b) *Critical Theory, Marxism and Modernity*, Cambridge, England, Polity Press.

KELLNER, D. (1989c) *Jean Baudrillard: From Marxism to Postmodernism and Beyond*, Cambridge, England, Polity Press.

KITCHEN, M. (1976) *Fascism*, London, Macmillan.

KLEIN, J. (1989) *Interdisciplinarity: History, Theory and Practice*, Detroit, Wayne State University Press.

KLINE, S. and LEISS, W. (1978) 'Advertising, Needs and "Commodity Fetishism"', *Canadian Journal of Political and Social Theory*, **2**, pp. 5–32.

KLINKOWITZ, J. (1988) *Rosenberg/Barthes/Hassan: The Postmodern Habit of Thought*, Athens, GA, University of Georgia Press.

KNORR-CETINA, K. (1981) *The Manufacture of Knowledge: An Essay on the Constructivist and Contextual Nature of Science*, New York, Pergamon.

KOLAKOWSKI, L. (1968) *The Alienation of Reason*, Garden City, NY, Anchor Books.

KOLAKOWSKI, L. (1969) *Marxism and Beyond*, London, Pall Mall.

KOLAKOWSKI, L. (1978) *Main Currents of Marxism*, Oxford, Clarendon Press.

KORSCH, K. (1970) *Marxism and Philosophy*, New York, Monthly Review Press.

KOSIK, K. (1976) *Dialectics of the Concrete*, Dordrecht, D. Reidel.

KRISTEVA, J. (1980) *Desire in Language*, New York, Columbia University Press.

KROKER, A. and COOK, D. (1986) *The Postmodern Scene*, New York, St. Martin's.

KUHN, T. (1970) *The Structure of Scientific Revolutions*, 2nd ed., Chicago, University of Chicago Press.

LAMANNA, M.A. (1988) 'The Author and Her Friends: The Small World of Textbook Publishing', *Teaching Sociology*, **16**, pp. 416–9.

LAMONT, M. (1987) 'How to Become a Dominant French Philosopher: The Case of Jacques Derrida', *American Journal of Sociology*, **93**, pp. 584–622.

LASCH, C. (1977) *Haven in a Heartless World: The Family Besieged*, New York, Basic Books.

LASCH, C. (1979) *The Culture of Narcissism*, New York, Norton.

LASCH, C. (1984) *The Minimal Self*, New York, Norton.

LATOUR, B. and WOOLGAR, S. (1979) *Laboratory Life: The Social Construction of Scientific Facts*, Beverly Hills, Sage.

LEISS, W. (1972) *The Domination of Nature*, New York, Braziller.

LEISS, W. (1976) *The Limits to Satisfaction: An Essay on the Problem of Needs and Commodities*, Toronto, University of Toronto Press.

LEISS, W., KLINE, S. and JHALLY, S. (1986) *Social Communication in Advertising: Persons, Products and Images of Well-Being*, Toronto, Methuen.

LEMERT, C. (1980) *Sociology and the Twilight of Man: Homocentrism and Discourse in Sociological Theory*, Carbondale, IL, Southern Illinois University Press.

LEMERT, C. and GILLAN, G. (1982) *Michel Foucault: Social Theory and Transgression*, New York, Columbia University Press.

LENHARDT, C. (1972) 'Rise and Fall of Transcendental Anthropology', *Philosophy of the Social Sciences*, **2**, pp. 231–46.

LENHARDT, C. (1975) 'Anamnestic Solidarity: The Proletariat and its Manes', *Telos*, **25**, pp. 133–54.

LENHARDT, C. (1976) 'The Wanderings of Enlightenment', in O'NEILL, J. (Ed.) *On Critical Theory*, New York, Seabury.

LENIN, V. (1952) *Materialism and Empirio-Criticism*, Moscow, Foreign Languages Publishing House.

LENIN, V. (1973) *What is to Be Done?*, Moscow, Progress Publishers.

LENIN, V. (n.d.) *State and Revolution*, Moscow, Foreign Languages Publishing House.

LENTRICCHIA, F. (1980) *After the New Criticism*, Chicago, University of Chicago Press.

LEWIS, L. (1975) *Scaling the Ivory Tower: Merit and its Limits in Academic Careers*, Baltimore, Johns Hopkins University Press.

LEWIS, L. (1988) *Cold War on Campus*, New Brunswick, NJ, Transaction.

LICHTHEIM, G. (1961) *Marxism*, London, RKP.

LUKÁCS, G. (1971) *History and Class Consciousness*, London, Merlin.

LUKE, A. (1988) *Literacy, Textbooks and Ideology*, London, Falmer Press.

LUKE, T. (1989) *Screens of Power: Ideology, Domination and Resistance in Informational Society*, Urbana, IL, University of Illinois Press.

LUKE, T. (1990) *Social Theory and Modernity: Critique, Dissent and Revolution*, New Park, CA, Sage.

LUKE, T. (1991) 'The Discourse of "Development": A Genealogy of

"Developing Nations" and the Discipline of Modernity', *Current Perspectives in Social Theory*, **12**, 11, pp. 271–93.

LYOTARD, J-F. (1984) *The Postmodern Condition: A Report on Knowledge*, Minneapolis, University of Minnesota Press.

LYOTARD, J-F. (1989) *The Differend: Phrases in Dispute*, Minneapolis, University of Minnesota Press.

MACPHERSON, C.B. (1962) *The Political Theory of Possessive Individualism*, Oxford, The Clarendon Press.

MANDEL, E. (1975) *Late Capitalism*, London, New Left Books.

MARCUS, G. and FISCHER, M. (Eds) (1986) *Anthropology as Cultural Critique: An Experimental Moment in the Human Sciences*, Chicago, University of Chicago Press.

MARCUSE, H. (1955) *Eros and Civilization*, New York, Vintage.

MARCUSE, H. (1960) 'Preface: A Note on Dialectic', in MARCUSE, H., *Reason and Revolution: Hegel and the Rise of Social Theory*, Boston, Beacon Press.

MARCUSE, H. (1964) *One-Dimensional Man*, Boston, Beacon Press.

MARCUSE, H. (1968) 'The Struggle Against Liberalism in the Totalitarian State', in MARCUSE, H., *Negations*, Boston, Beacon Press.

MARCUSE, H. (1969) *An Essay on Liberation*, Boston, Beacon Press.

MARCUSE, H. (1972) *Counterrevolution and Revolt*, Boston, Beacon Press.

MARCUSE, H. (1973) 'The Foundations of Historical Materialism', in MARCUSE, H. *Studies in Critical Philosophy*, Boston, Beacon Press.

MARCUSE, H. (1978) *The Aesthetic Dimension*, Boston, Beacon Press.

MARCUSE, H. (1978–79) 'Theory and Practice: A Discussion', *Telos*, **38**, pp. 123–52.

MARCUSE, H., WOLFF, R.P. and MOORE, JR. B. (1965) *A Critique of Pure Tolerance*, Boston, Beacon Press.

MARKOVIĆ, M. (1974) *From Affluence to Praxis*, Ann Arbor, University of Michigan Press.

MARSHALL, B. (1988) 'Feminist Theory and Critical Theory', *Canadian Review of Sociology and Anthropology*, **25**, 2, pp. 208–30.

MARX, K. (n.d.) *Capital*, Vol. 1, Moscow, Progress Publishers.

MARX, K. (1961) *Economic and Philosophic Manuscripts of 1844*, Moscow, Foreign Languages Publishing House.

MARX, K. and ENGELS, F. (1947) *The German Ideology*, New York, International Publishers.

MARX, K. and ENGELS, F. (1964) *The Communist Manifesto*, New York, Washington Square Press.

MASLOW, W.D. (1981) 'Academic Sociology as a "Classist" Discipline: An Empirical Inquiry into the Treatment of Marx in the Textbooks of North American Sociology, 1890–1965', *Humanity and Society*, **5**, pp. 256–75.

McCARTHY, E.D. and DAS, R. (1985) 'American Sociology's Idea of Itself: A Review of the Textbook Literature from the Turn of the Century to the Present', *History of Sociology*, **5**, pp. 21–43.

McCarthy, T. (1978) *The Critical Theory of Jurgen Habermas*, Cambridge, MA, MIT Press.

Mehan, H. and Wood, H. (1975) *The Reality of Ethnomethodology*, New York, Wiley.

Merleau-Ponty, M. (1964a) *Sense and Non-Sense*, Evanston, IL, Northwestern University Press.

Merleau-Ponty, M. (1964b) *Signs*, Evanston, IL, Northwestern University Press.

Merleau-Ponty, M. (1972) *Humanism and Terror*, Boston, Beacon Press.

Merleau-Ponty, M. (1973) *Adventures of the Dialectic*, Evanston, IL, Northwestern University Press.

Miliband, R. (1973) *The State in Capitalist Society*, London, Quartet Books.

Miller, M.C. (1988) *Boxed In: The Culture of TV*, Evanston, IL, Northwestern University Press.

Mills, C.W. (1951) *White Collar*, New York, Oxford University Press.

Mills, C.W. (1959) *The Sociological Imagination*, New York, Oxford University Press.

Mills, C.W. (1962) *The Marxists*, New York, Dell.

Misgeld, D. (1976) 'Critical Theory and Hermeneutics: The Debate Between Habermas and Gadamer', in O'Neill, J. (Ed.) *On Critical Theory*, New York, Seabury.

Morgan, J.G. (1983) 'Courses and Texts in Sociology', *Journal of the History of Sociology*, **5**, pp. 42–65.

Morrow, R. (1991) 'Critical Theory, Gramsci and Cultural Studies: From Structuralism to Poststructuralism', in Welxer, P. (Ed.) *Critical Theory Now*, London, Falmer Press.

Mueller, C. (1973) *The Politics of Communication*, New York, Oxford University Press.

Mulvey, L. (1989) *Visual and Other Pleasures*, Bloomington, IN, Indiana University Press.

Neumann, F. (1942) *Behemoth*, London, Gollancz.

Neumann, F. (1957) *The Democratic and the Authoritarian State*, Glencoe, IL, Free Press.

Newman, C. (1985) *The Postmodern Aura: The Act of Fiction in an Age of Inflation*, Evanston, IL, Northwestern University Press.

Norton, T.M. and Ollman, B. (Eds) (1978) *Studies in Socialist Pedagogy*, New York, Norton.

O'Connor, J. (1973) *The Fiscal Crisis of the State*, New York, St. Martin's.

Offe, C. (1984) *Contradictions of the Welfare State*, Cambridge, MA, MIT Press.

Offe, C. (1985) *Disorganized Capitalism*, Cambridge, MA, MIT Press.

O'Neill, J. (1972a) 'The Hobbesian Problem in Parsons and Marx', in O'Neill, J. *Sociology as a Skin Trade*, New York, Harper and Row, pp. 177–208.

References

O'Neill, J. (1972b) 'Public and Private Space', in O'Neill, J., *Sociology as a Skin Trade*, New York, Harper and Row, pp. 20–37.

O'Neill, J. (1972c) *Sociology as a Skin Trade*, New York, Harper and Row.

O'Neill, J. (1974) *Making Sense Together: An Introduction to Wild Sociology*, New York, Harper and Row.

O'Neill, J. (1976) 'Critique and Remembrance', in O'Neill, J. (Ed.) *On Critical Theory*, New York, Seabury, pp. 1–11.

O'Neill, J. (1981) 'Marxism and the Two Sciences', *Philosophy of the Social Sciences*, **11**, pp. 281–302.

O'Neill, J. (1982) *For Marx Against Althusser*, Washington, DC, University Press of America.

O'Neill, J. (1986) 'The Disciplinary Society: From Weber to Foucault', *British Journal of Sociology*, **37**, 1, pp. 42–60.

O'Neill, J. (1991) 'Is There a Class in This Text?', Unpublished manuscript.

Paci, E. (1972) *The Function of the Sciences and the Meaning of Man*, Evanston, IL, Northwestern University Press.

Papp, W.R. (1981) 'The Concept of Power: Treatment in 50 Introductory Sociology Textbooks', *Teaching Sociology*, **9**, pp. 57–68.

Parsons, T. (1937) *The Structure of Social Action*, New York, Free Press.

Parsons, T. (1951) *The Social System*, Glencoe, IL, Free Press.

Parsons, T. (1990) 'Prolegomena to a Theory of Social Institutions', *American Sociological Review*, **55**, pp. 319–33.

Perrucci, R. (1980) 'Sociology and the Introductory Textbooks', *American Sociologist*, **15**, pp. 39–49.

Persell, C.H. (1988) 'Reflections on Sociology Textbooks by a Teacher, Scholar, and Author', *Teaching Sociology*, **16**, pp. 399–402.

Petrovic, G. (1967) *Marx in the Mid-Twentieth Century*, Garden City, NY, Anchor Books.

Piccone, P. (1971) 'Phenomenological Marxism', *Telos*, **9**, pp. 3–31.

Piccone, P. (1976) 'Beyond Identity Theory', in O'Neill, J. (Ed.) *On Critical Theory*, New York, Seabury.

Piccone, P. (1978) 'The Crisis of One-Dimensionality', *Telos*, **35**, pp. 43–54.

Porter, J.N. (1981–82) 'Radical Sociology Textbooks: A Review Essay', *Humboldt Journal of Social Relations*, **9**, pp. 298–306.

Portoghesi, P. (1983) *Postmodern, the Architecture of the Postindustrial Society*, New York, Rizzoli.

Poster, M. (1989) *Critical Theory and Poststructuralism*, Ithaca, NY, Cornell University Press.

Poulantzas, N. (1973) *Political Power and Social Classes*, New York, RKP.

Rachlin, A. (1988) *News as Hegemonic Reality*, New York, Praeger.

RANSOM, J.C. (1941) *The New Criticism*, Norfolk, CT, New Directions.

RAULET, G. (1984) 'From Modernity as a One-Way Street to Postmodernity as a Dead End', *New German Critique*, **30**, pp. 155–77.

RICHARDSON, L. (1988) 'The Collective Story: Postmodernism and the Writing of Sociology', *Sociological Focus*, **21**, pp. 199–208.

RICHARDSON, L. (1990a) 'Narrative and Sociology', *Journal of Contemporary Ethnography*, **19**, pp. 116–35.

RICHARDSON, L. (1990b) 'Speakers Whose Voices Matter: Toward a Feminist Postmodernist Sociological Praxis', *Studies in Symbolic Interactionism*, in press.

RICHARDSON, L. (1990c) *Writing Strategies: Reaching Diverse Audiences*, Newbury Park, CA, Sage.

RICHARDSON, L. (1991) 'Value Constituting Practices, Rhetoric and Metaphor in Sociology: A Reflexive Analysis', *Current Perspectives in Social Theory*, **11**, pp. 1–5.

RITZER, G. (1975) *Sociology: A Multiple Paradigm Science*, Boston, Allyn and Bacon.

RITZER, G. (1988) 'Problems, Scandals and the Possibility of "Textbookgate": An Author's View', *Teaching Sociology*, **16**, pp. 198–206.

RULE, J.B. (1978) *Insight and Social Betterment*, New York, Oxford University Press.

RYAN, M. (1982) *Marxism and Deconstruction*, Baltimore, Johns Hopkins University Press.

RYAN, M. (1989) *Politics and Culture*, Baltimore, Johns Hopkins University Press.

SAID, E. (1979) *Orientalism*, New York, Vintage Books.

SARUP, M. (1989) *An Introductory Guide to Post-Structuralism and Postmodernism*, Athens, GA, University of Georgia Press.

SARTRE, J-P. (1963) *Search for a Method*, New York, Vintage Books.

SARTRE, J-P. (1965a) *Situations*, Greenwich, CT, Fawcett.

SARTRE, J-P. (1965b) *What is Literature?*, New York, Harper and Row.

SARTRE, J-P. (1976) *Critique of Dialectical Reason*, London, New Left Books.

SAUSSURE, F. DE (1960) *Course in General Linguistics*, London, Peter Owen.

SCHAFF, A. (1970) *Marxism and the Human Individual*, New York, McGraw-Hill.

SCHOOLMAN, M. (1980) *The Imaginary Witness: The Critical Theory of Herbert Marcuse*, New York, Free Press.

SCHROYER, T. (1973) *The Critique of Domination: The Origins and Development of Critical Theory*, New York, Braziller.

SCHUTZ, A. (1967) *Phenomenology of the Social World*, Evanston, IL, Northwestern University Press.

# References

SENNETT, R. (1978) *The Fall of Public Man*, New York, Vintage.

SHELTON, B.A. and AGGER, B. (1991) 'Shotgun Wedding, Unhappy Marriage, No-Fault Divorce?: Rethinking the Feminism-Marxism Relationship', in ENGLAND, P. (Ed.), *Feminism on Theory/Sociology on Gender*, Boston, Aldine.

SHORTER, E. (1975) *The Making of the Modern Family*, New York, Basic Books.

SILVERMAN, H. and WELTON, D. (Eds) (1988) *Postmodernism and Continental Philosophy*, Albany, SUNY Press.

SINGER, B. (1979) 'Early Castoriadis: Socialism, Barbarism and the Bureaucratic Thread', *Canadian Journal of Political and Social Theory*, **3**, 3, pp. 35–56.

SINGER, B. (1980) 'Later Castoriadis: Institution under Interrogation', *Canadian Journal of Political and Social Theory*, **4**, 1, pp. 75–103.

SLATER, P. (1977) *Origin and Significance of the Frankfurt School*, London, RKP.

SMART, B. (1983) *Foucault, Marxism and Critique*, London, RKP.

STALIN, J.V. (1940) *Dialectical and Historical Materialism*, New York, International Publishers.

STOCKMAN, N. (1984) *Antipositivist Theories of the Sciences*, Dordrecht, D. Reidel.

STOJANOVIĆ, S. (1973) *Between Ideals and Reality: A Critique of Socialism and its Future*, New York, Oxford University Press.

STRYKER, S. (1983) 'Editors' Reports', *American Sociological Review, ASA Footnotes*, **11**, 6, p. 13.

TAYLOR, F. (1919) *The Principles of Scientific Management*, New York, Harper and Brothers.

TAYLOR, F. (1947) *Scientific Management*, New York, Harper.

TISCHLER, H.L. (1988) 'Textbooks are a Reflection of the Discipline', *Teaching Sociology*, **16**, pp. 370–2.

TOCQUEVILLE, A. (1961) *Democracy in America*, New York, Schocken Books.

TURNER, B.S. (Ed.) (1990) *Theories of Modernity and Postmodernity*, Newbury Park, CA, Sage.

WALBY, S. (1986) *Patriarchy at Work*, Minneapolis, University of Minnesota press.

WALTERS, S.D. (1992) 'Material Girls: Feminism and Cultural Studies', *Current Perspectives in Social Theory*, **12**, in press.

WEBER, M. (1947) *The Theory of Social and Economic Organization*, Glencoe, IL, Free Press.

WEBER, M. (1968) *The Methodology of the Social Sciences*, New York, Free Press.

WEEDON, C. (1987) *Feminist Practice and Poststructuralist Theory*, Oxford, Basil Blackwell.

WELLMER, A. (1976) 'Communications and Emancipation: Reflections on the Linguistic Turn in Critical Theory', in O'NEILL, J. (Ed.) *On Critical Theory*, New York, Seabury, pp. 231–63.

WELLS, A. (1979) 'Conflict Theory and Functionalism: Introductory Sociology Books, 1928–1976', *Teaching Sociology*, **6**, pp. 429–37.

WERNICK, A. (1983) 'Advertising and Ideology: An Interpretive Framework', *Theory, Culture and Society*, **2**, pp. 16–33.

WEXLER, P. (1987) *Social Analysis of Education: After the New Sociology*, London, RKP.

WILLIAMSON, J. (1978) *Decoding Advertisements*, London, Marion Boyars.

WITTGENSTEIN, L. (1953) *Philosophical Investigations*, Oxford, Basil Blackwell.

WITTGENSTEIN, L. (1981) *Tractatus Logico-Philosophicus*, London, RKP.

WOLIN, R. (1984) 'Modernism versus Postmodernism', *Telos*, **62**, pp. 9–30.

WRIGHT, E.O. (1976) 'Class Boundaries in Advanced Capitalist Societies', *New Left Review*, **98**, pp. 3–41.

WRIGHT, E.O. (1978) *Class, Crisis and the State*, London, New Left Books.

WRIGHT, E.O., COSTELLO, C., HACHEN, D. and SPRAGUE, J. (1982) 'The American Class Structure', *American Sociological Review*, **47**, 6, pp. 709–27.

WUTHNOW, R. (1987) *Meaning and Moral Order: Explorations in Cultural Analysis*, Berkeley, University of California Press.

# Index

*The Falmer Press*

# Related Titles

**The Labyrinths of Literacy:**
**Reflections on Literacy Past and Present**
**Harvery J. Graff,** *University of Texas at Dallas, USA*

'. . .*yet another book from Falmer Press that breaks new ground*. . .*Readers who don't want their current assumptions about literacy's place in the world to be challenged should* not *read this book. Those who want to engage with a text, tussling with and reflecting upon important philosophical, historical and social issues should buy this book.'* **Discourse Processing Forum**

'. . .*throws up many important new points and questions accepted "truths", thus making a valuable contribution to the development and understanding of the subject.'* **History of Education**

275pp
Cloth ISBN 1 85000 163 4
Paper ISBN 1 85000 164 2

**Literacy, Texbooks and Ideology:**
**Postwar Literacy Instruction and the Mythology of Dick and Jane**
Allan Luke, *James Cook University of North Queensland, Australia*

'. . .*of considerable interest not only to those involved in the critical curriculum community, but to all those who care about reading and literacy instruction, textbooks, and the politics of the classroom.'*
**Michael W. Apple, Teachers College Record**

'*Luke's work sets new standards in scholarly commentary on school texts and provides a new,* improved *methodology for analysis which makes previous attempts to explain texts of the past seem very thin indeed.'* **Garth Boomer, Australian Journal of Reading**

**Literacy, Schooling and Revolution**
Colin Lankshear, *University of Auckland, New Zealand* with Moira Lawler

'*What makes this book valuable is not only its exceptionally useful conceptual and political clarification of what literacy has meant and might actually mean in the search for what Marcus Raskin has called "the common good". The volume goes considerably further. It provides us with a series of detailed pictures of significant historical and contemporary struggles to engage in "proper literacy".'* **Michael W. Apple, University of Wisconsin-Madison, USA**

'*A challenging introduction to the politics of literacy.*' **Curriculum Perspectives, Australia**

'*. . .provides a sombre background to the underlying question; "What is all this education for?"*' **Times Educational Supplement**

'*The authors challenge assumptions and practices that are no longer useful; they also point the way to a more just and equitable society. It's a fine, powerful and timely book.*' **New Zealand Listener**

**Winner of the 1988 American Educational Studies Association Critics Choice Award**

274pp
Cloth ISBN 1 85000 239 8
Paper ISBN 1 85000 589 3

## Language and Literacy in the Primary School
Edited by Margaret Meek, *University of London Institute of Education, UK* and Colin Mills, *Worcester College of Higher Education, UK*

'*. . .represents the most important collection so far available of views reflecting a new and influential way of looking at literacy development.*' **David Wray, *LINKS***

310pp
Cloth ISBN 1 85000 352 1
Paper ISBN 1 85000 357 2

## Language, Authority and Criticism:
## Readings on the School Textbook
Edited by Suzanne de Castell, *Simon Fraser University, Canada* and Allan and Carmen Luke, *James Cook University of North Queensland, Australia*

'*. . .essential background reading to any study of the role of interactively produced texts in education. Coupled with other books in the series such as* Literacy, Textbooks and Ideology, *it should form an important part of the library of all educators.*' **Bob Young, Australian Journal of Educational Studies**

'*. . .a useful and important study of the process by which textbooks are made, marketed, and utilized.*' **Interchange**

'*These essays look at the content, form, production and language of textbooks. They raise pertinent questions about insidious censorship and the authority mistakenly still given to some textbooks.*' **Times Educational Supplement**

322pp
Cloth ISBN 1 85000 365 3
Paper ISBN 1 85000 366 1